INDIVIDUAL EMPLOYMENT DISPUTES

Individual Employment Disputes

DEFINITE AND INDEFINITE TERM CONTRACTS

Donald W. Brodie

Q

QUORUM BOOKS

New York • Westport, Connecticut • London

Library of Congress Cataloging-in-Publication Data

Brodie, Donald W.
    Individual employment disputes : definite and indefinite term
contracts / Donald W. Brodie
      p. cm.
    Includes bibliographical references and index.
    ISBN 0-89930-512-1 (lib. bdg. : alk. paper)
    1. Labor contract—United States. 2. Employees—Dismissal of—Law
and legislation—United States. I. Title.
KF898.B76   1991
344.73'0189—dc20
[347.304189]   90-40701

British Library Cataloguing in Publication Data is available.

Library of Congress Catalog Card Number: 90-40701
ISBN: 0-89930-512-1

First published in 1991

Quorum Books, 88 Post Road West, Westport, CT 06881
An imprint of Greenwood Publishing Group, Inc.

Printed in the United States of America

∞

The paper used in this book complies with the
Permanent Paper Standard issued by the National
Information Standards Organization (Z39.48-1984).

10 9 8 7 6 5 4 3 2 1

Contents

Figures

Preface

These materials discuss the individual contract of employment at a time of significant changes in the judicial case law and the growing number of employment related statutes. In the face of these changes, these materials identify some of the themes that remain constant. Paramount among these constant elements are the doctrines of judicial restraint and employer rights, and the concept of just cause. Contract interpretation requires knowledge about the nature of contracts as well as knowledge about the nature of the dispute resolution forums. Contract disputes are resolved through the interplay of these elements. These materials provide background and discussion of this interplay among forums, contracts, and statutes. The background research involves court decisions at the state and federal level and arbitration awards.

These materials are aimed at public and private sector professionals involved in employment relations, including attorneys, personnel administrators, human resource managers, employee relations specialists, and union representatives. In addition, they are directly useful to employers and employees.

Chapter 1 identifies some of the elements that must be considered in determining whether an employment relationship exists. Preliminary definitions of the employer, employee, quit, and discharge are considered.

Chapter 2 discusses courts, arbitration, due process, in house grievance mechanisms, and government agencies as possible dispute resolution forums for employment disputes. Special attention is given to the doctrine of forum self-restraint.

Chapter 3 examines various facets of the doctrine of employer rights. This doctrine is identified as the predominant element to consider in any employment contract dispute.

Chapter 4 looks at the process of creating, modifying, and ending the employment relationship and contract. Oral contracts and employee handbooks are major topics.

Chapter 5 identifies and discusses specific clauses in the contract subject to frequent disputes. Terms of duration, releases and waivers, noncompetition clauses, and terms in an at will contract are among the clauses considered. Individual clauses and individual clauses in collective bargaining contracts are discussed.

Chapter 6 considers the just cause concept and the process of evaluation. Cause is a critical issue because it provides a defense for the employer in most contract disputes.

Chapter 7 looks at the interplay between statutes and employment contracts. Proposals for statutory change in the employment at will doctrine are considered.

Chapter 8 is the author's conclusions, grouped into three categories: employer, employee, and public interest. General themes and likely future directions are identified.

Acknowledgments

Special thanks go to Ms. Joyce Drops, word processing specialist, who prepared the manuscript, and thanks to others on the University of Oregon Law School staff who worked on portions of the manuscript. The book is dedicated to Linda, a new employer, and Emily, a new employee.

INDIVIDUAL EMPLOYMENT DISPUTES

Employment Relationship

INTRODUCTION

The American workplace went through a tumultuous period in the 1980s. One continuing element of the upheaval is the decline in the number of employees represented by unions.[1] Another major event was the growing number of lawsuits brought by discharged, non-union employees. A result of these events has been the increased attention given to the individual, nonunion employee and his or her relationship with the employer.

The individual employment relationship is governed by a number of different legal relationships, such as the individual contract of employment, tortious conduct, constitutional rights, and statutory applications. The primary focus of this book is on the individual contract of employment between the employee and employer. Understanding the individual contract of employment requires looking not only at the terms of the contract, but also looking at some of the implied terms, such as employer rights, and the impact of existing and proposed employment statutes on the contract. The central focus of these materials will be on the creation, interpretation, modification, and enforcement of the individual contract of employment. Proposals for changing the contractual relationship are also considered.

The workplace is a highly varied one. There are public sector and private sector differences. There are individual contracts in both union and nonunion workplaces. The jobs that employees perform range from entry level, manual labor to executive level, policy making positions. The conditions under which employees work range from relative isolation to public contact to the executive suite. The terms under which employees work range from subminimum wage to multimillion-dollar salaries. Employers range from the bankrupt to the highly profitable, from providing traditional products and services to providing the highest technology.

Despite all of these variations, the essential employment relationship springs from the employment contract. The contract is common to all workplaces. These materials identify issues common to most individual contracts, rather than emphasizing the differences between different employment relationships. Identifying similarities makes it easier to reach generalized conclusions. For effective day to day employment decision making in the workplace, it is necessary to identify broad generalizations that can be of general help to employers and employees.

There is much that is common in the workplace. Certainly the discharged employee feels just as discharged whether it occurred under an individual or a collective contract, or whether it occurred in the public or the private sector. Similarly, an employer committed to or required to give "fairness" or "due process" should be able to rely on general standards rather than on some peculiar definition that fits only a particular workplace situation. This is not to suggest that all of the generalizations discussed throughout are true in every situation. For example, when looking at individual situations, courts and arbitrators may find profound differences between the public and private sector employment relationships, or between the collective and individual contracts. Nonetheless, the all too frequent emphasis on differences in workplaces obscures many of the similarities that can lead to useful generalization.

Information about the individual contract of employment can be gained from many sources, ranging from the contracting parties to arbitrators to the courts of last resort. Each source views the contract from its own, special perspective. The primary sources that are used here are the reported decisions of courts and arbitrators. The court and arbitration decisions of most interest here are those primarily related to issues of job security and discipline, although other employment issues also arise.

In summary, these will look at court decisions and arbitration awards that discuss the individual contract of employment.

THE BASIC CONTRACT

The employment contract is the basic element in any employment relationship.[2] Employment contracts can be generally categorized as individual contracts or collective bargaining contracts. The major focus here is on individual contracts, which can be characterized as falling into two primary categories, definite term or indefinite term. A definite term contract is for a fixed period of time, such as a month or a year or five years. An indefinite term contract has no agreed upon duration. It may end in the next moment or last for 40 years. Indefinite term contacts are frequently called at will contracts. Both definite term and indefinite term contracts are covered in these materials.

The individual contract may be written or oral, although most are probably oral. There probably was little or no negotiation about the terms of the contract. Without a history of negotiations and without a writing, there is little concrete evidence concerning the details of the agreement, and the courts may use presumptions about what the parties meant. The employer's offer may have been "accepted" by the employee's action of simply beginning to work, rather than by an elaborate exchange of promises.[3]

Most employees are not covered by collective bargaining contracts, but a significant number of them are. The presence of a collective bargaining contract does not necessarily preclude using individual contracts that go beyond the collective bargaining contract terms. For some topics, such as employee assistance programs, last chance agreements, and drug or alcohol testing consents, there is a growing use of individual contracts in the collective bargaining context. Both collective and individual contracts contain terms that are central to these materials, such as duration, job security, grievance mechanisms, waivers, and consents, to identify a few. In addition, it is useful to compare how courts react so differently to the collective contract compared to the individual contract, even though the workplaces may be identical in all other respects.

The individual contract of employment is usually oral and often is not the product of real negotiations. It may have a definite or indefinite term. It may be found in the union and nonunion workplace.

CONTRACT TERMS

The individual contract of employment may contain express terms and implied terms. Those that may come to mind first are such terms as wages, hours, duties, and benefits, if any. However, the contract frequently gets much more complicated than that. The contract may be viewed as being created at the time of hire and then be essentially static until the employment relationship is ended. Again, the contractual relationship is frequently more dynamic. The employee may be asked to consent or be compelled to consent to a variety of contract clauses during the life of the ongoing employment relationship.

Wages, hours, and duties may be among the foremost terms of the individual employment contract, but negotiations or the contract may go far beyond these obvious clauses. Sometimes the additional clauses are the product of traditional negotiations and sometimes the they are the product of sign or be discharged negotiations. Employees may be "asked" to consent to a polygraph or other test, which includes a waiver of challenges to the test.[4] The results of a drug test may not be given to the police or others unless the employee consents.[5] An employer may not use an employee patent without paying compensation unless the employer contracts the employee's consent.[6] A contract of waiver and settlement of statutory employment claims may be involved.[7] The employee may have to sign a contractual covenant not to compete.[8] Contracts may convert indefinite term (at will) status to fixed term status, or vice versa.[9] Employees may have to sign acknowledgments of receipt of an employer manual, such manual being used by the employer to evidence the terms of employment and usually imposing at will terms of duration.[10] An employee in the securities industry may be required to agree to arbitrate all employment disputes.[11] Employees may be required to sign false statements attesting, for example, to the correctness of their pay as a contract agreement condition to receiving their paychecks.[12] Errant employees may be requested, in lieu of discharge, to sign individual, last chance agreements that waive just cause provisions in collective bargaining contracts.[13] Agreements on the purchase of stock options may be part of the employment contract.[14]

The employment relationship may impact beyond the traditional bounds of the individual employment contract. An employee may have to sign a *pre*-employment agreement to submit to polygraph testing.[15] Statutes may require that employers obtain written consent from spouses of retiring workers who choose certain types of pension benefits payouts.[16]

In summary, the individual employment contract contains not only clauses on basic wage and hour terms, but also may contain a variety of waivers, settlements, agreements to test, agreements involving untrue statements, and agreements not to compete, to name only a few examples. In addition, the individual employment contract process is ongoing; it may begin at the pre-employment stage and continue to be modified throughout the employment relationship. Some clauses may represent actual negotiations, whereas other clauses may represent sign or be discharged negotiations. As discussed below, courts and arbitrators may take different, even contradictory, approaches to the different clauses with the same contract or they may treat all clauses in the same way.

EMPLOYER AND EMPLOYEE

In order to have an employment contract, the parties must have an employment relationship. Not all work relationships are employment relationships.

An independent contractor is not an employee, although the work that is being done by the independent contractor may be similar to the work commonly done by an employee.[17] The legal relationship between an independent contractor and the employer is not an employment relationship.[18] An independent contractor may be generally described as a worker whose method of performance is not dependent upon the supervisory control of the person for whom the service is being performed.[19]

The shareholder in a professional corporation usually has an employment contract with the corporation. Many professional workers, such as lawyers, doctors, accountants, and others are organized in this manner. The existence of the employment contract, however, does not mean that the shareholder will be treated as an employee for all purposes. The shareholder is more often treated as an owner or employer, rather than as an employee.[20]

A partner is not an employee of the partnership. The partner is an owner-employer.[21] The relationship between the partnership and the partner is different from the relationship between an employee and the partnership. The partner has those rights that are incorporated into the partnership agreement.[22]

A statutorily defined employment relationship also consists of an employer and an employee. However, statutes may contain specialized definitions that exclude certain employers from coverage under the statute and therefore preclude employees from employment actions based on the statute. This issue may arise as a discharged employee seeks to combine contract and statutory claims in the discharge litigation. For example, Title VII of the 1964 Civil Rights Act defines an employer as one who employs 15 or more persons.[23] An employer of fewer persons is not bound by this federal statute. A number of states have similar antidiscrimination statutes, but they may define employer in a more comprehensive way. Some states, for example, define employer as a person who employs one or more employees.[24]

Many companies have multiple operating entities. They may be organized so that the parent company operates and controls the subsidiary organization more or less directly, or they may be structured so that the various organizations act in an essentially independent manner. When an employee sues an employer, the employee must properly identify the employer of that plaintiff employee.

The variety of complex relationships that can exist between a parent and a subsidiary may make this identification difficult. One test that is used is to determine whether the related companies constitute an "integrated enterprise."[25] Under this test the court will look to the interrelationship of operations, whether there is common management, whether there is centralized control of personnel, whether there is common ownership, and whether there is common financial control. For example, in one case, the question was whether the employee was an employee of the credit union (where the employee worked) or whether the employee was an employee of the power company to which the credit union was attached. Based on the use of a similar test, the employee was found to be the employee only of the credit union.[26]

The fact that one company may be able to exercise some control over the personnel policies of a second company does not necessarily make the first company the employer, when an employee of the second company sues. A company can bring economic pressure on other companies without becoming an employer of the subordinate company's employees.[27] Where the employee incorrectly identifies the employer, the named company owes no legal obligation to the mistaken employee. An operationally separate, but wholly owned, subsidiary owes no obligations to employees of the parent company.[28]

An "economic reality" test may be used to determine whether an individual is an employee. One court described this test as follows: "This requires viewing an employment situation as a whole. . . . Control of the worker's duties, payment of wages, authority to hire and fire, and responsibility for the maintenance of discipline are all factors to be considered, but no one factor is controlling."[29]

In summary, the finding of an employment relationship is critical to any discussion of an employment contract. There are a variety of work relations that may be contractual but do not involve an employment contract, such as the independent contractor or partnership. Where an employment relationship exists, care must be taken to properly identify the employer, which is not always obvious in the face of complex corporate structures. Where a dispute arises over the meaning of an alleged employment contract, the employer's first line of defense may be to challenge the existence of an employment relationship or to challenge the employee's identification of the proper employer. If the employer is successful in these defenses, the complaining employee will not be able to get to the substance of the contract dispute.

PUBLIC OR PRIVATE EMPLOYER

A determination must frequently be made as to whether the employer is in the public or private sector. In many circumstances, the correct answer will be obvious. The employer will clearly be the state or will be a private corporation or sole proprietorship. The public or private question is most likely to arise where an otherwise private employer is supported, in part, by funding from some level of government. The public-private distinction is essential because, for example, the public employer is constrained by constitutional due process hearing considerations, whereas the private employer is not so constrained. In one such case, the court stated: "The receipt of some federal funding (36 percent) by defendants is not sufficient government participation to consider plaintiff's discharge as state action, i.e., public employer."[30] Another case found that the federally funded Legal Services Corporation was not a government employer.[31]

In summary, some contract disputes will turn on whether the employer is public or private. The public employer may have obligations or immunities under constitutions or statutes that the private employer does not share.

QUIT, DISCHARGE, AND CONSTRUCTIVE DISCHARGE

The employment relationship may be terminated in a variety of ways. A definite term contract may expire, the employee may unilaterally quit, or the employee may be discharged. A termination may give rise to a dispute over whether the termination was a breach of the terms of the employment contract. This problem may arise, for example, in a dispute over whether the employee quit or whether the employee was discharged. If the employee voluntarily quits, the employee has no further recourse under the contract. There can be no claim of breach of contract. If the employee was discharged, the employee may claim that the discharge was a breach of the contract.[32]

Where a contract has definite or fixed term, and that term expires, the person no longer has employee status unless the contract is renewed. This situation is often characterized as not involving a discharge, but as involving only the failure to renew or rehire.[33] Whatever the characterization, the person no longer has employee status.

An employee may decide to quit or resign and thereby lose employee status and no longer be a party to an employment contract.[34]

A quit may be obvious or may be inferred from the circumstances, such as when an employee fails to contact the employer for several weeks.[35]

The employee may be discharged by the employer. "There are no magic words required to discharge an employee."[36] If the discharge is valid, the employment contract is terminated, but if the discharge is a breach of the employment contract the employee may be entitled to remedies.

Between the voluntary quit and the discharge lies the complex doctrine of "constructive discharge." Under this doctrine, an employee who, on the surface, appears to have quit, will seek to prove that the employee was actually discharged and that the discharge was a breach of the contract. If the employee cannot show that the apparent quit was involuntary, the employee will have no further rights or remedies under the contract.

There are a number of approaches to constructive discharges. One is the reasonable person approach. "In judging whether a resignation is truly involuntary, the courts have applied an objective standard; the test is not whether the particular employee felt it was necessary to resign, but whether 'a reasonable person in the employee's shoes would have felt compelled to resign.'"[37] Another approach requires that the employer deliberately create the conditions that lead to the quit or resignation.[38]

Within the reasonable person test, there are many distinctions. Mere humiliation or loss of prestige resulting, for example, solely from a demotion or reduction in supervisory duties, is unlikely to be so intolerable as to enable a court to find a constructive discharge.[39] A quit following the failure to receive an expected or "deserved" promotion or a pay raise will generally be treated as a quit, and not a constructive discharge.[40] Courts are willing to give employers wide latitude. "In the course of most, if not all, people's employment a wide variety of disappointments, and possibly some injustices occur. Most of these are normal incidents of employment that would not lead a reasonable person to quit."[41] It is not the employee's subjective feelings that matter; it is how a mythical reasonable person would react.[42] It is more likely to find a constructive discharge where the employer's action results in a decrease of salary, hours, or benefits.[43] A "resign or be fired" scenario can result in a constructive discharge if the employee "resigns."[44]

Where the employee quits in the face of intolerable conditions, a court may find a constructive discharge. It is unclear how soon an employee must quit once the intolerable conditions arise. For example, in one situation the employee claimed that a transfer gave rise to the intolerable situation. However, the employee sued only after taking early retirement five years later. The court said the employee need not resign immediately after the intolerable circumstance arises, but waiting five years was too long.[45] The employee may feel that a transfer to a changed circumstance is intolerable, but some courts have indicated that a failure to inquire or determine all of the details of the new situation may preclude a finding of constructive discharge.[46]

Many constructive discharge situations involve allegations of discrimination. Most courts seem to say that the mere presence of workplace discrimination does not constitute constructive discharge.[47] However, more aggravated forms of discrimination combined with adverse employment opportunities may permit a finding of constructive discharge.[48]

Resignations and attempted withdrawal of resignations can also involve complexities. An employee may resign in the emotion of the moment, but later, in a cooler moment, may seek to rescind the resignation. The results in such cases are mixed. In one such case, an agent of the employer accepted the employee back, but later the employer ordered the employee to clean out the employee's locker and sent the employee a final paycheck because the employee had quit. An arbitrator found that the voluntary resignation was converted into an involuntary resignation.[49]

A resignation need not take a specific form, in the absence of rules to the contrary. It may be oral or written, so long as it indicates the employee's intent.[50] Rules or statutes may require written resignations.[51] Where formal action is required to accept a resignation, a withdrawal before formal action may be effective.[52] However, rules may permit resignations to become effective without formal action.[53] A resignation may be so written as to show an unconditional intent to become effective immediately upon tender. In such a situation, the court may find no acceptance action need be taken.[54]

Another scenario involves an employee who is told that if the employee acts in a certain manner, the employee will be considered to have quit. For example, an employee driver with health concerns turned the truck around and returned to the home terminal rather than completing the run. The employer treated it as a quit. The court used the following test. "The proper inquiry in determining whether he was discharged is whether the employee voluntarily left his position, not whether he chose to do an act for which he knew his employer would fire him."[55]

Related to this is the situation where the employer tells the employees that they will receive certain benefits if they quit, but they will not receive the benefits if they are discharged. Based on the representation, the employees quit but then find that they do not receive the benefits. This may be treated as a discharge rather than a quit.[56]

When an employee is laid off, it is usually the end of the employment relationship, but there may be exceptions to this general rule. One court has stated: "A person who has ordered his life around a particular job, built up experience and seniority in the position, and has a reasonable expectation of being recalled to that position stands in a far different position than an employment applicant."[57] The court may have found an implied clause in the employment contract about recall rights.

CONCLUSION

Identification of an actual employment relationship and identification of the proper employer and the proper employee to the contract are critical preliminary questions that must be confronted by persons seeking to exercise rights under an individual employment contract. Where the employer and employee do not match, there is no employment relationship and no employment contract. Where an employment relationship once existed, the parties must look to doctrine of quits, discharge, and constructive discharge to determine where there are any possible rights that might be claimed under the employment contract.

A number of elements must be considered in determining whether an employment relationship exists. If an employment relationship is found, other characteristics must be identified. Paramount among these other characteristics is the public sector - private sector distinction. Figure 1.1 summarizes some of these issues.

From this point on in these materials, it is generally assumed that there is or was an employment relationship between the parties, and

Figure 1.1 Is There an Employment Relationship?

EMPLOYMENT RELATIONSHIP	OTHER RELATIONSHIP
Employment Contact	Independent Contractor
Statutory Definition, Public Sector	Statutory Definition Not
Statutory Definition, Private Sector	Met
Constructive Discharge Claim	Public Sector Financial
Public Sector Financial Support	Support
Parent, Subsidiary Structure	Discharge For Cause
	Voluntary Quit
	Parent, Subsidiary
	Structure
	Partner, Shareholder

proper identification of the employer has been made. It is important, however, to keep in mind that these issues of identification are powerful defenses for employers who have disputes with employees. Both sides must give close attention to these vital, preliminary matters.

NOTES

1. L. Merrifield, T. St. Antoine, and C. Craver, Labor Relations Law 42 (1989).
2. Darlington v. General Elec., 2 Indiv. Empl. Rights (BNA) 1666 (Pa. Super. Ct. 1986).
3. Hishon v. King & Spalding, 104 S. Ct. 2229, 2233 (1984).
4. Quinn v. Limited Express, Inc., 715 F. Supp. 127 (D. Pa. 1989).
5. Nat'l Treasury Employees Union v. Von Raab, 109 S. Ct. 1384 (1989).
6. Moore v. American Batmag Corp., 710 F. Supp. 1050 (D. N.C. 1989).
7. Wall v. U.S. Dept. of Health and Human Services, 871 F.2d 1540 (10th Cir. 1989).
8. In re Hearing Centers of America, Inc., 106 B.R. 719 (Bankruptcy Ct., Fla. 1989).
9. Moraine Indus. Supply, Inc. v. Sterling Rubber Products Co., 891 F.2d 133 (6th Cir. 1989).
10. Adams v. Bainbridge - Decatur Co. Hospital Auth., 888 F.2d 1356 (11th Cir. 1989).
11. Utley v. Goldman Sachs & Co., 883 F.2d 184 (1st Cir. 1989).
12. Dole v. Haulaway, Inc., 29 Wage & Hour Cas. (BNA) 873 (D. N.J. 1989).
13. Pettypool v. Ariz. Dep't of Economic Security, 777 P.2d 230 (Ariz. Ct. App. 1989).
14. Keating v. Burton, 545 N.E.2d 35 (Ind. Ct. App. 1989).
15. City of Warrensville Heights v. Jennings, 1989 WL 117301 (Ohio Ct. App. 1989) (Text in Westlaw).
16. Retirement Equity Act of 1984, 29 U.S.C.A. 1055.
17. Dake v. Mutual of Omaha Ins. Co., 35 Empl. Prac. Dec. (CCH) 34,881 (D. Ohio 1984).
18. Donovan v. Brandel, dba Jerry Brandel Farms, 101 Lab. Cas. (CCH) 34,555 (6th Cir. 1984).
19. North American Van Lines, Inc. v. NLRB, 111 Lab. Cas. (BNA) 10,982 (D.C. Cir. 1989); Rosenfeld v. Thirteenth St. Corp., 4 Indiv. Empl. Rights (BNA) 770 (Okla. Sup. Ct. 1989). Sisters of St. Mary v. Blair, 2 Indiv. Empl. Rights (BNA) 866 (Mo. Ct. App. 1987). C. Morris, II The Developing Labor Law 1464–1474 (1983).
20. EEOC v. Dowd & Dowd, 736 F.2d 1177 (7th Cir. 1984); Note, "Coming of Age in the Professional Corporation: Liability of Professional Corporations for Dismissal of Members Under the Age Discrimination In Employment Act," 48 Univ. Pitt. L. Rev. 1185 (1987).
21. Holland v. Ernst & Whinney, 35 Empl. Prac. Dec. (CCH) 34,653 (D. N.C. 1984).
22. E.g., ORS 68.010–68.650 (1985).

23. Civil Rights Act of 1964, 42 U.S.C. 2000(e)(b).

24. ORS 659.020(6) (1985).

25. Brenimer v. Great Western Sugar Co., 567 F. Supp. 218 (D. Colo. 1983).

26. Perrin v. Florida Power & Light Co., 34 Empl. Prac. Dec. (CCH) 34,413 (D. Fla. 1984). See also Curto v. Sears, Roebuck & Co., 34 Empl. Prac. Dec. (CCH) 34,579 (D. Ill. 1984).

27. Hague v. Spencer Turbine Co., 28 Empl. Prac. Dec. (CCH) 32,575 (D. N.C. 1982).

28. Lang v. El Paso Nat. Gas Co., 35 Empl. Prac. Dec. (CCH) 34,646 (D. Tex. 1984).

29. Falls v. Sporting News, 2 Indiv. Empl. Rights (BNA) 1241 (6th Cir. 1987).

30. Coopwood v. Res-Care, Inc., 37 Empl. Prac. Dec. (CCH) 35,264 at 37,826 (D. Ind. 1984).

31. Newman v. Legal Services Corp., 628 F. Supp. 535 (D. D.C. 1986).

32. Morton v. Spectrum Fabrics Corp., 2 Indiv. Empl. Rights (BNA) 856 (Cal. Ct. App. 1987).

33. D'Ulisse-Cupo v. Bd. of Directors, 2 Indiv. Empl. Rights (BNA) 948 (Conn. S. Ct. 1987).

34. Grey v. First Nat'l Bank of Chicago, 3 Indiv. Empl. Rights (BNA) 504 (Ill. App. Ct. 1988); Bd. of Trustees v. Fineran, 3 Indiv. Empl. Rights (BNA) 1651 (Md. Ct. App. 1988).

35. Naes Fuel v. Wash, 90 Lab. Arb. (BNA) 149 (O'Grady, Arb. 1988).

36. Hinthorn v. Roland's of Bloomington Inc., 3 Indiv. Empl. Rights (BNA) 434 (Ill. S. Ct. 1988).

37. Beye v. BNA, 2 Indiv. Empl. Rights (BNA) 1843 (Md. Ct. App. 1984). See also, Sivel v. Readers Digest Inc., 2 Indiv. Empl. Rights (BNA) 1880 (D. N.Y. 1988).

38. Bulaich v. AT&T Information Systems, 778 P.2d 1031 (Wash. Sup. Ct. 1989).

39. Thompson v. John L. Williams Co., 3 Indiv. Empl. Rights (BNA) 623 (D. Ga. 1988).

40. Morton v. Spectrum Fabrics Corp., 2 Indiv. Empl. Rights (BNA) 856 (Cal. Ct. App. 1987), but see Carroll v. Pennsylvania, 2 Indiv. Empl. Rights (BNA) 1878 (Pa. C'Wealth Ct. 1988) where the benefit was conditioned on taking an illegal polygraph test and the employee quit.

41. Rutan v. Republican Party of Ill., 4 Indiv. Empl. Rights (BNA) 445, 451 (7th Cir. 1989).

42. Lombardo v. Oppenheimer, 701 F. Supp. 29 (D. Conn. 1987).

43. Garner v. Wal-Mart Stores, Inc., 807 F.2d 1536 (11th Cir. 1987); Lombardo v. Oppenheimer, 701 F. Supp. 29 (D. Conn. 1987).

44. Sheets v. Knight, 779 P.2d 1000 (Or. Sup. Ct. 1989).

45. Panopulos v. Westinghouse Electric Corp., 264 Cal. Rptr. 810 (Cal. Ct. App. 1989).

46. Fischhaber v. G.M.C., 436 N.W.2d 386 (Mich. Ct. App. 1989).

47. Missouri Comm. On Human Rights v. City of Sikeston, 769 S.W.2d 798 (Mo. Ct. App. 1989); Snell v. Montana-Dakota Utilities Co., 643 P.2d 841 (Mont. Sup. Ct. 1982); Glasgow v. Georgia Pacific Corp., 693 P.2d 708 (Wash. Sup. Ct. 1985).

48. Bruhwiler v. Univ. of Tenn., 859 F.2d 419 (6th Cir. 1988); Jenkins v. Southeastern Mich. Chapter, American Red Cross, 369 N.W.2d 223 (Mich. Ct. App. 1985).

49. International Mill Service, Inc., 88 Lab. Arb. (BNA) 118 (McAlpin, Arb. 1986). See also Burrow v. Westinghouse Elec. Corp., 2 Indiv. Empl. Rights (BNA) 1725 (N.C. Ct. App. 1988).

50. Wylie v. The Marley Co., 891 F.2d 1463 (10th Cir. 1989).

51. Petrella v. Siegal, 534 N.E.2d 41 (N.Y. Ct. App. 1988).

52. Borough of California v. Horner, 565 A.2d 1250 (Pa. C'Wealth Ct. 1989).

53. Sinkevich v. School Comm. of Raynham, 530 N.E.2d 173 (Mass. Sup. Ct. 1988).

54. Rose v. Green, 536 N.Y.S.2d 822 (N.Y. App. Div. 1989).

55. Burrow v. Westinghouse Elec. Corp., 2 Indiv. Empl. Rights (BNA) 1725 (N.C. Ct. App. 1988).

56. Staggs v. Blue Cross of Md. Inc., 2 Indiv. Empl. Rights (BNA) 1018 (Md. Ct. App. 1985).

57. Rutan v. Republican Party of Ill., 4 Indiv. Empl. Rights (BNA) 445, 457 (7th Cir. 1989).

Forums and Remedies for Individual Contract Disputes

INTRODUCTION

Most individual contract disputes are probably never litigated. However, an increasing number of these disputes are being considered in a variety of dispute resolution forums.[1] This chapter looks at some of the characteristics of some of the forums and the commonly available remedies. The forums considered are courts, arbitration, in house non-union grievance mechanisms, due process, hearings and agencies. In addition, the problem of remedies is discussed. The emphasis is on the forums as they relate to disputes involving individual employment contracts.

It is important to be aware of some of the major characteristics of the various dispute resolution forums. In some situations there may be a choice of forums available to the complaining party, usually the employee. Selection of the initial forum will involve balancing various tactical elements. Where there is no choice of initial forum, the complaining party must determine whether that forum will make resolution of the dispute worth the time and expense that it may entail. For the defending party, usually the employer, the employee's choice of forum may dictate some of the defensive arguments and tactics that may be used to defeat or wear down the other side.

Several questions are common to the contract dispute resolution forums considered in this chapter. These questions include the extent of forum restraint when dealing with individual contract disputes, procedure, burden of proof, presumptions, period of limitations, exhaustion, and scope of judicial review. One aspect of review of forum restraint is to identify any descriptions given by the forum about how the forum views its role vis-à-vis the employer and the employee. This may manifest itself in expressions of greater or lesser self-restraint on how far the forum should intrude into the employment relationship when interpreting the contract. There may be statements to the effect that business-employment decisions are primarily an employer or management right. Procedure is an important aspect of forum review. Procedural rules of the forum will identify who has the evidentiary burden of proof. Presumptions favoring one side, usually the employer, may affect the outcome. There will be a period of limitations or time after which the forum will no longer consider the dispute. The employee may be required to use or "exhaust" preliminary forums or steps before being permitted to appeal to a higher decisional level or to the courts. Whether an employer or employee considers the forum to be fair may depend largely upon the procedures being used.

The following sections discuss various forums and remedies for employment disputes. Figure 2.1 gives a brief overview of some of these matters.

COURTS

Diversity: State, Federal

The first characteristic of the judicial system, for these purposes, is its diversity. Fifty different state court systems are deciding similar

Figure 2.1 Dispute Resolution Forums

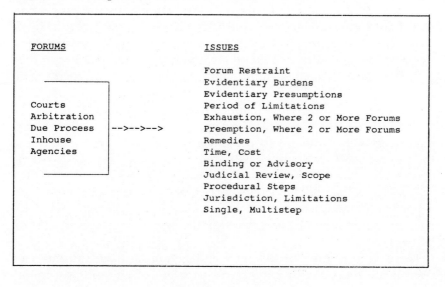

```
FORUMS                    ISSUES

                          Forum Restraint
                          Evidentiary Burdens
                          Evidentiary Presumptions
Courts                    Period of Limitations
Arbitration               Exhaustion, Where 2 or More Forums
Due Process   -->-->-->   Preemption, Where 2 or More Forums
Inhouse                   Remedies
Agencies                  Time, Cost
                          Binding or Advisory
                          Judicial Review, Scope
                          Procedural Steps
                          Jurisdiction, Limitations
                          Single, Multistep
```

employment contract disputes. Different states often reach dissimilar results on similar facts. In addition, individual contract disputes may go into the federal court system, again with varying results in different federal districts or circuits. The federal courts may handle combination federal and state claims. The federal courts may have to interpret and apply the state law to those parts of mixed federal and state claims being made by the employee.

The judge made or common law must be identified or created in each separate state jurisdiction, unless the jurisdiction has an applicable statute. A court in one state need not recognize a rule from another state, and in this individual employment area, many do not. Similarly, the rule in one federal circuit is not necessarily going to be followed in another federal circuit.

One result of this diversity is that employees and employers may have significantly different rights depending upon the jurisdiction in which the claim is made. Some courts will read employer rights in a broad manner; others will be more restrictive. In addition, the area of individual employment contract law is undergoing reanalysis, and the rules are changing in many jurisdictions. Neither employers nor employees can be entirely certain of their rights at a given time and place without researching the latest decisions in their particular jurisdiction. Many states are also considering legislation that will modify the way in which disputes involving individual employment contracts are handled.

Statutes will also contribute to diversity at the state level. Each state's statutory scheme is likely to have some approaches that differ from other states. Statutes may require that the plaintiff employee use or exhaust statutory forums and procedures before proceeding to court with the dispute. By way of comparison, in private sector collective bargaining contracts, federal law (National Labor Relations Act) is paramount. This single statute and its forum, the National Labor Relations Board, tend to make it a more unified body of practice than the diverse law of individual, noncollective employment contracts.

The judicial diversity must be kept in mind when reading these materials, which attempt to present a broad summary of views of individual contract disputes gathered from many state and federal courts. This generalized approach will identify many important issues and concepts that will have relevance in most jurisdictions. However, a particular jurisdiction must be examined to determine what its particular rule might be on any one of the general concepts discussed below.

The diverse nature of the state and federal judicial forums may complicate the plaintiff employee's problem of choosing an initial forum. This complication may provide the employer with procedural defenses against the employee's action in court.

JUDICIAL RESTRAINT AND INDIVIDUAL CONTRACTS

One of the most important characteristics of the judicial forum is the doctrine of self-imposed judicial restraint under which the courts decide individual employment claims. The role of the courts in employment disputes is significantly limited by the court's self-created concept of judicial restraint. The courts discuss these limitations at greatest length in cases involving individual employment contracts, particularly when an indefinite term or at will contract is at issue. However, the doctrine of judicial restraint also applies to judicial approaches to disputes involving collective bargaining contracts.

Judicial restraint is manifested primarily in the statements of appellate courts that are reviewing decisions made at the trial level. Trial judges must give weight to these statements. The fact that juries may occasionally return large verdicts in favor of plaintiff employees does not diminish the impact of the judicial admonitions about judicial restraint.

Numerous reasons are given for the existence of the doctrine of judicial restraint. The reasons all tend in the same direction. That direction is one of deferring to the employer in close or doubtful cases. A variety of rationales are given for the doctrine of judicial restraint. These rationales are based on the court's view of the appropriate public policy to be applied to employment disputes. One of the reasons given for the court's reluctance to delve deeply into the employee's individual contract complaints against the employer is that courts say that they do not want to "weigh" the evidence concerning employee conduct for themselves. They do not wish to substitute their judgment on the "weight" of the evidence for the judgment of the employer. In the common situation of a dispute over whether there was adequate performance by the employee, the court is unlikely to make its own independent evaluation of how poor or good the performance of the employee was. The court will not expand its role merely because the employee claims the employer made a mistake. In the context of public employment, the Supreme Court has stated a general judicial rule applicable to disputes in the employment area: "We must accept the harsh fact that numerous individual mistakes are inevitable in the day-to-day administration of our affairs."[2]

The Supreme Court has also warned courts to be cautious when the courts review the business judgment decision of the employer, unless the courts are required by statute to conduct a more extensive review.

"Courts are generally less competent than employers to restructure business practices, and unless mandated to do so by Congress they should not attempt it."[3] However, even the presence of a statute is not to be seen as an open invitation to the court to redetermine the facts concerning, for example, the employer's judgment about the employee's performance. Under Title VII, for example, courts state that the lawsuit is not about the defendant employer's business judgment.[4]

Additional reasons are given by the courts for their reluctance to fully review or "second guess" the employer's rationale. One of the additional reasons is said to be the complex nature of the employment relationship, with its "multifarious" aspects.[5] The court may perceive itself to be ill equipped to resolve "complex" employer - employee disputes. The courts express a desire not to second guess the employer. They do not want to impose an outsider's judgment on the employment relationship,[6] "unless mandated to do so by Congress."[7]

Some courts say that they do not want to become the "bargaining agent" for the nonunion employee.[8] This "bargaining agent" argument is one example of some of the many inconsistencies found in the statements of various courts. The inconsistency arises because some courts have also noted that one of the factors favoring individual contract employment law reform is that the bargaining power between the employer and the employee may be inequitably distributed.[9]

Courts say that they do not want to foment unwarranted employee versus employer litigation.[10] The rationale apparently is that by providing the employee with only limited rights in dispute resolution, the employees will be generally discouraged from seeking any redress against employers. Courts indicate that they do not want to foment litigation when they are unable to correct managerial deficiencies, even though the decisions may adversely affect the employee.[11] The courts do not want to be seen as trying to run the business and they cannot turn poor managers into good managers.

Courts are quick to pass the buck and urge that such complex matters as the reform of the mechanism for handling employment disputes should be left to legislative resolution.[12] The courts do not discuss whether this is because the problem is inherently legislative or whether, having created a judicial rule concerning individual contract disputes that is increasingly under challenge, some courts now wish to back away from the problem.[13] Legislation does have the advantage of being able to mandate either a broader or a narrower role for the court in overseeing how the employer operates the business and the employment relationship.[14]

The effect of the court's reluctance to deeply scrutinize the employer's personnel actions is a major factor that increases the employer's rights in a individual contract discharge situation. Employees are given a double burden. One burden is to overcome the court's self-imposed restraint and show that the employee's claim is not an unwarranted intrusion into employer decesion making. Then the employee must focus on the actual dispute and demonstrate that the employer's actions were a violation of the individual contract of employment, or a violation of some other duty owed to the employee. If the court feels that it should not second guess the employer as a matter of judicial restraint based on public policy considerations, the merits of the employee's claim will not be considered.

Many feel that the restrained judicial approach is the proper public policy action in a free enterprise economic system. The courts have been warned about "restructuring" business practices unless mandated by legislation.[15] The Supreme Court has also noted that "we know from our experience that more often than not people do not act in a totally arbitrary manner, without any underlying reasons, especially in a business setting."[16] If the limited judicial role is seen as a requirement of the capitalist, free enterprise economic system, then legislative rather than judicial reform becomes the necessary route for change, if any. Where the court is operating under a statute, it may be somewhat less reluctant to examine the reasons given by the employer because the public policy balance between employees and employers has been debated and resolved.

In summary, courts have made a major public policy choice in adopting the doctrine of judicial restraint in employment disputes. This is a longstanding doctrine that protects employer's personnel decisions that are challenged by employees. The courts base the public policy of judicial restraint on a combination of economic doctrine and institutional self-doubt. It is likely that the economic doctrine is the paramount consideration.

Burden and Presumption

Judicial procedure can play an important role in the resolution of the employment dispute in court. Judicial procedure is formal and complex. The goal here is to illustrate a few of the procedural issues that may have direct impact on the discharge dispute. It is not an attempt to consider all of the relevant procedural issues that can arise. Burden of proof is always a major consideration. In any trial situation, the overall burden of proof is upon the complaining party, who will usually be the employee.[17] The burden of proof is especially important in close cases, and many discharge cases are close. A common circumstance that gives rise to close cases is where the facts on each side are essentially in balance and the result will depend on which side has the greater credibility. In a close case where the evidence is otherwise more or less equally balanced, the party with the burden of proof, usually the employee, is likely to lose because the employee may be seen as not carrying the burden of proof. The Supreme Court has stated this idea in a related situation involving job qualifications and safety issues. "When the employer's argument has a credible basis in the record, it is difficult to believe that a jury of lay persons . . . would not defer in a close case to the (employer) airline's judgment."[18] Judicial restraint is an additional consideration in the close case that may help tip the balance against the employee with the burden of proof.

A presumption used by most courts plays a very important role in individual employment discharge disputes. In the absence of a provable fixed term contract, the court will presume that the individual employment relationship involves an at will contract.[19] Generally, presumptions are rebuttable with proper proof. However, some courts will treat the at will presumption as though it were virtually irrebuttable. Once the court has invoked this presumption, the employee has the burden of attempting to overcome it, but the employee is often unable to do this because the usual, unwritten employment contract is so informal that objective proof of specific terms, such as duration, cannot be shown. Thus where the employee has no written contract, the employee will be presumed to be an at will employee. The unrebutted at will presumption justifies the arbitrary discharge of the employee.

The procedural stage at which many discharge cases are decided by the courts is on the defendant employer's motion to dismiss. This motion is usually made at the end of the employee's initial presentation. The plaintiff employee is required to initially put forward enough evidence to show the existence of a potentially provable claim, or a prima facie case. If the employee fails to put forward this initial prima facie case (e.g., evidence that might rebut the at will presumption), the court may rule in favor of the employer's motion to dismiss because the employee is at will. If the employee puts forth a sufficient opening case, the motion to dismiss may be denied and the matter will proceed to the merits. Frequently, the employee can only show the existence of an unwritten contract, which is then presumed to be an at will agreement. Because the employer can arbitrarily discharge the employee under an at will agreement, the court may then grant the employer's motion to dismiss.

These procedural moves make it important to carefully read the discharge cases to determine what the court really ruled. In many reported cases in which the court appears to rule for the employee, frequently all that the court has ruled is that the employer's motion to dismiss has been denied. Such a ruling does not mean that the employee will win the case on the merits, it only means that the employee is entitled to go forward and attempt to factually prove the claim. Carrying the overall burden of proof is usually difficult.

In summary, courts take a very restrained approach to the exercise of their power in individual employment contract disputes. Courts are reluctant to second guess the employer. Court procedures such as the use of the at will presumption and the amount of evidence needed to meet the complaining employee's burden of proof are additional elements that tip the scale in the employer's favor in close cases. The diversity of the various state court systems means that the plaintiff employees in different states may experience very different outcomes, in part depending upon the degree of judicial restraint and the strength of the presumption of at will status. The diversity of judicial forums makes it difficult to determine employee rights in the different states. Employers who have multistate operations may find themselves faced with a variety of different rules, or even a variety of conflicting rules. Judicial procedures may make it difficult for the employee to present his or her case fully once the employer has made a motion to dismiss. The difficulty of getting consideration of their full story may make courts a frustrating forum for many employees.

ARBITRATION

Individual and Collective Contracts

Grievance arbitrators are commonly used in employer-employee disputes that are based on a collective bargaining contract.[20] Collective bargaining contracts rarely provide for at will employment. The collective contract usually has a definite duration or term, as well as a cause requirement for discharge. Arbitrators therefore work in a contractual system that puts more mutually agreed upon limits on the employer than does the individual contract, at will system in which the courts usually work. It is useful to look at arbitration even though currently it rarely applies in individual contract cases because arbitration is the most frequently suggested alternative to the current judicial approach to individual contract disputes.

Arbitration and Courts

Many higher level employees are not eligible for collective bargaining coverage because they are supervisors or otherwise excluded from coverage under the National Labor Relations Act.[21] As a result of these restrictions, arbitrators will not be involved in cases involving them. Arbitrators, therefore, do not commonly deal with as wide a range of employment contracts or with the full range of the class of all employees that courts do. Nonetheless, the arbitrator's comments are important in helping to describe the nature of the employment relationship and to identify their views on deference to the employer's judgment.

The role of the courts and the role of the arbitrators are substantially different.[22] Despite these differences, arbitrators, like courts, often talk about the limitations on their powers. They state that they do not want to second guess an employer's judgment.[23] One arbitrator has expressed the following view of the role of the arbitrator:

> He (the arbitrator) might say to the employer: I think you have acted unwisely, and if I had been in your place I would have acted differently. But the fact is, I am not in your place. It is your responsibility, not mine, to manage the enterprise, and I will not substitute my judgment for your own as to the wisdom of what you did. I will, however, subject it to the test of reasonableness— review your exercise of managerial discretion to determine whether it has been arbitrary, capricious, or discriminatory.[24]

Despite the disclaimers, the arbitrator will usually be less restrained than a court in reviewing a discharge decision. As the foregoing quotation states, arbitrators are authorized to test the reasonableness of the employer's determination under the terms of the collective bargaining contract. A reasonableness test usually requires some evidence to support a discharge decision and collective bargaining contracts usually have some form of a just cause requirement for discharge.

The arbitrator is more likely than a court to exercise an expanded review of the employer's decision. The collective bargaining contract empowers the arbitrator to exercise his or her review judgment. The collective bargaining contract puts the arbitrator in a different position, relative to the parties, than a court.[25] One commentator has given the following description of some of the differences:

> The [U.S. Supreme] Court forcefully reaffirms that the parties have selected the *arbitrator* to interpret their agreement. It is the

arbitrator's interpretation that they have bargained for. The courts must honor the award if its essence is drawn from the agreement even though a court could reach and may prefer a different interpretation: provided, however, that the award must not order the performance of an unlawful act or one that would violate a strong public policy.[26]

There are additional differences between courts and arbitrators. The arbitrator is invited into the conflict by the parties. The parties have voluntarily contracted to be bound by the decision of the arbitrator. The contract with the agreement to be bound by the decision of the arbitrator is presumably the result of a mutual agreement between the parties. A court is not selected by both parties as a forum for dispute resolution; rather, it is selected by the unilateral action of the plaintiff employee. The selection of an individual arbitrator is also a mutual decision by the employer and union. The arbitrator decides on the basis of a written contract, but the court frequently must decide when there is no written contract. The court is frequently dealing with an at will situation, whereas the arbitrator is dealing with a contract with a cause requirement for discharge. "The arbitrator . . . considers all the evidence and decides whether management's determination should be upheld as being reasonably supported by the evidence and as not having been influenced by improper elements such as arbitrariness, caprice, or discrimination."[27]

In summary, the arbitrator is working in a system where the employer has agreed to limitations on the employer's entrepreneurial rights, while the court is frequently dealing with an at will contract that places no or few restrictions on the employer's entrepreneurial rights. Whereas arbitration rarely applies to an individual contract, it is the most commonly suggested alternative to the current system of judicial contract dispute resolution. It is uncertain whether the proposed use of arbitration in individual contract cases will involve the same procedures as arbitration under collective bargaining contracts.

Court Review of the Arbitrator

The courts give the collective bargaining grievance arbitrator a great deal of latitude in resolving an employment dispute. The courts achieve this result through the process of severely limiting judicial review of an arbitrator's decision. The limited scope of review is the result of the Supreme Court's identification of the national labor policy favoring private dispute resolution found in the National Labor

Relations Act.[28] This greatly diminishes the relative role of the courts in collective bargaining contract disputes, which generally means that it is unlikely that a court will overturn a decision of the arbitrator.[29] For example, whereas courts feel themselves to be bound by their own judicial precedents, courts tolerate conflicting arbitral decisions on identical factual situations.[30] Courts will sustain an arbitrator's decision even if the decision was erroneous.[31] Courts permit the arbitrator to make a mistake, "even a mistake of law."[32]

> Insuring uniformity of arbitral decisions is not a compelled function of judicial review. The parties to the controlling contract may well have bargained for possibly disparate results on "identical factual situations" as a price willingly paid for the perceived virtues of the arbitral process.[33]

Another court gave the following reasons why courts are likely to defer to arbitrators:

> [T]he arbitration process is more flexible, efficient, expedient, and less expensive than litigation; the arbitrator has more expertise in resolving controversies that arise under the industrial law of the shop than does a court of law; the parties have voluntarily agreed to submit its dispute to final and binding impartial adjudication, and arbitration is a favored alternative to other nonpeaceful methods of conflict resolution, such as strikes, boycotts, etc.[34]

In the same vein, arbitrators need not explain their decisions, although in practice they usually write opinions in labor cases. "Arbitrators are not required to elaborate their reasoning supporting an award."[35] This broad latitude contributes to the finality of the award by further reducing the role that a court might play.

In summary, the court will defer to arbitrators' expertise and decisions in most situations. This gives the collective bargaining contract and the grievance mechanism contained in the contract a special status in the employment relationship between the employer, the union, and the individual employee. Whereas the collective bargaining contract is treated as a unique contract, the individual, nonunion employment contract is not recognized as having special characteristics. The nonunion, individual employment contract is treated as a traditional contract viewed in the context of judicial restraint, the presumption of at will status, and an elaborate theory of employer rights that are recognized in individual contract disputes.[36]

Arbitration is usually the final step in a multistep grievance procedure. The common expectation and experience are that most disputes will be settled at a prearbitral step. That settlement will commonly be made by the union and employer, with the possible involvement of the individual employee-grievant. A question of enforcement may arise where the individual employee never approved the settlement of the grievance. In one such case, a court said, "Courts are, and should be, extremely reluctant to set aside grievance settlements, even if never approved by the individual grievant. Our national labor policy is premised on an assumption that 'the employer and the union . . . will endeavor in good faith to settle grievances short of arbitration.'"[37]

Arbitration Procedure

The collective bargaining contract has a contract status different from that of the individual contract of employment. Given the legal uniqueness of the collective bargaining agreement, it is not surprising that the arbitration procedures differ from the judicial trial hearing procedures used for the standard individual contract.

Collective bargaining requirements imposed on employers in discipline situations are fairly complex. Common requirements in the collective bargaining context include the prior promulgation of standards of employee conduct, dissemination of the standards, progressive discipline for offenses, requirement of adequate investigation by the employer, and a determination of whether the severity of the discipline is appropriate for the offense. The collective bargaining grievance mechanism often provides for a "due process" type of hearing procedure at or near the worksite that is not available in the formalized, win-lose judicial discharge case. The employee (or union) is entitled to present the employee's side of the story. The burden of proof in discharge cases may be placed on the employer to show the existence of cause or just cause for the discharge.[38]

The common use of an arbitrator's power of mitigation is a unique and important element in collective bargaining contract arbitration. The employer's choice of discipline must be matched to the employee's transgressions.[39] If the discipline is disproportionately greater than the offense, many contracts give the arbitrator the power to mitigate the discipline. For example, a discharge may be reduced to a lesser penalty, such as a suspension. Courts, in contrast, usually do not require use of a just cause based standard for discharge and do not exercise a power of mitigation in reviewing the individual employment contract discharge. Courts also place the burden of proof on the employee as the complaining party.

Where a private sector collective bargaining contract is in effect, the contract will usually be governed by the federal National Labor Relations Act. Under the federal law, a dispute involving the contract must first be resolved through the grievance mechanism established in the contract.[40] An employee complainant must exhaust the grievance mechanism. If an attempt is made to go to court before using this mechanism, the federal courts are required to refer the parties back to the contract mechanism. This exhaustion requirement is also important because the contractual time period or the period of limitations to bring a claim under the contract is usually quite short,[41] a matter of days or weeks at most. If the complainant does not exhaust the contract mechanism within the contractual period of limitation, the contract claim is lost. Once the claim is lost under the contract period of limitations, it cannot be revived by raising the same issue in court.

Usually, the only claims that can be raised under the contract grievance mechanism are contract claims. An employment claim based on law or statutes outside of the contract usually will be rejected by the arbitrator.[42] If the contract does not incorporate outside law, the employee must rely on courts or agencies. This can lead to procedural complications where a discharged employee is making several claims, some based on the contract and some based on other sources of rights.

In summary, the collective bargaining grievance arbitration process leaves the employer, employee, and the union largely to their mutually agreed upon procedures to work out contract disputes. Judicial restraint in arbitration is manifested by limited review deferring to the judgment of the arbitrator rather than to the employer's judgment. The use of grievance arbitration is mostly found in collective bargaining contracts, not individual contracts. However, arbitration is occasionally used for individual contracts, and it is the most commonly suggested alternative dispute resolution forum for individual contracts. Where individual contract arbitration exists, the employee usually must exhaust it before attempting to proceed to court. One of the major remedial differences between collective bargaining grievance arbitration and courts is the arbitrator's power to mitigate a severe punishment. The popularity of the arbitration model, as shown by judicial deference, makes it an ideal model of comparison for other dispute resolution forums for individual contract disputes.

There are great differences in the treatment of individual contract and collective contract disputes. However, because a basic employment relationship lies at the heart of both disputes and contracts, the differences in treatment raise the question of whether the differences are warranted in fact.

A major question in the proposed reform of the at will doctrine is the role of arbitration. If the proposals for arbitration mean collective bargaining style arbitration, then reform will have one result. If the proposals for arbitration mean a lesser form of arbitration, then reform will have a far different result. It is incumbent upon those proposing reform to make clear in advance the nature of the arbitration that is intended.

DUE PROCESS, PUBLIC SECTOR

Hearing the Other Side

Under procedural due process hearing considerations, when a public employee has a protectable property interest (e.g., a contract) in a job, the Supreme Court has set the following as one standard for a pretermination hearing: "The tenured public employee is entitled to oral or written notice of the charges against him, an explanation of the employer's evidence, and an opportunity to present his side of the story."[43] The Supreme Court also stated that "the pretermination hearing need not definitely resolve the propriety of the discharge. It should be an initial check against mistaken decisions—essentially a determination of whether there are reasonable grounds."[44] This statement means that the due process hearing is not expected to be totally error free.

The employer also has due process rights in the discharge of an employee when government action is involved. The Supreme Court gave the following description of the due process rights of an employer who sought to discharge an employee under the terms of a contract. The government sought to delay the discharge under the whistleblower provisions of a statute.

> We conclude that minimum due process for the employer in this context requires notice of the employee's allegations, notice of the substance of the relevant supporting evidence, an opportunity to submit a written response, and an opportunity to meet with the investigator and present statements from rebuttal witnesses. The presentation of the employer's witnesses need not be formal, and cross examination of the employee's witnesses need not be afforded at this stage of the proceedings.[45]

Due process does not necessarily require an error free procedure nor does it necessarily require second guessing the employer. The purpose is to establish the reasonableness of the action.

When the judicial presumption of at will status is compared with the collective bargaining or due process model, the judicial model stands alone with its obstacles to the consideration of the employee's side of the employment dispute. Similarly, both the arbitration and due process models implicitly reject the more extreme judicial statements given in justification of the doctrine of judicial restraint. The arbitration and due process models provide for a reasonableness or fairness review of the employment dispute, whereas the judicial model gives a win-lose or right-wrong type of response. Due process and the arbitration model give both parties an opportunity to be heard; the judicial model may terminate at the earlier time of the employer's motion to dismiss based on the presumption of at will status.

In summary, due process procedures are generally what the courts describe, namely *minimal* due process. One of the most important aspects, for these purposes, of due process is the idea that the procedure is intended to be a check of the reasonableness of the employer action and not a redetermination of all factual issues. Too frequently in the case law it is easy to find employees who are basically arguing that the dispute forum should make a de novo decision. If this is not required under the Constitution, it is not likely to be required in other forums. Courts accurately point out that a dispute resolution process cannot right all wrongs in human relationships, especially in the workplace.

IN HOUSE GRIEVANCE MECHANISMS

In a collective bargaining contract context, most contracts contain a grievance mechanism culminating in binding arbitration. The grievance mechanism is specifically designed to permit the parties to resolve disputes over the meaning of the contract themselves rather than by going outside to use the courts. In the individual contract context, the use of in house grievance mechanisms is fairly new, but it is an area of growth.[46] The in house mechanism usually will not involve binding arbitration but it is a preliminary opportunity for both parties to attempt to resolve the dispute.

Various Procedures

There are a variety of inhouse grievance procedures that have been reported in the cases. A few employers provide for the arbitration of disputes in the nonunion situation.[47] A final and binding review panel may be used as the final step in a multistep grievance procedure.[48] The American Arbitration Association (AAA) has promulgated Model

Employment Arbitration Procedures for possible inhouse use in the nonunion, individual contract situation where the parties mutually agree to their use. The AAA procedures provide for an expeditious summary proceeding where the parties have agreed to summary procedures. A one day hearing process with no stenographic record would be held. Informal hearing procedures will be used. The arbitrator's award need not be accompanied by an opinion unless the parties agree otherwise. The expenses of the arbitration will be shared equally unless a different agreement is reached. The award itself will be far more summary than the traditional labor arbitrator's opinion.[49] The award may be submitted to a court for enforcement unless the parties agree that it would not be binding. Compared to traditional collective bargaining arbitration, the AAA proposal is likely to result in arbitration that is faster, cheaper, and involves less complex procedures. It may also be a little less thorough and complete.

An employer may not want final and binding arbitration, but the employer may be willing to use nonbinding, multistep appeals procedures, with the steps of appeal going up the usual employer chain of command within the workplace.[50] Some employers may follow a progressive discipline system that begins with informal counseling and ends in disciplinary probation or discharge.[51] Some inhouse systems may reflect the minimal due process considerations, such as notice and an opportunity to respond.[52] Some procedures involve group decisions where employee representatives may be permitted to sit on the reviewing committee.[53]

The event that may give rise to the use of the inhouse grievance mechanism may be narrowly or broadly defined. For example, one broadly defined mechanism is triggered "when an employee thinks or feels that any condition affecting his or her employment is unjust, inequitable, a hindrance to the satisfactory operation (sic) or creates a problem, the employee shall use the . . . procedures for the solution of such problems."[54]

A distinction should be drawn between proceedings for dispute resolution involving both the employee and the employer, and the employer's internal investigative procedures. Industrial due process considerations do not apply to internal investigative procedures that are used to determine what the company position should be in the dispute.[55] Fairness relates more to decision making than to investigation procedures.

Inhouse review bodies may only be empowered to make nonbinding recommendations to the final deciding officer. The final deciding officer may reject the recommendations. Where an employee sought to challenge such a rejection, one court stated that the employee would have to allege that the rejected recommendations were consistent with the employer's established policies and show that the policies constituted a contract with the employee. The mere fact of a favorable committee recommendation standing alone did not benefit the employee.[56]

Contract or Not

Inhouse grievance mechanisms are commonly found in employer promulgated manuals or handbooks. They raise the question of whether or not the use of the mechanism is contractually required. If the procedural manual is not found to be a binding contract, the use of the mechanism is optional with the employer. If the manual is found to be a binding contract, the employer's failure to follow the mechanism's procedures will constitute a breach of the contract. If there is no contract, the employer is free to use or ignore all or part of the procedure. The question of employee handbooks is discussed at greater length below,[57] but a brief summary would be that where the handbook has disclaimers[58] or where there is the use of words such as "may," it indicates that the procedures are nonbinding.[59] There may be no contractual obligation to use the grievance mechanism. Other cases have found the words and practices of a particular mechanism to be sufficient to have created a binding contract.[60] In numerous cases, courts have found that they need not directly answer the contract question because, whether binding or optional, evidence showed that the employer had complied with the handbook inhouse mechanism requirements.[61]

Several courts have found that the mere presence of an inhouse grievance mechanism does not necessarily imply that the mechanism must use "just cause" as the basis of the employment decision.[62] In other words, the mere availability of grievance procedures does not necessarily place a substantive restriction on the basis of the employer's exercise of discretion in making the employment discharge decision. The grievance procedures may simply provide for extended consideration.

Unanswered Issues

Several issues appear in the cases that should be noted. Although the case law is still slim, courts seem to be saying that where an inhouse grievance mechanism is available, the employee may have a duty to exhaust the mechanism before going into court.[63] This point should be watched carefully. Where one party claims that the grievance mechanism is part of an individual contract, that party will have to show that they complied with its terms.[64] If no contract exists, there would seem to be no reason why the employee should be required to exhaust the grievance mechanism.

Grievance mechanisms usually have short time limits within which they must be used.[65] Failure to use it within the limitation period may result in a forfeiture of rights if there is a contract. The time limit may be very short. For example, one clause required an employee to initiate a grievance within four days after discharge.[66] In another situation, an employee claimed that the employer discharged her as retaliation for using the inhouse grievance mechanism. The court found no public policy violation in this procedure.[67] It seems unfair, however, that one court would require an employee to exhaust a grievance mechanism as a prelude to further judicial action, and another court would permit the employer to discharge the employee in retaliation for the employee's use of the mechanism. The general issue of retaliation for use of an inhouse mechanism is also something that has to be carefully watched, because there is little case law to date.

Where an inhouse mechanism is used, there is always a question of what scope of review the court will employ, if the decision gets into court. In a case involving nonunion arbitration, the court gave the arbitrator's decision the same deferential and limited review that they would have given the decision of an arbitrator under a collective bargaining agreement.[68] Judicial restraint and deference to employer rights policies may favor finding that the outcome of a procedurally fair inhouse procedure is subject only to limited judicial review.

A recurring question in the cases is the due process related issue of how neutral the decisionmakers in an inhouse mechanism must be. For example, the claim may be made that employees who are on an inhouse grievance mechanism review committee may feel that they must vote in favor of the employer in order to keep their jobs or their benefits. By way of analogy, the usual inhouse constitutional due process hearing in the public sector does not require an impartial judge at the pretermination hearing.[69] Where a general claim of bias is made without any specific facts showing actual bias, a court is likely to reject the argument.[70] At this point, it seems clear that the inhouse grievance system need not show the relatively high level of impartiality required in collective contract grievance arbitration. Similarly, where an employee alleged that the detailed grievance mechanism was used to harass the employee, a court refused to review the claim because constructive discharge was not a viable concept in an action for retaliatory discharge.[71]

Courts will have to determine what weight to give a decision reached in a nonbinding inhouse grievance mechanism if the matter is appealed to court. The Supreme Court has considered the question of what weight to give to a collective bargaining arbitrator's award when the complaining party subsequently brought a court action on the same claim. The Court adopted "no standards as to the weight to be accorded an arbitral decision," but told the lower courts to look to such matters as procedural fairness and the competence of the arbitrator. The Supreme Court indicated that the arbitrator's decision might be given "great weight."[72] Statutory employment discrimination claims are probably entitled to greater judicial scrutiny than breach of individual employment contract claims. If the arbitrator's award in such a case might be entitled to "great weight," a fair and impartial inhouse decision on a mere contract claim should also be entitled to great weight, in appropriate circumstances.[73]

In summary, there has been new interest in the use of inhouse grievance mechanisms as forums to resolve disputes involving individual contracts of employment. It is likely that this trend will continue. The inhouse mechanisms may be binding or nonbinding and come in a great variety of procedural styles. There are a number of unanswered questions that are common to most systems. Paramount among those questions are issues of the neutrality of the decision-maker, the exhaustion of the mechanism before going to court, and the thoroughness of whatever judicial review might be available. In other words, a fundamental question is whether a fair and contractual inhouse system will be given a finality much like collective bargaining arbitration or will it be treated as simply a procedural step to be exhausted before proceeding to a judicial determination on the merits. Nonunion inhouse grievance mechanisms that are fair in procedure and reasonable in outcome can play an important role in individual contract dispute resolution. No other class of forums has the potential to reach so many employees at so many levels.

AGENCIES

Courts play the major role in resolving disputes under individual contracts. Arbitrators and inhouse grievance mechanisms play a lesser but growing role in the interpretation of the individual employment contract. State or federal government agencies are not likely to be major players in directly interpreting individual contracts. However, the employment statutes that the agencies administer may significantly affect the individual contract environment because they frequently limit the grounds upon which an employee may be discharged. For example, two or more private sector employees acting in concert to protect working conditions may be protected from discipline under the National Labor Relations Act whether or not they are at will.[74] The employer's otherwise unlimited contractual right to discharge an at will employee may be limited by the rights protected by the National Labor Relations Board. Employees may have a right to a work environment that is free from sexual harassment under guidelines promulgated by the Equal Employment Opportunity Commission.[75] Employees may have a right to refuse hazardous work under regulations promulgated by the Secretary of Labor under the Occupational Safety and Health Act.[76] Whereas agency action is not a major theme of these materials, many of the agency decisions limit the employer's exercise of arbitrary power otherwise available under the at will or other contractual status of the individual employee.

Agency Procedure

Agency hearing procedure will be controlled primarily by the organic legislation that created the agency and, perhaps, by a general administrative procedure act. Agencies created under a statute are likely to be the first forum to interpret the legislation and its impact on the individual contract employee. The agency may have the effect of modifying some terms of the individual contract in the process of interpreting the statute. The agency's interpretations may take the form of binding legislative rules, nonbinding interpretative rules, case by case adjudication, or investigative and settlement activity. The agencies share common procedural themes with the courts and arbitrators. These common themes include the period of limitations on bringing the action, the need to use or exhaust the agency procedure before going into court, and the scope of review offered by the courts.

The statutory agency procedure is likely to begin with an agency conducted investigation to determine if there is a basis for a proceeding. If a hearing is held, it is likely to be an adversarial hearing using lawyers on both sides. Hearing procedures are likely to be similar to judicial procedures, but less formal than those used in the courtroom. Either the employee or the agency is likely to be the complaining party and they will have the burden of proof. The presumption of at will contract status is unlikely to play a major role because it is overridden by the public policy of the statute. Like arbitration and due process, the agency hearing is more likely to hear the full story from both sides than is a court because the at will presumption does not lead to a motion to dismiss by the employer. The agency decision will be subject to limited judicial review.

Where a statute provides a remedy and a forum for the complaint of the employee, the employee may be obliged to use the agency forum before using any other forum. This requirement is generally referred to as a requirement that aggrieved individuals "exhaust" their administrative remedies.[77] Failure to exhaust may mean that the court cannot consider the employee's claim and the claim may be lost.[78] Once the individual has exhausted the agency forum, the courts may be willing to conduct limited judicial review of the agency decision.

Some contract or other claims may overlap with statutory rights. Courts will attempt to balance the policies behind the statutory and nonstatutory claims to answer the exhaustion question.[79] In these cases, the relationship between the contract of employment and the role of agency must be resolved in order to determine the impact of the employment agreement.

The presence of statutory rights is giving rise to a major new individual contract issue. This new issue is the rapidly expanding question of the conditions under which the employer can require or urge the employee to agree to waive the statutory protections. The waiver question is most acute where the employer seeks to have the employee sign an unsupervised blanket waiver of rights.[80] The employer seeks the waiver as a defense against postemployment charges brought by the employee. The employer may attempt to condition special benefits or employment itself on the employee's agreement to sign the waiver.

Compared to individual contract or tort claims that the employee may use in court, the period of limitations for bringing a statutory action before an agency is usually relatively short. One of the more common periods of limitations in the federal legislation is six months.[81] If the complaint is not brought within that time limit, the statutory claim will be lost and the agency or the court will not have jurisdiction to hear the dispute thereafter.

The employee may try to combine individual contract claims with statutory claims. This can lead to difficult procedural issues that may send the employee to the agency before proceeding further in court. The presence of statutory claims may compel the court to exercise somewhat less judicial restraint than it would exercise on an individual contract claim standing alone. The public policy of the statute may require the court to override prohibited employer personnel decisions.

In summary, the major forum for resolving disputes over individual contracts of employment is likely to be a court. The individual employee in the judicial forum must contend with the serious obstacles of the doctrine of judicial restraint and the presumption of at will contract status. The other major forums, arbitration, due process, and agencies, do not use these obstacles with the same rigor as the courts. Inhouse grievance mechanisms vary widely as to the amount of restriction the employer is willing to put on his or her discretion. Forums other than courts share a number of basic issues, including exhaustion, period of limitations, and scope of judicial review. Agencies may not have to directly interpret contracts of employment, but they may override some employer powers granted under the at will doctrine.

Agencies are likely to be an increasingly popular forum for employee disputes as the number of statutes granting rights to employees increases. When courts say that reform of the at will doctrine is a legislative issue, they may be indirectly correct. The common law gives employees few rights in today's workplace. Statutes, although often subject matter specific, provide relief from some employer actions. Statutes also may provide an agency forum that not only must be used before going to court, but the agency may provide expert staff to help handle the employee's complaints. The unintended result of the judicial forum unwilling to respond to employee concerns may be the creation of large numbers of agencies that infringe deeply into the employer's rights that courts often seek to protect. A major limitation on the agency forum is narrow subject matter jurisdiction. As the number of statutes and agencies grow, the amount of procedural complication and problem of choice of forums expands. As a model of study, the arbitration forum deserves increased study because of its apparent ability to handle a wide range of subject matters of dispute. In contrast, the expertise of a specialized agency is also a powerful attraction. However, dilution of employer and employee concerns through an excessive proliferation of single subject agencies is probably not in the public interest.

CHOICE OF FORUM

Forum selection between courts, arbitrators, inhouse mechanisms, or agencies can become complex. All or most of the employee's claims are likely to arise out of the single act of discipline or discharge. Contract, tort, and statutory claims may all be involved. A variety of factors may be involved in making the selection of the forum.

Time

A major factor in any employee's consideration of whether to bring a lawsuit in the judicial forum is the time that it takes to reach resolution. A number of years can pass between the event and the final resolution of the dispute in court.[82] Discovery of evidence and trial preparation can take a long time. Courts are frequently backlogged on trial dates. Agencies may also be slow to respond. Some agencies are months or years behind in investigating and processing statutory complaints. Arbitration is often the better choice where time is of the essence and where arbitration is available, although arbitration can easily take a year or more before the matter is finally resolved.[83] Where final and binding arbitration exists, the employee's only choice is to exhaust the contractual grievance - arbitration procedures. One of the reasons for the relative popularity of arbitration is the savings in time and money that can occur compared to a lawsuit.[84] However, many higher level employees are not eligible for collective bargaining and, therefore, do not have arbitration as a choice.

Cost

The cost factor is such that the most likely employee to sue, or be able to find a lawyer to take the case for a contingent fee, is the higher level employee who has the potential for a significant monetary recovery. The costs of a lawsuit include the investigation, preparation for the hearing, the cost of the actual hearing, and perhaps the cost of an appeal. This may help to explain the disproportionately large number of long-term, higher level employees who are represented in the court cases, as compared to other types of employees. The combination of years, seniority, and higher salaries makes the potential recovery significant enough to warrant the suit, which will often be undertaken on a contingent fee contract. However, higher level employees have a very difficult case because the courts often show greater deference to the employer's decisions in disputes involving these higher level employees.

The average employee may find that the potential recovery does not warrant the expense of a lawsuit or that a lawyer may not wish to take the case on a contingent fee. If the employee can take the complaint to a state or federal agency, the agency and its expert staff may investigate, prepare, and prosecute the case at little or no immediate, direct expense to the employee. However, the employee will have little to say about the manner in which the agency operates and makes its decisions. The union or unit member employee who goes to arbitration usually has the dispute handled by the union, without immediate, direct expense to the employee.

Period of Limitations

The period of limitations may be an important factor in choice of forum. The time period for many statutory actions is six months. Once that period has passed, the statutory action is lost. Contract and tort claims often have a period of limitations measured by years.[85] In-house and contract procedures may have very short limitation periods.

Control over Process

Where the employee has a choice between several forums, one factor that the employee may consider is which forum gives the employee the most control over the possible outcome. This may be especially important where a group is sponsoring the litigation as a "test case" on some point of law. If the claim is before the agency, often the agency does the investigation and drafts the charge to reflect the violations it sees, which may not be the same view as that of the employee. If the employee goes to court with the employee's own lawyer, the employee can direct the lawyer to proceed according to the employee's desires.

One Bite, Two Bite Remedies

Another difficulty in forum choice is determining whether the first choice of forums is also the final choice, or whether, if the employee loses in the first forum, the employee can continue to pursue the same claim in another forum. If the first choice is the final choice, it is sometimes said that the employee only gets "one bite" at the remedial apple. If the employee can take a claim lost in the first forum into a second forum, it is sometimes said that the employee has a "two bite" remedy.

Where there is a collective bargaining contract, most contract claims are required to be processed through arbitration by the terms of the contract. There is no other choice, unless the claim raises statutory issues tryable before an agency. The court will not determine whether the collective bargaining contract has been breached when there is an arbitrator who can make that determination. In contrast, an employee may grieve alleged employment discrimination that may violate either a contract or a statute through arbitration, and then take the same claim to EEOC and the courts, even if the employee lost in arbitration.[86] In summary, the initial choice of forums may be a very critical decision.

Federal or State Courts

Closely related to the choice of the initial forum is the problem of choosing between state or federal courts. A discharged employee's claims may be based on an individual employment contract, which raises statute of limitations and other questions of state contract law. A claim may be based on a collective bargaining contract, which usually raises questions of federal law under the NLRA. If a private sector collective bargaining contract issue is sought to be raised in state court, it will usually be removable to the federal courts.[87] One court illustrated a common forum problem in the following manner:

> [E]mployees frequently attempt to avoid federal law by basing their complaint on state law, disclaiming any reliance on the provisions of the collective bargaining agreement. Nevertheless, many of the cases are in fact section 301 suits [NLRA] and as such are governed by federal law. In such cases the "artful pleading" doctrine requires that the state law complaint be recharacterized as one arising under the collective bargaining agreement.[88]

The discharged collective bargaining employee may seek to avoid contract claims because, for example, the contract period of limitations may have passed. The employee may attempt to characterize the claim as one arising in tort to avoid the at will presumption, which will usually be decided under state law. However, the courts have the authority to look behind the claim and determine its actual basis. If the alleged tort claim is found to be actually based on collective bargaining contract clauses, for example, the state court action will be dismissed and the employee relegated to federal law.[89]

Federal courts may also become involved in cases where the parties to the action are from different states. The federal courts may be a forum of choice for plaintiffs who seek to have a federal court try an issue when the state level precedents are against the plaintiff's position. The federal courts, however, are bound to apply state law where it is applicable.

> The historical basis for diversity-of-citizenship jurisdiction is to ensure a fair forum to noncitizens of the state in which the federal court sits. Congress has seen fit to extend jurisdiction beyond the need for a fair forum, so one could argue that the federal courts sit as a frequently available alternative to the state courts in order to derive the benefits of competing court systems. No rational view of the purposes of diversity supports the notion, however, that a district court should disregard established state law because of a perceived trend not yet manifested even in the state's appellate courts.[90]

Federal courts may have to apply state and federal law where there are mixed state and federal claims. "Since the (federal) court has jurisdiction over a substantial federal claim, it retains pendent jurisdiction over the state claims of breach of contract and retaliatory termination."[91]

> Pendent jurisdiction, of course, is a doctrine of discretion. We (federal courts), recognize that in appropriate circumstances dismissal of the state claims without prejudice is proper. Such circumstances may exist, for example, where the trial judge finds that the state issues predominate in terms of the comprehensiveness of the remedy sought, or that there is a sufficient likelihood of jury confusion in treating divergent legal theories of relief to justify separating state and federal claims.[92]

Employees may feel that the federal court forum may exercise somewhat less judicial restraint than the state court forum. Thus there are a variety of tactical as well as legal issues involved in initially deciding to try a state court forum or a federal court forum.

In summary, the choice of forums, where more than one is available, can be a difficult tactical decision. The employee must consider a variety of factors. The employer may face a multiplicity of actions, where consecutive two bite actions are permitted. Once the employee has chosen a forum, the employer's first line of defense may be to challenge that choice as being improper. An employer may wish to consider the use of a contractual inhouse grievance mechanism. Such a mechanism may first permit the employer to argue that the employee must first exhaust that mechanism and, second, permit the argument that the court should perform only limited judicial review of the grievance mechanism decision.

The employee must realistically consider what the employee is seeking from the forum. Many employees seem to want the dispute resolution forum to redecide all aspects of the employer's decision. They want the forum to substitute the forum's judgment for the judgment of the employer. This will be very difficult to accomplish. In contrast, if the employee wants a review of the employer's decision based on reasonableness or fairness, this goal can be accomplished in more than one forum. It must be noted, however, that a review of fairness or reasonableness does not guarantee error free decision making. Reasonableness does not necessarily mean rightness.

REMEDIES

A variety of remedies are potentially available to a winning employee for breach of the individual employment contract, depending upon the nature of the breach. Different violations will warrant different types of remedies. The most common claim of breach of contract being considered here is discharge of the employee. Traditional judicial remedies for unlawful discharge are compensatory damages (back pay) and reinstatement. Traditional judicial remedies for violation of a tort duty to the employee may include compensatory and punitive damages. In arbitration, reinstatement with back pay or reinstatement without back pay are common remedies in discharge cases. The arbitrator may also exercise the power to mitigate, and, for example, reduce a discharge to a suspension. Punitive damages are generally not available in arbitration.

A major controversy has arisen over whether punitive damages should be awarded where the claim is basically one involving a discharge claimed to be in violation of the contract. Punitive damages can be high, occasionally passing the million dollar amount. One argument in favor of punitive damages is that it is difficult to adequately compensate an employee for the "devastating effect on their economic and social status"[93] that an unlawful discharge might have. It may be difficult, however, to use back pay or lost wages as a measure for an at will employee who had no legal justification for expecting long-term employment.[94] In contrast, if the "cost" to the employer of an illegal discharge is low—only back pay, for example—the employer may feel little hesitation in arbitrarily dismissing employees.[95] A back pay remedy may simply be viewed as a cost of doing business, despite the personal and social impact on the employee. A recent decision from the bellwether state of California has adopted an approach rejecting punitive damages in most individual contract cases and permitting only recovery for contract damages.

> We therefore conclude that the employment relationship . . . (does not) warrant judicial extension of the proposed additional tort remedies in view of the countervailing concerns about economic policy and stability, the traditional separation of tort and contract law, and finally, the numerous protection against improper terminations already afforded employees.[96]

Reflecting a general business attack against many forms of punitive damages, recent legislation in Nevada caps punitive damages in many discharge cases at three times the compensatory damages (back pay). In addition, a variety of procedural requirements must be met where punitive damages are sought.[97]

Where the employer's actions go "well beyond the bounds of ordinary liability of breach of contract," however, some courts may make an exception to their general rule and may permit punitive damages.[98] Employees seeking damages must also give attention to their duty to mitigate damages resulting from the breach of contract.[99]

Arbitration is the result of an agreement between the parties, unlike a court action. The parties' agreement may set forth the power and authority of the arbitrator to give remedies. The agreement and, therefore, the remedial authority, can be as broad or narrow as the parties agree.[100]

Reinstatement is a common remedy for an unlawful discharge. Its effectiveness is unclear. In one study on reinstatements under the National Labor Relations Act, it was reportedly found that only about 40 percent of potential reinstatees actually accepted reinstatement and that 80 percent of those left within two years. If these figures are representative of remedies for individual employment contract disputes, then it may mean that financial damages are the only effective remedies.[101]

In summary, choice of forum issues are as much a choice of remedies as anything else. Where courts are involved, the judicial forum may be effectively removed where remedies do not provide enough inducement to obtain the lawyer that the employee always needs. The combination of judicial restraint and limited remedies may remove courts as effective forums. The effectiveness of available remedies is largely unstudied, but the issue of effectiveness seems critical to any reform that is suggested. For example, if reinstatement usually does not provide stability either for the employer or the employee, a dispute resolution procedure that relies on reinstatement may be fatally flawed. Choice of forum and choice of remedy are two sides of the same coin.

FUTURE FORUMS AND REMEDIES

Recent legislation in Montana and the draft legislative proposal by the National Conference of Commissioners on Uniform State Laws will impact on individual employment contract litigation and on the remedies issued in individual contracts. Although these two matters have limited current application, they provide insight into what the future may hold. The new Montana Wrongful Discharge Statute limits lost wages and benefits to a period not to exceed four years, with a duty to mitigate that recovery, and provides for punitive damages only where the employer engaged in actual fraud or malice.[102] The discussion Draft Employment Termination Act of the Commissioners on Uniform State Laws provides for an arbitrator's possible award of back pay less any mitigation and for liquidated damages for discharges lacking good faith not to exceed the amount of back pay, and a possible two year severance pay recovery where there is no reinstatement.[103]

Reading enacted legislation, draft legislation, and recent cases together, several things emerge. Damages or wage recovery is being limited to the contract and punitive damages are being limited or made unavailable in many situations. Fraud or malice or similarly based actions by the employer might permit recovery of some punitive damages. Arbitration is a commonly preferred forum for the resolution of individual contract disputes.

CONCLUSION

Courts are the primary forum that interpret individual at will contract employment disputes, whereas arbitration is the primary forum for collective bargaining contract disputes. Courts are very reluctant to substitute their decisions for those of the employer on the meaning of the contract. Where a statute authorizes judicial review, such as under antidiscrimination legislation, the courts may review the employer's decisions somewhat more thoroughly because the public policy of the statute overrides the powers granted employers under the at will doctrine.

Arbitrators will be generally restrained in their interpretation of the contract, recognizing contractual and inherent employer rights. They will usually be authorized by the arbitration clause to go further than a court in determining the reasonableness of the employer's actions. The arbitrator's decisional and remedial authority, however, can be limited to whatever terms the parties agree to put into the arbitration contract. Courts generally defer to an arbitrator's award. Agencies also give considerable deference to the employer's judgment, unless the action falls plainly within the statutory directive.

Several generalizations are possible. Courts are reluctant to go deeply into the issues in these disputes because of the doctrine of judicial restraint. They usually will not second guess the employer and they will also generally defer to an arbitrator's award. Nonjudicial resolution of employment disputes seems to be preferred by courts, as evidenced by their use of limited judicial review of these decisions. Similarly, statutes and proposed legislation dealing specifically with individual contract disputes are beginning to appear and they also show a strong preference for nonjudicial dispute resolution. These factors provide encouragement for the extensive use of contractual inhouse grievance mechanisms. Where inhouse or government agency forums are available, courts seem inclined to require that these forums be exhausted (used) before there is recourse to the courts. In much of the case law and in the statutory approaches and proposals, there are trends toward limiting the employee's remedies for breach of contract, preferring nonjudicial approaches and providing greater access to some dispute resolution forum. It is likely that judicial review of the nonjudicial dispute resolution forum will be limited. It is uncertain whether the proposed statutory methods of nonjudicial dispute resolution will include use of the extreme version of the doctrine of judicial restraint used by courts in individual employment contract disputes.

Ironically, courts show the greatest reluctance of all forums to second guess the employer, but courts provide the largest source of financial remedies where punitive damages are permitted. Arbitrators are empowered to show less reluctance to test the reasonableness of the employer's action, but they also provide less financial recovery for a winning employee. However, the arbitration forum stands alone with its unusual authority to mitigate the discipline imposed by the employer.

Judicial restraint is the hallmark of the way in which courts approach disputes involving individual contracts. This judicial restraint is based on asserted limitations of the court to understand all of the elements of the employment relationship, certain economic principles concerning the fundamental rights of a capitalistic system, and a desire to minimize the volume of disputes. The court's statements of economic principles are never justified by the court on the basis of evidence in the case and usually is not subject to attack if the employee tries to offer evidence. Without question, there are some irreducible minimum employer rights inherent to our economic system. If courts are going to use these arguments, however, it would seem desirable that reasoned statements be used rather than bald pronouncements. Perhaps the at will doctrine does contribute to a state's program of economic development, but it is not a self-evident conclusion. It seems more likely that the court's references to unverified economic theory may be the result of an inability or unwillingness to develop a comprehensive doctrine of just cause for discharge. Just cause concepts can include many of the economic protections courts seek for employers. Cause concepts are more amenable to rational dialogue than unilateral pronouncements, as arbitrators have long demonstrated in their awards.

A great deal of attention is given to the structure and procedure of dispute resolution forums. A similar amount of attention should be given to the remedies issue. For example, retraining, additional training, or new job placement may be more effective remedies than reinstatement. Remedies may tie closely to the availability of forums, as is shown by the relationship between potential punitive damages and lawyer availability through contingent fee contracts. The public interest in the employment dispute in most cases probably lies in permitting the employee to get employment stability, not in getting even.

NOTES

1. J. Dertouzos, E. Holland, P. Ebener, *The Legal and Economic Consequences of Wrongful Termination* (Rand Corp., The Institute For Civil Justice 1988).

2. Bishop v. Wood, 426 U.S. 341, 349–50 (1976).

3. Furnco Const. Corp. v. Waters, 438 U.S. 567, 578 (1978).

4. Criddle v. Hickory Hill Furniture Co., 34 Empl. Prac. Dec. (CCH) 34,547 at 34,443 (D. Miss. 1984).

5. Magnan v. Anaconda Indus. Inc., 101 Lab. Cas. (CCH) 55,485 at 76,182 (Conn. Sup. Ct. 1984).

6. Criddle v. Hickory Hill Furniture Co., 34 Empl. Prac. Dec. (CCH) 34,547 at 34,443 (D. Miss. 1984); Mellitt v. Schrafft Candy Co., 115 L.R.R.M. (BNA) 4195, 4198 (D. N.H. 1981).

7. Furnco Const. Corp. v. Waters, 438 U.S. 567, 578 (1978).

8. Magnan v. Anaconda Indus. Inc., 101 Lab. Cas. (CCH) 55,485 at 76,182 (Conn. Sup. Ct. 1984).

9. Sheets v. Teddy's Frosted Foods, Inc., 115 L.R.R.M. (BNA) 4626, 4628 (Conn. Sup. Ct. 1980).

10. Sheets v. Teddy's Frosted Foods, Inc., 115 L.R.R.M. (BNA) 4626, 4628 (Conn. Sup. Ct. 1980); Wilson v. Vlasic Foods, Inc., 116 L.R.R.M. (BNA) 2419, 2422 (D. Cal. 1984).

11. Furnco Const. Corp. v. Waters, 438 U.S. 567, 578 (1978); Reed v. May Dep't Stores, 28 Empl. Prac. Dec. (CCH) 35,531 at 24,359 (D. Mo. 1981).

12. Magnan v. Anaconda Indus. Inc., 101 Lab. Cas. (CCH) 55,485 at 76,182 (Conn. Sup. Ct. 1984).

13. See ch. 7 for a discussion of some statutory proposals.

14. Furnco Const. Corp. v. Waters, 438 U.S. 567 (1978).

15. Id. at 578.

16. Id. at 577.

17. E.g., ORS 40.105 (1985).

18. Western Air Lines, Inc. v. Criswell, 472 U.S. 400 (1985).

19. Ch. 4, fn. 6.

20. F. Elkouri and E. Elkouri, *How Arbitration Works* 6 (4th ed. 1985).

21. C. Morris, II *The Developing Labor Law* 1450–1488 (1983).

22. F. Elkouri and E. Elkouri, *How Arbitration Works* 7–9 (4th ed. 1985).

23. Diamond Power Specialty Co., 83 Lab. Arb. (BNA) 1277, 1280 (Kindig, Arb. 1984); Tryco Mfg. Co., Inc., 83 Lab. Arb. (BNA) 1131, 1137 (Fitzsimmons, Arb. 1984).

24. Lucky Stores, Inc., 83 Lab. Arb. (BNA) 760, 766 (Sabo, Arb. 1984).

25. Pugh v. See's Candies, Inc., 115 L.R.R.M. (BNA) 4002, n.26 at 4010 (Cal. Ct. App. 1981).

26. F. Elkouri and E. Elkouri, *How Arbitration Works* 598 (4th ed. 1985).

27. Id. at 617.

28. Id. at 27–29.

29. Id. at 87–89.

30. Conn. Light and Power Co. v. Local 420, IBEW, 114 L.R.R.M. (BNA) 2770 (2d Cir. 1983); Westinghouse Elevators of Puerto Rico, Inc. v. S.I.U. of Puerto Rico, 583 F.2d 1184 (1st Cir. 1978).

31. Cape Elizabeth School Bd. v. Teachers Ass'n, 116 L.R.R.M. (BNA) 2812, 2818 (Me. Sup. Ct. 1983).

32. Iowa City School Dist. v. Educ. Ass'n, 116 L.R.R.M. (BNA) 2832, 2836 (Iowa Sup. Ct. 1983).

33. Clinchfield Coal Co. v. Local 1098, UMW, 101 Lab. Cas. (CCH) 11,081, fn. at 22,346–347 (4th Cir. 1984).

34. Hoteles Condado Beach v. Local 901, Union DeTronquistas De Puerto Rico, 116 L.R.R.M. (BNA) 2900, 2903 (D.P.R. 1984).

35. Action Electric, Inc. v. Local 292 IBEW, 109 Lab. Cas. (BNA) 10,739 at 22,966 (D. Minn. 1987).

36. Ch. 3, infra.

37. Borg v. Greyhound Lines, Inc., 109 Lab. Cas. (BNA) 10,504, at 21,973 (D. Cal. 1984).

38. F. Elkouri and E. Elkouri, *How Arbitration Works* 661 (4th ed. 1985).

39. Id. at 664–67.

40. C. Morris, II *The Developing Labor Law* 1294–1299 (2d ed. 1983).

41. BNA Collective Bargaining, Negotiations and Contracts, Basic Patterns, Clausefinder 51:81 (1985).

42. F. Elkouri and E. Elkouri, *How Arbitration Works* 369–380 (4th ed. 1985).

43. Cleveland Bd. of Educ. v. Loudermill, 470 U.S. 532, 546 (1985).

44. Id. at 545–46.

45. Brock v. Roadway Express, Inc., 107 S. Ct. 1740, 1748 (1987).

46. See generally, F. Foulkes, *Personnel Policies in Large Nonunion Companies* (1980).

47. NuVision Inc. v. Dunscombe, 3 Indiv. Empl. Rights (BNA) 756 (Mich. Ct. App. 1987); ZDEB v. Shearson Lehman Bros., 2 Indiv. Empl. Rights (BNA) 1460 (D. Colo. 1987).

48. Dahlman v. Oakland Univ., 3 Indiv. Empl. Rights (BNA) 1765 (Mich. Ct. App. 1988).

49. Resolving Employment Disputes, Model Employment Arbitration Procedures, American Arbitration Association, 140 West 51st Street, New York, NY 10020–1203. For other references, see "Lawyers Examine Growing Phenomenon of Arbitration in Non-union Settings," 7 Employee Rel. Weekly (BNA) 1094 (1989).

50. Skirpan v. United Airlines, 4 Indiv. Empl. Rights (BNA) 924 (D. Ill. 1988); Hill v. City of Kinston, 4 Indiv. Empl. Rights (BNA) 100 (N.C. Ct. App. 1988); Pagdilao v. Maui Intercontinental Hotel, 3 Indiv. Empl. Rights (BNA) 1628 (D. Haw. 1988); Jackson v. ABCD, 3 Indiv. Empl. Rights (BNA) 1102, fn. 1 (Mass. Sup. Ct. 1988); Melnick v. State Farm, 3 Indiv. Empl. Rights (BNA) 730 (N.M. Sup. Ct. 1988); Arnold v. Diet Center Inc., 2 Indiv. Empl. Rights (BNA) 1531 (Idaho Ct.

App. 1987); Schnelting v. Coors, 2 Indiv. Empl. Rights (BNA) 1451 (Mo. Ct. App. 1987); Bratt v. IBM Corp., 785 F.2d 352 (1st Cir. 1986).

51. St. Yves v. Mid State Bank, 2 Indiv. Empl. Rights (BNA) 1550 (Wash. Ct. App. 1987).

52. Mandelblatt v. Perelman, 3 Indiv. Empl. Rights (BNA) 857 (D. N.Y. 1988).

53. Loftis v. G.T. Products Inc., 3 Indiv. Empl. Rights (BNA) 641 (Mich. Ct. App. 1988); Schnelting v. Coors, 3 Indiv. Empl. Rights (BNA) 1451 (Mo. Ct. App. 1987); Churchey v. Adolph Coors Co., 2 Indiv. Empl. Rights (BNA) 314 (Colo. Ct. App. 1986).

54. Skeets v. Johnson, 2 Indiv. Empl. Rights (BNA) 96, 97 (8th Cir. 1987).

55. Northrup Corp., 90 Lab. Arb. (BNA) 728–29 (Weiss, Arb. 1987).

56. Morris v. Lutheran Medical Center, 115 L.R.R.M. (BNA) 4966 (Neb. Sup. Ct. 1983).

57. Ch. 4, fn. 64–129.

58. Buttler v. Westinghouse Elec. Corp., 3 Indiv. Empl. Rights (BNA) 1430 (D. Md. 1987).

59. Reilly v. Stroehmann Bros. Co., 2 Indiv. Empl. Rights (BNA) 1244 (Pa. Super. Ct. 1987).

60. Churchey v. Adolph Coors Co., 3 Indiv. Empl. Rights (BNA) 1032 (Colo. Sup. Ct. 1988).

61. Therrin v. United Air Lines, 2 Indiv. Empl. Rights (BNA) 1572 (D. Colo. 1987); Churchey v. Adolph Coors Co., 2 Indiv. Empl. Rights (BNA) 314 (Colo. Ct. App. 1986).

62. Darlington v. General Electric, 2 Indiv. Empl. Rights (BNA) 1666 (Pa. Super. Ct. 1986); Reilly v. Stroehmann, 2 Indiv. Empl. Rights (BNA) 1244 (Pa. Super. Ct. 1987); Skeets v. Johnson, 2 Indiv. Empl. Rights (BNA) 96 (8th Cir. 1987).

63. Jiminez v. Colo. Interstate Gas Co., 3 Indiv. Empl. Rights (BNA) 1646 (D. Wyo. 1988); Suarez v. Ill. Valley C.C., 3 Indiv. Empl. Rights (BNA) 1450 (D. Ill. 1988); Schnelting v. Coors, 2 Indiv. Empl. Rights (BNA) 1451 (Mo. Ct. App. 1987). See also, A. Westin and A. Feliu, *Resolving Employment Disputes Without Litigation* 275 (1988).

64. Dahlman v. Oakland Univ., 3 Indiv. Empl. Rights (BNA) 1765 (Mich. Ct. App. 1988).

65. Myers v. Western-Southern Life Ins. Co., 3 Indiv. Empl. Rights (BNA) 723 (6th Cir. 1988).

66. Johnson v. Armored Transport of Cal., 2 Indiv. Empl. Rights (BNA) 954 (9th Cir. 1987).

67. Miller v. Sevamp Co., 2 Indiv. Empl. Rights (BNA) 1202 (Va. Sup. Ct. 1987).

68. NuVision Inc. v. Dunscombe, 3 Indiv. Empl. Rights (BNA) 756 (Mich. Ct. App. 1987).

69. Duchesne v. Williams, 3 Indiv. Empl. Rights (BNA) 715 (6th Cir. 1988).

70. Dahlman v. Oakland Univ., 3 Indiv. Empl. Rights (BNA) 1765 (Mich. Ct. App. 1988).

71. Grey v. First Nat'l Bank of Chicago, 3 Indiv. Empl. Rights (BNA) 504 (Ill. App. Ct. 1988).

72. Alexander v. Gardner-Denver Co., 415 U.S. 36, fn. 21 at 60 (1974).

73. A. Westin and A. Feliu, *Resolving Employment Disputes Without Litigation* 271–72 (1988).

74. NLRB v. City Disposal Systems, Inc., 465 U.S. 822 (1984).

75. Meritor Savings Bank, FSB v. Vinson, 477 U.S. 57 (1986).

76. Whirlpool Corp. v. Marshall, 445 U.S. 1 (1980).

77. Butz v. Hertz Corp., 115 L.R.R.M. (BNA) 4044 (D. Pa. 1983).

78. Presnell v. Pell, 115 L.R.R.M. (BNA) 4856 (N.C. Sup. Ct. 1979).

79. Hentzel v. Singer Co., 115 L.R.R.M. (BNA) 4036, 4043 (Cal. Ct. App. 1982).

80. Ch. 5, fn. 73–100.

81. C. Morris, II *The Developing Labor Law* 1616–1617 (2d ed. 1983).

82. Perry v. Sindermann, 408 U.S. 593 (1972) (discharged in 1969, case remanded by Supreme Court).

83. D. Brodie and P. Williams, *School Grievance Arbitration* 14–15 (1982).

84. F. Elkouri and E. Elkouri, *How Arbitration Works* 7–9 (4th ed. 1985).

85. E.g., ORS 12.080 (1985) (contract, 6 years); ORS 12.110 (1985) (listed torts, 2 years) and ORS 12.115 (1985) (negligent injury, 10 years).

86. Alexander v. Gardner-Denver Co., 415 U.S. 36 (1974).

87. Turner v. General Motors Corp., 115 L.R.R.M. (BNA) 4016 (D. Mich. 1982).

88. Olguin v. Inspiration Consol. Copper Co., 117 L.R.R.M. (BNA) 2073, 2076 (9th Cir. 1984).

89. Buscemi v. McDonnell Douglas Corp., 101 Lab. Cas. (CCH) 11,112 (9th Cir. 1984).

90. Boniuk v. New York Medical College, 115 L.R.R.M. (BNA) 4643, 4645 (D. N.Y. 1982); see also Bruffett v. Warner Communications, 115 L.R.R.M. (BNA) 4117 (3d Cir. 1982); Crocker v. Chamber of Commerce, 115 L.R.R.M. (BNA) 4067 (D. D.C. 1983). The Supreme Court has recognized this point. "A property interest in employment can, of course, be created by ordinance, or by an implied contract. In either case, however, the sufficiency of the claim of entitlement must be decided by reference to state law." Bishop v. Wood, 426 U.S. 341, 344 (1976).

91. Kay v. North Lincoln Hospital Dist., 115 L.R.R.M. (BNA) 4238, 4242 (D. Or. 1982).

92. Cancellier v. Federated Dep't Stores, 115 L.R.R.M. (BNA) 4111, 4115 (9th Cir. 1982); see also Carrillo v. Illinois Bell Tel. Co., 115 L.R.R.M. (BNA) 4467, 4471 (D. Ill. 1982); Hovey v. Lutheran Medical Center, 115 L.R.R.M. (BNA) 4796 (D. N.Y. 1981).

93. Foley v. Interactive Data Corp., 3 Indiv. Empl. Rights (BNA) 1729, 1751 (Cal. Sup. Ct. 1988).

94. Sterling Drug Inc. v. Oxford, 3 Indiv. Empl. Rights (BNA) 1060 (Ark. Sup. Ct. 1988).

95. Rodriguez v. Eastern Airlines, Inc., 2 Indiv. Empl. Rights (BNA) 92 (1st Cir. 1987); Vigil v. Arzola, 2 Indiv. Empl. Rights (BNA) 377 (N.M. Ct. App. 1983); Rodriguez v. Eastern Airlines, 2 Indiv. Empl. Rights (BNA) 92 (1st Cir. 1987).

96. Foley v. Interactive Data Corp., 3 Indiv. Empl. Rights (BNA) 1729, 1747 (Cal. Sup. Ct. 1988); see also Stering Drug Inc. v. Oxford, 3 Indiv. Empl. Rights (BNA) 1060 (Ark Sup. Ct. 1988).

97. Law Capping Punitive Damages Signed into Law In Nevada, 7 Employee Rel. Weekly (BNA) 711 (1989).

98. K Mart Corp. v. Ponsock, 2 Indiv. Empl. Rights (BNA) 56 (Nev. Sup. Ct. 1987).

99. Ortiz v. Bank of America, 2 Indiv. Empl. Rights (BNA) 1068 (9th Cir. 1987).

100. F. Elkouri and E. Elkouri, *How Arbitration Works* 285–290 (4th ed. 1985).

101. "Professor urges Remedies to Reverse Firings, Refusals to Bargain with Unions," 7 Employee Rel. Weekly (BNA) 315 (1989).

102. Mont. Code Ann. 39-2-905, Lab. Rel. Rep. Indiv. Empl. Rights Manual (BNA) 567:5 (1989).

103. Model Uniform Employment Termination Act 6 (Draft 1989), Lab. Rel. Rep. Indiv. Empl. Rights Manual (BNA) 540:51 (1989).

3

Employer Rights

EMPLOYER RIGHTS: ENTREPRENURIAL CONTROL

The single most important element in the resolution of an individual contract employment dispute is the doctrine of the employer (or management) rights. In general, the broader the range of employer rights, the less relative importance is likely to be given to a claim of employee. The purpose of this chapter is to consider how judges, and to a lesser extent arbitrators, describe some of the aspects of the doctrine of employer rights.

Courts use broad language to describe employer rights in individual contract litigation. One court stated that "the legal protection of the employee interests in job security is the exception, rather than the rule, in this state."[1] Another said, "an employee is just as terminable at will after 24 years as he was on his first day of work."[2] Another used "the presumption that in all but the rarest cases an employee has no right to the job itself."[3] Yet another court stated " we must weight the employer's interest in running his business more heavily than all the other interests. Inherent in the at will presumption itself is an important public policy—that the employer should be master of his business."[4]

Although statements of the foregoing type are used to justify arbitrary discharge decisions, courts do not believe that most employers run their personnel systems on the basis of arbitrary action. The U.S. Supreme Court has noted: "[W]e know from our experience that more often than not people do not act in a totally arbitrary manner, without any underlying reasons, especially in a business setting."[5] The court seems to be saying that although the at will individual contract system

permits arbitrary decision making, the permitted arbitrariness is rarely used. That is not the experience of many employees.

The doctrine of judicial restraint in employment cases, identified
earlier,[6] provides additional support to the employer rights doctrine.
The doctrine of judicial restraint should also be kept in mind when
considering any aspects of employer rights.

Collective Bargaining and Individual Contracts

In addition to general statements about judicial restraint and
employer authority, courts have identified a number of more specific
areas of employer decision making that have been reserved for
unilateral employer decision making despite the impact on individual
employment contracts. In particular, the United States Supreme Court
has identified areas of reserved employer rights that are defined as
essential to our system of economic organization. The context in which
many of the Court's statements have been made relates to collective
bargaining. The major topic of these materials is individual contracts,
not collective contracts. However, the Court's statements appear to be
based on its concept of the fundamental nature of our economic
system. This makes them applicable to either collective or individual
contracts. Accordingly, little distinction is drawn between individual
and collective employment contracts in this chapter.

Many types of employer decisions affect the job security of the
employees. These decisions include whether or not to stay in business,
whether to use human employees or robots on an assembly line, and
a variety of other types of decisions. More fundamentally, the courts
frequently note that the employer has the unilateral, protected right
to go out of business regardless of the impact on the employee. Courts
will then compare other employer decisions that are deemed to be
analogous to the decision to quit business and conclude that the
employer has unilateral rights in these analogous areas.

The U.S. Supreme Court has categorized three basic types of
decisions that employers make. The Court stated the following:

> Some management decisions, such as choice of advertising and
> promotion, product type and design, and financing arrange-
> ments, have only an indirect and attenuated impact on the
> employment relationship. Other management decisions, such as
> the order of succession of layoffs and recalls, production quotas,
> and work rules, are almost exclusively "an aspect of the relation-
> ship" between employer and employee. The present case con-
> cerns a third type of management decision, one that had a direct

impact on employment, since jobs were inexorably eliminated by the termination, but had as its focus only the economic profitability of the contract with Greenpark, a concern under these facts wholly apart from the employment relationship. This decision, involving a change in the scope and direction of the enterprise, is akin to the decision whether to be in business at all, "not in (itself) primarily about conditions of employment though the effect of the decision may be necessary to terminate employment." At the same time, this decision touches on a matter of central and pressing concern to the union and its members of employees: the possibility of continued employment and the retention of the employees' very jobs.[7]

The employer is given great deference to make the two (product and designing scope and direction of business) of the three types of decisions without having to bargain with the union. In other words, the employer has the power to make unilateral decisions based on fundamental business considerations involving product, promotion, profitability, and scope and direction of the enterprise. The employer may look only to the business impact of these decisions and need not balance the interests of the employees. The same types of business decisions must be made by an employer subject to a collective bargaining contract or by an employer with individual contracts of employment. An individual nonunion employee whose job security is affected by one of these decisions is not likely to receive greater job protection than the collective bargaining employees do. Thus the Supreme Court has identified a range of decisions that are solely within the power of any employer to make, regardless of the impact on the employees. Where the business decision results in job losses, the employer's business justification apparently serves as just cause for the discharges.

The Supreme Court has identified a number of other concepts which are used to describe basic and essential employer rights in our economic system. Again, it must be noted that although these comments have frequently arisen in the collective bargaining context, these concepts appear to be more related to the basic nature of our economic system than to the collective bargaining contract. They can, therefore, be considered to have some application to both individual and collective bargaining contracts.

The Supreme Court has stated, as a general proposition, the following guidelines:

Management must be free from the constraints of the bargaining process to the extent essential for the running of a profitable business. It also must have some degree of certainty beforehand as when it may proceed to reach decisions without fear of later evaluations labeling its conduct an unfair labor practice.[8]

If one were to substitute references to individual employment contract ligation for the bargaining and unfair labor practice references in the foregoing quotation, it would be an accurate description of the individual, noncollective cases bargaining in these materials.[9]

Where the employer makes "a significant change" in operations, the employer has the unilateral power to make the decision. The employees are unlikely to have legal redress in the event that their job security is impaired by the decision. "The decision to halt work at this specific location represented a significant change in petitioner's operations, a change not unlike opening a new line of business or going out of business entirely."[10]

The employer has unilateral decision making powers where there is a need for "speed, flexibility, and secrecy."

> At other times, management may have great need for speed, flexibility, and secrecy in meeting business opportunities and exigencies. It may face significant tax or securities consequences that hinge on confidentiality, the timing of a plant closing, or a reorganization of the corporate structure. The publicity incident to the normal process of bargaining may injure the possibility of a successful transition or increase the economic damage to the business. The employer also may have no feasible alternative to the closing, and even good-faith bargaining over it may both be futile and cause the employer additional loss.[11]

Decisions akin to shutting down or starting up a business are fundamental employer rights in our economic system.

> We conclude that the harm likely to be done to an employer's need to operate freely in deciding whether to shut down part of its business purely for economic reasons outweighs the incremental benefit that might be gained through the union's participation in making the decision, and we hold that the decision itself is not part of 8(d) "terms and conditions" over which Congress has mandated bargaining.[12]

Decisions that lie at the "core of entrepreneurial control" are matters reserved exclusively for management.

Nothing the Court holds today should be understood as imposing a duty to bargain collectively regarding such managerial
decisions, which lies at the core of entrepreneurial control.
Decisions concerning the commitment of investment capital and
basic scope of the enterprise are not in themselves primarily
about conditions of employment, though the effect of the decision
may be necessary to terminate the employment. If, as I think clear,
the purpose of 8(d) is to describe a limited area subject to the
duty of collective bargaining, those management decisions which
are fundamental to the basic direction of a corporate enterprise
or which impinge only indirectly upon employment security
should be excluded from that area.[13]

Courts will not impose job security responsibilities on employers
that will "discourage and inhibit the transfer of capital."[14]

The employer has the power to make fundamental business
decisions in a unilateral manner and can expect to be generally free
from liability if those decisions impair the employment contracts of
individual employees. Such freedom does not permit the employer to
get away with simply labeling everything as "entrepreneurial control." The courts can look behind the employer's statements to determine if the reasons given for the decisions are the real reasons. "An
employer may not simply shut down part of its business and mask its
desire to weaken and circumvent the union by labeling its decision
'purely economic.'"[15] An undefined element of good faith seems to be
required by some courts.

Again, the context of most of these comments is collective bargaining contracts. However, the individual contract employees generally
have less protection than their collective bargaining counterpart. The
individual contract employees cannot expect any more protection
than their collective contract counterparts. They will usually receive
less protection. In the words of one court, "principles of freedom of
contract and the importance of economic growth" are involved.[16]
These are important public policy considerations that weigh against
individual employee contract claims.

Statements concerning the "core of entrepreneurial control" take on
added meaning in the light of the increasing attention being given to
proposed legislation that would modify the traditional common law
approach to individual employment contracts. The Montana statute
and Commissioners on Uniform State Laws draft will be discussed
later.[17] Courts will interpret those statutes with an eye toward judicial
statements about the fundamentals of the economic order and
entrepreneurial control. Absent an extremely clear legislative statement, courts are likely to interpret such legislation in the light of the

significant deference given to employer rights that is a long and well established element in American employment law.

In summary, courts have reserved broad areas of economic business decision making that directly impact on employee jobs as being reserved for unilateral employer decision making. The courts base these reserved, unilateral decision-making powers on the important public policy of permitting an employer to run a profitable business. For these purposes, no distinction need be drawn between collective bargaining contracts and individual contracts of employment. The statements concern entrepreneurial aspects of being an employer, regardless of the status of the employees of that employer. The economic fundamentals of running a business are the same in either the individual or collective contract situation. Court decisions concerning collective bargaining contracts can be used to help understand individual contracts of employment. This close relationship between the union and nonunion workplace is too frequently ignored.

An employer's rights are greatest when a particular decision can be shown to be akin to the decision to stay in business. The employer has a unilateral right to make fundamental decisions concerning the scope and direction of the business. The employer has a right to the product, its design, and the financial arrangements. Management needs the certainty to decide without fearing litigation. Business decisions require speed and flexibility. The free flow of capital must be protected. Sometimes these decisions are summarized by references to decisions that lie at the core of entrepreneurial control. The impact of these decisions on job security provisions of individual contracts will be viewed as incidental, given the stronger public policy basis of entrepreneurial control.

SPECIAL EMPLOYMENT RELATIONSHIPS

The individual employment contract may consist of many express or implied terms. Few individual contracts of employment are actually negotiated, so most of the terms will be implied. There are a variety of special contract employment terms found in the implied terms of the individual contract of employment. These implied terms describe special employment relationships that are recognized by both courts and arbitrators. The special relationships tend in the general direction of increasing management's rights to make decisions that lessen any job security that the special employees may otherwise have had. The special employment relationships of primary concern here relate to job security status. They include probationary status, higher level jobs, jobs with special characteristics, and contingent employees.

Probationary Status

One status that the employee may hold is that of probationary employee. The primary job security characteristics of the probationary employee are usually twofold: the employee can be discharged at any time for any reason, and the duration of the probationary period is usually relatively short. The probationary employee usually is a new employee, but not always. A probationary employee may have some job security rights, but they will usually be minimal. There are several subcategories within the overall category of probationary employees.

Probationary status is the subject of increasing attention in court and arbitration cases. However, it is important to note that there is little or no judicial, arbitral, or legislative movement to limit the unilateral power of the employer over the probationary employee. The ongoing flood of "wrongful discharge" litigation and reform discussion is concerned with employees who are long past their probationary period. It remains to be seen whether employers will use some form of reversion to probationary status to escape limitations that may be imposed on the treatment of nonprobationary employees.

New Probationary Employee. A new probationary employee is a beginning employee who is in a trial period of employment. The employee may be a younger or an older person, but the employment relationship is new. The probationary employee usually has the least job security of any employee and is commonly hired under an explicit and mutual understanding giving the employer this unilateral power. Usually the employee knowingly accepts these short-run terms. The mutually recognized purpose of probationary status is to give the employer an opportunity to determine if the employee will perform satisfactorily, to determine if the employee will "fit in."[18] The employer usually does not need to give a reason if the employee is discharged during this probationary period. Probationary status is usually the same regardless of whether the employee is under an individual or collective contract.

A probationary employee who is without a contract other than the probationary term and who feels that he or she was improperly discharged during the probationary period is not likely to have much effective recourse against the employer. If there is recourse, it will probably be under a general statute that provides a remedy for violation of some legal status other than the probationary status. For example, if the probationary discharge were alleged to be based on prohibited discrimination, the employee's suit would cite that statutory basis for action. That claim is not necessarily related to the probationary status.[19] The recognized purpose of the probationary status is to permit the employer to have a broad discharge power, and it is expected that there is little direct recourse if the employer exercises that power. The courts will give a broad reading to the intent of the probationary contract.

A long-term employee with one employer might revert to the status of a new probationary employee if that employee is lawfully discharged or quits, and takes a new job. There is no indication that such an older, probationary employee would be treated by courts or arbitrators in any manner different from other probationary employees, absent statutory considerations.

A probationary employee who does not pass the employer's scrutiny during the first probationary period may be offered an opportunity to go through the probationary cycle again.[20] There is no indication in the case law how many times an employer can keep renewing probationary status by recycling the employee through a series of consecutive probationary stages.[21] Whereas the number of cases is small, there is an increasing number of cases where the employee has been put through the probationary cycle several times. The employees in these cases may be new or may be experienced in the job market, but they hold a probationary status.[22] There has apparently been no case to date successfully proving bad faith in renewing the probationary cycle. However, this may change as the number of employees increase who face a new probationary cycle. For example, employees testing positive for drugs or alcohol and who are retained by the employer are often put into a special, probationary status.[23]

In summary, employees may have a special employment contractual relationship that gives the employer unilateral and largely unreviewable power to discharge the employee. The probationary contract is an example of this unprotected employment status. Probationary contracts are well recognized and not subject to serious challenge today. Increasing numbers of employees may be recycled through the probationary status as a result of such things as workplace drug and alcohol testing. Probationary status is a concept that is usually understood by both the employee and the employer. New employees and experienced employees may both end up in a probationary status.

Other Terms of Probationary Contract. The major term of the probationary contract gives the employer the arbitrary power to discharge. Like any other part of the employment contract, most courts seem to agree that the conditions of a probationary period can be set by agreement between the parties.[24] Among the job security terms that might be included in a probationary contract are notice period before the discharge takes place, severance pay, procedural requirements to be followed in event of unsatisfactory work, or a list of limitations on the causes for discharge under the probationary contract. Few probationary new employees, however, will have the bargaining strength to negotiate some job security protection during their probationary period.

In addition to being subject to summary discharge, a new probationary employee may experience limitations on other rights in the workplace. One case suggested that a probationary employee might have "a diminished expectation of privacy such as to remove the . . . (drug) tests from the category of Fourth Amendment searches."[25] Undoubtedly there will be increased attention focused on the use of probationary status. There are numerous circumstances under which experienced employees may become subject to substantially diminished rights of the probationary employee.

Experienced Probationary Employee. An employee who is beyond the new or initial hiring probationary period may sometimes find him- or herself returned to a probationary status. This may occur where there is a promotion, or transfer, or as the result of discipline, especially after testing positive for drugs or alcohol.

When an experienced, regular employee is promoted, the new position may be subject to a probationary period. In the absence of an agreement concerning what happens if the employee does not satisfy the terms of this new probation, the employer may be permitted to discharge the employee from the new position if the promotion does not work out. There seems to be no automatic right to return to the old position. Where there is an agreement concerning the failure to meet the probationary standard for the new position, the employee may be entitled to be returned to the employee's prior, nonprobationary position.[26]

An experienced employee who is well past the initial probationary period may be evaluated as performing poorly and be disciplined by being put on a probationary status.[27] The disciplinary probation period will be used to see if the employee can once again shape up. Despite the prior period of service, the employee may then be treated like any other probationary employee. One court stated it as follows: "Finding the manual to be silent as to the specific rights of employees on disciplinary probation, the court applied the usual and accepted meaning of 'probation' in an employment context. . . . We find the district court's interpretation of the contract to be well reasoned."[28]

A common expectation might be that where an experienced employee is put on probation, at the end of the designated period the employee would revert to nonprobationary status or be discharged.

In some cases, however, the employee may be recycled through another probationary period.[29] Extending a probationary period might make some sense from an employer's perspective where the initial period is relatively short, for example, 90 days or less.[30] However, some employers may use a much longer period of probation, such as 12 months.[31] Where long probationary periods are used, putting the employee through successive probationary periods might be tested by allegations of bad faith action where the doctrine is available.

There is a considerable amount of effort being given to reforming the harshness of the at will presumption and doctrine, which permits the employer to discharge an employee for any reason or no reason. These reform efforts do not include changing the status of the probationary employee. For example, the new Montana wrongful discharge statute does not cover probationary employees, and the statute does not distinguish between new and experienced probationary employees.[32] Presumably both would be outside of the protections of the statute.

Probationary status for an experienced employee may be imposed in an arbitrator's award as a condition of reinstatement.[33] Where an employer has an employee assistance plan (EAP) covering drug or alcohol abuse, probation is often a condition of returning to work.[34] During these periods, the employees may be subject to such things as unannounced testing, successful completion of the EAP, and have "to cooperate with any and all company medical authorities."[35]

In summary, the probationary status is used for a great many different purposes beyond seeing if the new employee fits in. The assumption in these probationary situations is that the probationary employee can be subject to all manner of special conditions that limit commonly assumed rights. The growing use of testing for drugs and alcohol in the workplace will make this a much more important issue where testing positive leads to probationary status. In addition, an experienced employee may revert to probationary status as the result of a promotion, transfer, or the imposition of discipline. Nothing indicates that probationary status cannot be renewed at the end of a probationary period.

Postprobationary Status. The existence of a short term, unprotected probationary status as the initial employment relationship suggests that a more permanent, postprobationary status will follow. The probationary period, or at least the new employee probationary period in the private sector, is usually of short duration. The employee is usually aware of the probationary period and has the expectation that a different job security status will follow. In point of fact, the postprobationary status is likely to be that of an at will contract status. Under the at will contract, the employee can be discharged for any reason, just as the employer could during the probationary status. Thus from a job security perspective, there is little to distinguish probationary and postprobationary at will status. In a dissenting opinion, a Supreme Court Justice noted this contradiction and indicated that a probationary period implies a postprobationary period that includes a measure of job security.

> For example, petitioner was hired for a "probationary" period of six months, after which he became a "permanent" employee. No reason appears on the record for this distinction, other than the logical assumption, confirmed by a reasonable reading of the local ordinance, that after completion of the former period, an employee may be discharged only for cause.[36]

The fact that the argument was noted in dissent demonstrates its weakness when used in court. Most courts find that there is no contradiction between finding that an employee can be subject to arbitrary discharge during the probationary period and can be equally subject to arbitrary at will discharge during the postprobationary period.[37] One rationale that is used to distinguish probationary and postprobationary status is to look at contract benefits other than job security. The postprobationary employee may be eligible for such benefits as sick leave and wage increases, although still be subject to arbitrary discharge.[38] Occasionally a court will find sufficient other evidence beyond the end of the probationary period; to find an implied contract clause that the existence of a probationary period implies that discharge in the postprobationary period must be based on cause.[39]

If there is a written contract, the postprobationary status may be spelled out. The terms of a postprobationary period can be "set by the agreement between the parties,"[40] if the employee has bargaining power. The employee may be able to bargain some other probationary protections, such as requiring certain procedures be followed prior to a discharge. Most employees probably have no bargaining power and no written contract terms, especially if they are new employees. An experienced employee put on disciplinary probation usually will have no bargaining power. The employee who is transferred or promoted may have some bargaining power to negotiate on postprobationary status if the employee has a real choice about whether to accept or reject the promotion.

A new employee probationary period is often included in collective bargaining agreements. Those contracts frequently spell out the details for the probationary employee.[41] Usually the collective bargaining contract provides that a regular employee can be discharged only for good cause once the employee has passed the probationary period. As indicated, most courts are unwilling to imply such a postprobationary status in individual contracts of employment.

In summary, probationary status contract clauses give the employer the maximum amount of authority to discharge the probationary employee. There is little judicial recognition of any differences between newly hired probationary employees and experienced employees who have reverted to a probationary status. However, the probationary status is a contract status, and there is no doctrinal reason why a probationary contract cannot have some clauses relating to job protection. Courts generally see no contradiction between an at will probationary contract period and a postprobationary contract status that is at will, that is, has no job security provisions. The major differences between probationary status and postprobationary status may lie in employee benefit clauses other than the job security clauses.

Higher Level Employees

A characteristic of some employment positions is their higher level job status. This may be evidenced by the blue collar, white collar distinction, although usually higher level job status cases involve the upper end of the white collar group. In general, the courts say that the higher the status or level of the job, the greater the discretion of the employer to discharge. There is no clear definition of higher level, but the job security characteristics of such an employee are relatively clear.[42] The result of this doctrine is an enhancement of employer rights.

Many persons fall into the category of higher level employees. The range may include executives with six or seven figure incomes, as well as more modestly paid supervisors, and managers.[43] Many of these higher level positions will be filled by trained professionals.

The identification of the higher level category is important for job security purposes. The courts give the employers great latitude to discharge persons in this higher level status. There are various reasons for this. The higher level employee may hold a position of trust, and the court may permit a discharge when that "feeling" of trust is destroyed.[44] The employer will not be required to articulate the criteria for evaluation for higher level employees in as definite and objective a manner as might be expected for other employees. "Many criteria for higher level jobs are not easily articulable, and their conversion to writing does little to stop employers who desire to discriminate."[45] This permits the employer to use a more subjective, less reviewable, basis of evaluation with less fear that a court will overturn the decision.[46] In other words, the scope of just cause for discharge purposes is expanded. The employer can require a greater level of performance and expect greater responsibility from the higher level employee.[47]

The employer can demand from supervisors a higher level of loyalty, and can require that supervisors and the employer speak with one voice.[48] The employer can require great cooperation.[49] An employer can discipline a supervisor where there is doubt about that person's future effectiveness, as when a supervisor spoke before a group of illegal strikers with whom the supervisor had worked.[50] The employer can expect that the supervisor will be "personable."[51] Higher level employees may be subject to a greater loss of personal privacy than other employees.[52] Higher level employees may owe the employer a higher level of loyalty.[53]

Between judicial and arbitral forums, the criteria for discharge of higher level employees are set primarily by the courts. Arbitrators will not have as much opportunity as courts to consider these cases because the higher level employees will not be eligible for collective bargaining status under the National Labor Relations Act. They fall into the group of supervisors, confidential employees, managerial employees, or other types of employees who are excluded from protection under the NLRA.[54]

Some of the highest level employees may negotiate very beneficial individual contracts. An example of this is the "golden parachute" contract held by some top level corporate executives.[55] However, most of the higher level employees are middle range executives who probably have no written employment or benefits contract, who are in an at will status, and who are not eligible for collective bargaining status (even if there were sufficient employee interest).[56]

Any single employer is not likely to have very many higher level employees. Because there are few employees in this category for any given employer, a discharged employee in this category for any given employer will be less able to show that the employee has been treated in a disparate manner. Disparate treatment analysis requires a number of similar circumstances to identify the norm. This means that the employee will not be able to rely upon statistical arguments concerning patterns that may emerge from discharge statistics.[57] Small numbers may be found to be not statistically meaningful. This may, for example, make claims of discrimination more difficult to prove. Where there are few employees in a class, there are also probably very few discharge examples. The employee who is discharged may have a more difficult time showing that cause did not exist for the discharge because there are too few examples of what cause might mean in that particular workplace context.[58] The employer's definition of cause is more likely to be accepted.

Discharge cases should be read carefully to determine the level of the employee. The employer may have greater discretion to discharge a higher level at will employee than other at will employees. A discharge case involving a higher level at will employee will not necessarily be a clear precedent for the discharge of a lower level at will employee. The expectations and demands can be greater for a higher level employee than for a lower level employee. The effect of these doctrines is to enhance employer decision-making rights concerning higher level employees.

In summary, higher level employees have less job security than many other employers. Courts recognize that the nature of the jobs makes it difficult to establish objective criteria for higher level positions. This gives the employer greater discretion to make adverse personnel decisions based on a finding of cause. A larger range of subjective criteria will be permitted to be used. In addition, the relatively small number of higher level positions makes it more difficult to demonstrate disparate treatment. A small number of personnel decisions may not be statistically significant. Employee status as a higher or lower level employee greatly affects management rights in individual contracts.

Special Characteristics of the Job

When a job has special characteristics, the employer can discharge the employee for cause when the employee is unable to perform in a manner satisfactory to meet the special job characteristics. This is an indistinct, but important job category that is recognized by the courts. Arbitrators may also be important sources of definition of these special characteristics, because many of these employees are eligible for collective bargaining under the labor legislation. Jobs with special characteristics give the employer a greater range decision making criteria, which has the effect of increasing employer rights.

Where the employee can be arbitrarily discharged under an at will individual contract, the employer may have little interest in trying to identify special job characteristics. However, where the employer has to justify a discharge on the basis of cause, the failure of the employee to perform to meet the special employment characteristics may give rise to cause as a lawful justification for the discharge. There seems to be surprisingly little effort in the litigation to date to identify special job characteristics. In the future, when there may be greater statutory emphasis on showing a cause basis for discharges, special job characteristics will doubtlessly play a larger role.

As already suggested, higher level jobs may have special requirements (e.g., trust) which may enhance the employer's discretion to discharge for cause if the special requirements are not met. In addition, many "lower" level jobs are recognized as having special characteristics that also give the employer greater discretion to deal with the employee and increase employer rights to make for cause adverse decisions affecting the employee's contractual status.

A job with public safety overtones may be found to have special characteristics. A passenger bus driver has a special responsibility for safety that extends to both the passengers and the public at large.[59] An over the road truck driver may be required to show "extreme caution" concerning levels of health, care, and ability.[60] A delivery person may have special duties in regard to courtesy and honor, because the delivery person represents the employer in the public's eye and may handle the employer's money.[61] A supervisor should be personable.[62] Food checkout clerks have a special responsibility of trust and accurate work because they handle all of the money for the employer. They may be subject to discharge for a first time infraction, whereas the discharge of other employees may require multiple infractions.[63] An employer can take actions that will limit the employer's potential liability to third parties, such as disqualifying a bus operator who had experienced a heart attack.[64] Other examples of jobs with unusually unique characteristics include persons filling a pastoral position[65] or court officers.[66]

Special attributes of jobs are recognized in arbitration. The attributes were described in the following manner:

> Special requirements of the job may call for particular attributes . . . in the employee. . . . For example, the job may require qualities of leadership, initiative, responsibility for independent judgment or self-reliance, the ability to get along with others; or it may involve dealing with a 'special class' of customers, or require that the employee be physically available for emergency work.[67]

Individual contract case decisions should be read carefully to determine if any special job characteristics are involved. If they are, the decision may not be a valid precedent where special characteristics are not required.

In summary, a job may have special characteristics that must be met by the employee. If the employee cannot meet the job characteristic requirements, there will be cause for discharge. The expansion of the

scope of good cause resulting from identifying special job characteristics gives greater rights to the employer over these employees
than over employees who must meet no special requirements. Examples of special characteristics include higher level positions,
employees who interact directly with the public, and employees who
handle the employer's money. Where an employer seeks to identify
cause as a basis of discharge, the characteristics of the job should be
carefully analyzed.

Other Job Categories

Other categories of jobs give the employer enhanced decision-
making rights. Temporary and part-time employees (contingent
workforce) are other examples of indistinct classes of employees.
These employees have few contract protections, which means that the
employer has a maximum amount of rights. There is little reported
litigation concerning most of them and they may not be covered by
protective labor legislation. Few are likely to have written agreements.

There are also some special categories of temporary positions. For
example, "relief supervisors are essentially bargaining unit
employees temporarily assigned the limited supervisory capacity and
function."[68] Presumably such an employee should be judged by the
characteristics of the regular position, not the temporary position. An
employee may also be hired to temporarily fill a position until a
thorough job search can be conducted.[69] Such an employee may have
no special claims that can be advanced when the time comes to
permanently fill the position, despite the accrued experience.

A temporary employee may not be protected by protective employment statutes, which may lead to a dispute over whether the employee
is temporary. The Vietnam Era Veterans' Readjustment Assistance Act
protects full time employees from a discharge based on their military
reserve obligation. In a case involving this statute, there was a question concerning the full time status of a student employee. It seemed
likely that the student would leave after graduation. The court found
that the student should not be considered to be a temporary employee
merely because the student might change jobs after graduation.[70] The
court noted that most employees would change jobs if a better opportunity arose. Because he was not temporary he was protected by the
statute.

The Draft Employment Termination Act of the Commissioners on
Uniform State Laws defines an "employee" as an individual who
works for an average of at least 20 hours a week.[71] Anything less than
that presumably would be temporary, and not covered by the

proposal. Employment legislation must be carefully reviewed for language of this nature.

In summary, the employer has a broad range of general rights to manage the business and its employees. Within the class of all employees, some of the employees will be subject to special conditions of employment. The general effect of these special conditions will be to enhance employer right to discharge them for cause.

Probationary employees are the major example of a special employment relationship. They may be discharged at will or for cause during their probationary period. The most common class of probationary employees is the new employee who is probationary. However, experienced or senior employees may revert to a probationary status as the result of discipline or a promotion to a new position. Employees in higher level jobs have a special employment relationship compared to other employees. This special relationship permits employers to discharge them with less objective justification than nonhigher level employees. Some jobs require special characteristics that the employee must possess or perform. These special characteristics again enhance the employer's right to discharge for cause because the employee must meet both the general job requirements and, in addition, meet the special job requirements. Another example of a special employment characteristic is the de minimus status held by temporary or part time employees. Special employment relationships have the effect of expanding the basis upon which an employer might find that cause exists for a discharge.

Judicial decisions and arbitration awards, to a lesser extent, do not frequently identify special job characteristics, except in the most obvious circumstances. Existing case law permits the recognition of a wide range of identifiable special characteristics. Attention to this issue might shift many disputes away from an at will analysis toward a for cause discharge analysis. Where there is discussion of the special character of a job at the time of employment, employees might be able to use the discussion as a basis for arguing that more than an at will relationship was intended.

GENERAL EMPLOYEE DUTIES

One aspect of employer rights is the power of the employer to make unilateral business related decisions that affect employees. This right can be summarized under the heading of entrepreneurial control. Another aspect of employer rights involves the duties owed by the employee to the employer. In addition to some of the special duties of an employee, there are a number of identified general duties owed by all employees. An employee owes a number of duties to the employer as his or her side of the employment contract. These duties may be implied or expressed, but most of them are implied by courts and arbitrators because there is no written contract. If the employee breaches the obligations, the employer may have just cause to take adverse personnel action or other actions against the employee. Where the employer has just cause for the personnel action, the just cause reason will be a valid defense in either an at will or in a fixed term contract discharge dispute.

The general duties owed by the employee could be considered in a discussion of discipline and cause (Chapter 6), or in a discussion of contract terms (Chapter 5), or as part of the present discussion of employer rights. The relationship between these duties and the other topics should be kept in mind.

These implied terms to the employment contract apply to both individual contracts and collective bargaining contracts of employment. They are another example of an area where individual and collective contracts share many common characteristics. These implied duties are an obligation on the employee and a benefit to the employer. In other words, the employer has a right to insist on them without having to negotiate. This gives them the characteristic of an employer right.

Viewed as a matter of contractual mutuality, there is no similar length list of implied duties that is commonly owed by the employer to the employee. This again makes the essentially one sided employee duties look like fundamental employer rights.[72] The employee's general duties may add little to the employer rights where the employer already has the authority to arbitrarily discharge the employee, as under an at will contract. However, where the employer seeks to justify a discharge on the basis of cause, both the general duties owed to the employer and the special characteristics of the job should be given close scrutiny.

Basic Duties

One of the most basic of the general duties is regular attendance at the workplace.[73] Equally basic is the obligation that the employee perform the assigned tasks.[74] The employee should arrive at work on time, not be tardy and properly perform. These employee duties complement the employer's rights to make decisions on product choice, promotion of the product, and economic profitability mentioned earlier.[75] A tardy or absent employee interferes with productivity. The general rule on absences is such that even if an absent employee takes employer approved absences, the employee has still been held subject to discharge.[76] Clearly, unearned absences can result in discharge.[77] Stealing from the employer is obviously a major offense.[78] Fights among the employees cannot be tolerated,[79] but exceptions may be made for moments of isolated anger.[80]

Following orders given by the employer is a basic requirement. Where an assignment or procedure is not carried out, the employee may be under an obligation to report that fact to the employer and to report the reason why it was not carried out.[81] A plaintiff employee who was discharged for not following orders may have had an honest belief in the validity of the employee's reasons for disobeying, but that belief will not aid the employee.

> It is clear that plaintiff did not share the hopes of other company officials on the performance of the more expensive (mailing) lists. . . . However, plaintiff's view of the potential effectiveness of the subject lists is irrelevant. It is undisputed that the other officers considered this a viable alternative, and plaintiff was under direct orders to procure such lists for testing.[82]

The employee may believe that a work order is foolish, but that belief will not help the disobedient employee either.

> I can appreciate these sentiments from employees faced with a seemingly unnecessary assignment given with little advance notice. The assignment may have been a touch cavalier. It may be open to the criticism that it was a waste of public money in light of the work load. These are judgments for the (employer). . . . The arbitrator is limited to the terms of the contract and the principles of just cause. It is not my function to disallow the assignment if it offends my business judgment.[83]

The employee is under a general duty to first obey orders and later grieve the matter, if a grievance mechanism is available. The self-help technique of refusal is a dangerous decision.[84]

Loyalty

The employee owes a duty of loyalty to the employer.[85] It is not always clear in discussions of this topic whether the duty of loyalty is a phrase that summarizes the total of all duties owed to the employer or whether the duty of loyalty is only one of several other distinct obligations owed to the employer. For present purposes, the duty of loyalty will be considered to be one of several distinct, individual duties owed to the employer. Failure to abide by this duty can result in adverse employee action. A number of different elements may be involved in the duty of loyalty.

The duty of loyalty means, in part, that the actions of the employee should enhance and not detract from the employer's business. This includes an obligation not to disparage the employer's product.[86] The employee should follow company policy and not substitute the employee's own personal preferences for those of the employer.[87] For example, an employee cannot choose to emphasize quality over quantity where the employer has quantity as the goal.[88] The employee must work on those projects assigned by the employer.[89] The employee has no right to demand that the employer meet the employee's choice of work that the employee finds acceptable.[90] For example, an employee is not privileged to refuse to work on nuclear power related projects because of moral objections concerning nuclear power.[91] Where the employer adopts a new marketing strategy over the contrary recommendation of the employee, the dissenting employee is still obliged to carry out the new policy.[92] The employee may not make personal business use of the employer's confidential information or customer lists.[93]

The requirement applies equally to professionally trained employees. A doctor may be required to conduct a distasteful research project assigned by the employer.

> Chaos would result if a single doctor engaged in research were allowed to determine, according to his or her individual consciences, whether a project should continue. An employee does not have a right to continued employment when he or she refuses to conduct research simply because it could contravene his or her personal morals.[94] Higher level employees may have a higher level of duty owed to the employer.[95]

Breach of the duty of loyalty may give the employer cause for discharge. In such a case where there is cause for discharge, a claim for unemployment compensation may be denied.[96] The disloyal employee may not have a claim for wages from the employer during the period of disloyalty.[97]

Frequently, the loyalty cases involve situations in which the employee subsequently opens a business that is competitive with the former employer. In some of these circumstances, the employer may be entitled to a limited injunction that, for example, prohibits the employee from soliciting customers of the former employer.[98] The fact that employer may also have breached part of the employer's side of the employment contract will not necessarily be a defense that is available to an employee who is charged with breaching the employee's duty of loyalty.[99]

In summary, the duty of loyalty is a broad obligation on the employee. It ranges from following employer policy to not competing for the employer's special customers. Remedies for breach of the duty of loyalty may range from discharge to loss of compensation to injunctive restrictions.

Code of Ethics

Reliance on a professional code of ethics may not give the professional employee a basis upon which to refuse an employer's order. The code may provide the employee with a defense to the insubordination charge if the order is clearly unethical.[100] In other situations, the code may not. An arbitrator described the issue in the following manner:

> No matter how appropriate bodies may interpret the Code with respect to individual responsibility and a practitioner's obligations thereunder . . . this Grievant (lawyer), as an employee and as a member of the Union that negotiated an explicit professional responsibility providing for the benefit of all in the unit, was obligated to follow its procedures. Moreover, as a Staff Attorney assigned to clients of the Society (the employer), not his own, he had an obligation to apprise the Society of his purpose, something he did not do.[101]

A code of ethics may be viewed as an expression of public policy or it may be viewed as serving the more narrow interests of the profession. Where a provision is viewed as serving solely the interests of the profession or viewed as an administrative regulation concerned with technical or administrative matters, an employee who relies on the ethical code in a discharge case might find that it provides no protection.[102]

In summary, a code of ethics, whether personal or professional, is unlikely to provide a defense for an insubordinate employee, except in the clearest cases. However, a code of ethics might overlap with a whistleblower statute, and the statute might give relief to the employee.

Best Efforts, Employees

The employee is obligated to do the employee's best work. The employee should help the employer remain competitive.[103] The employee should not endanger or compromise the interests of the employer. The employee is not privileged to conduct the employee's personal business while being paid to work for the employer.[104]

The employee must be able to recognize and prepare for changes in the nature of the employer's business.[105] This might involve learning new techniques or obtaining other training.[106] Where there is a compelling business reason, the employee might be obligated to perform overtime.[107] Where the employer demands a higher level of efficiency, the employee who fails to respond cannot defend on the notion that past practices were to accept sloppy or less efficient work.[108] The long-term employee is obviously going to experience more changes in the job and workplace than the short-term employee. The stereotype of the older employee, who is more likely to be long term, is that the employee is less adaptable and more difficult to train.[109] Older employees must nonetheless adapt to changing times. "In the new industrial experience, the employee will have to anticipate greater and greater changes."[110]

In summary, an employee owes a duty of best efforts to the employer. The duty of best efforts includes changing and upgrading skills to meet the employer's changing conditions. When a new owner takes over, the employee must meet the demands of that new employer.

Follow Policies

Courts recognize that employers have a legitimate interest in requiring employee's to follow company policy. An outspoken dissenter who does not go through regular channels may be discharged in the best interests of the business. The dissenter may become a nuisance because of the manner in which the dissent is expressed. The employer is entitled to preserve the administrative procedures for doing things that has been established.[111] An employer has a legitimate interest in preserving normal operating procedures.[112] An employee may be subject to discipline for going outside of these channels. An example is the employee who goes over the head of the immediate supervisor to present complaints.[113] The employee is also expected to accommodate his or her professional view and objectives to those of the employer.[114]

A long-term employee is expected to know company policy and procedures. An employee with 13 years of experience should know about product specifications and should be able to read blueprints.[115] Many years of prior compliance with the rules will demonstrate that company procedures were well known by a employee and a sudden failure to follow the procedures puts the employee in jeopardy.[116] For example, five years of experience indicated that the employee knew that he needed a property pass to properly remove company property from the premises.[117]

A special problem is presented by the whistleblower. The whistleblower may go outside of the employer before reporting internally or the employee may not follow a promulgated internal procedure for bringing such issues to the attention of the employer through the chain of command. Legislation may long-term how the employer can treat such an employee.[118] Special issues may arise where an issue of employer product safety and public safety is involved. Some courts have distinguished cases where the employer tried to hide the defect from situations where the employer had made no effort to disguise the problem. In the former instance, the employee may be more privileged to go outside of company channels.[119]

A long-term employee who fails to follow proper procedure may be in a more serious situation than a shorter term employee. The experience coming from long service may show that the long-term employee knew or should have known company policy and indicate that going outside of established procedure was a deliberate act. A deliberate violation of the rules may receive more serious discipline than where a new employee did a similar thing but did not know the proper procedure. The long-term employee's false sense of security about job tenure may also help lead the long-term employee astray.[120] Absent a contract, seniority does not protect an at will employee.

The employee has a duty to respect the authority of the employer and the employer's representative.[121] Adverse personnel action may be properly taken where the employee seeks to challenge or intimidate the supervisor.[122] The offense becomes much more serious where the challenge or intimidation takes place in presence of other employees.[123] The duty is a heavy one. As one arbitrator said, "there is no such thing as a little defiance."[124] Familiarity bred by long service does not substantially change the requirement, although a few courts may require a duty of extra care in dealing with a long-term employee.[125]

In summary, employees are required to follow company procedures. Charges and complaints must go through the established chain of command, unless a whistleblower statute provides otherwise. Long-term employees are especially at risk here because their long service is evidence of knowing what should be done and how it should be done.

Attitude

Employee attitude is a legitimate matter of employer concern.[126] Many employees seem to be unaware or unconcerned with how important attitude can be. The employee has a duty to avoid demoralizing others in the workforce and a duty not to threaten the productivity of the workplace.[127] The employee cannot hold the job in disdain and expect to continue to work. Where the employee has an attitude toward the job that is detrimental or disruptive, the employer may take adverse action.[128] If the employee cannot get along, the employee is likely to be fired.[129]

Arbitrators give careful attention to employee attitude. The leading treatise on arbitration states, in part:

> An employee's attitude may be in issue and may be important, depending upon the nature of the job. It has been held that, in determining whether an employee is qualified for a job, supervision may evaluate the employee's attitude which may include "conscientious application, care for materials, concern for others in a group and response to instruction."[130]

There is nothing to suggest that the attitude of the long-term employee is treated in any more lenient manner than that of a new employee. "In another case, the employee's attitude toward the job and spirit of cooperation were said to be included in the word 'qualifications' as used in the seniority provisions; and the senior employee's uncooperative attitude could properly be considered in denying him a promotion to a better job."[131]

A long-term employee obviously has a greater number of chances at promotions and other benefits than the shorter term worker. Long service may breed a sense of false security or false expectations. When the employee fails to receive a benefit or promotion that was expected, the employee may develop an embittered attitude toward the employer.[132] Such an attitude may violate a duty owed to the employer. In one such case, the situation was described as follows:

> He was negligent in a variety of ways: 1. He allowed his disappointment over his failure to be promoted to seriously affect his job performance. 2. He performed his job functions totally inadequately, and exhibited a hostile attitude. . . . 3. He failed to heed a number of warnings which he did have that his job could be in jeopardy.[133]

The long-term employees may feel that their long service and past favorable evaluations may permit them to act in a more independent manner toward the employer or other employees. Such attitudes may also put the long-term employee at risk.[134]

In summary, the general duty owed by the employee under the individual employment contract is to perform the task for which the employee was hired. However, this obvious obligation carries with it a myriad of related duties. If the employee fails to adequately meet these obligations, the employer has cause to discharge. The employee duties give rise to a major employee right to take adverse action where the duties are not fulfilled. Employee duties include performance, timely presence, following orders and not challenging orders, loyalty, following the employer's preferences and not the employee's personal preferences, maintaining a positive attitude, and many other duties. Performance of some of these duties can be measured objectively, whereas others are judgmental. Courts will rarely second guess an employer's judgment as to the adequacy of the employee's performance of these duties. The skills and knowledge of procedures gained by long-term employees permit employers to judge them more critically than a new employee may be judged. Similarly, the false sense of security or the false sense of familiarity experienced by long-term employees may erroneously lead them to think that they will be judged less critically by the employer, which is not the true situation. If anything, it appears that long-term employees are frequently subject to greater scrutiny.

EFFICIENT OPERATIONS: BUSINESS JUDGMENT

The employer determines what product to produce or service to offer, how to produce it, what quantity and quality to produce, and a variety of related decisions.[135] The employer has the right to expand or reduce the business at any time.[136] These fundamental business decisions are deemed essential if the employer is to remain competitive. There is little question but that courts and arbitrators feel the employer must be given and is given great latitude in making these business decisions. "(A) corporate officer has the right to exercise his duties without liability even though the employment relations of others may be affected."[137] These employer rights may be summarized as essential elements of entrepreneurial control.

Efficiency

One hallmark of the American employer is the right to make decisions that will increase efficiency and will generate greater profits. The latitude given the employer to make business decisions concerning efficiency is very broad. This efficiency rationalization also covers the hiring and discharge decisions that immediately affect the employees. Efficiency becomes an argument that justifies basic product and production decisions, as well as personnel decisions.[138] Only an efficient business can survive.[139] "Courts . . . must avoid second-guessing employers' business decisions that are made on an appropriate economic basis."[140]

Both courts and arbitrators frequently defer to fundamental employment decisions that an employer states will enhance the efficiency of the business. The employment decisions might relate to the working in general, such as moving a plant or partially closing. The employment decisions might be more aimed at individuals, such as weeding out the inefficient. This deference is usually given without requiring factual proof of the relationship between the personnel decision and its demonstrable effect on efficiency of the operation.

In many of the court cases, the court is dealing with an at will situation where either no reasons or false reasons can be acceptable under the at will doctrine. Arbitrators will be dealing with few at will situations. The fact that both the courts and the arbitrators, operating in two different dispute resolution systems, emphasize the efficiency argument indicates the importance of the concept. It also suggests that the concept is equally related to individual employment contracts and collective bargaining contracts.

Efficiency has been described as a "clear, precise, and an appropriate standard."[141] Efficiency has been given statutory recognition in federal public sector employment. "Cause" for purposes of discharge has been statutorily defined in the federal public sector system in terms of the "efficiency of the service."[142] "Cause" has been described elsewhere in the public sector as shortcomings "detrimental to the . . . efficiency of the employer."[143]

Courts frequently permit a broad discretion to discharge when it is justified as being necessary to the business. "[T]he employer has an important interest in being able to discharge . . . whenever it would be beneficial to his business."[144] The right of discharge is "necessary to permit him to operate his business efficiently and profitably."[145] The general attitude of judicial restraint in employment litigation exhibited by the courts often means that the court will not require the employer to prove that the employment decision really increased or maintained the efficiency of the business. The employer's reliance on the efficiency rationale becomes, in effect, an unchallengeable conclusion accepted by the courts.

The employer has the right to expect that the employees will become increasingly efficient and to meet higher qualifications than they have in the past.

Sophistication of product and elegance of construction are making greater and greater demands on the people. It may not be enough in just any situation to be able to say "I learned mine the hard way in the shop" and then be taken by surprise by some highly technical development introduced on a new product. In the new industrial experience, the employee will have to anticipate greater and greater changes.[146]

Courts and arbitrators feel that the employer needs great personnel flexibility to meet the uncertainties of the business world. From this point of view, the age of the employee and the seniority of employment do not necessarily add to the qualifications of the employee. New economic and working conditions might result in making the experienced employee less efficient. Whereas the experienced employee may have been efficiently working under one set of job requirements, the introduction of new products, machines, processes, or managers may require a period of considerable adjustment by the employee. The period of adjustment may be a period of reduced efficiency even for experienced personnel.

There should be little question that a demonstrably inefficient employee has violated the employee's side of the employment contract. However, the efficiency argument not only permits the employer to replace demonstrably inefficient workers, but also permits replacement of workers who have a past record of good evaluations. Presumably, the good evaluations meant that the employee was efficient. This contradiction arises because the efficiency doctrine does not require the employer to show that there is an actual impact on efficiency or to show demonstrated inefficiency on the part of the employee. The efficiency rationale is arguably just another way of expressing a judicial reluctance to second guess the employer. This refusal to second guess is particularly obvious in at will employment cases where the employer need give no reason or basis for an action. When no reason is required, the efficiency argument may be relied upon to lessen the appearance of arbitrary employment decision making. However, even if the decision is arbitrary, it is lawful under the at will doctrine.

The question of requiring factual proof that an employee's retention would harm the employer has been raised directly. In one case, a competent supervisor was discharged for speaking before a group of illegally striking air controllers. The supervisor claimed that he was discharged on the basis of "undifferentiated speculation," not on the basis of evidence that harm would come to the government employer if he were retained. The court rejected the argument, stating in part, "In our view (plaintiff) Brown would place too great a burden on the (employer) agency to show harm in his case."[147] However, in arbitration, a different result might sometimes be reached because the burden of proving the grounds for discharge is usually put on the employer where there is a cause requirement.[148]

Even where an efficient employee is mistakenly discharged, the mistake may not avail the employee. The Supreme Court has noted in a related context that "we must accept the harsh fact that numerous individual mistakes are inevitable in the day-to-day administration of our affairs."[149] The judicial tolerance of error in employment decisions is the general rule, even though many employees seem unwilling or unable to accept it.

In summary, the employer's right to decide issues of efficiency permits the employer to make decisions about the workforce that will accomplish that goal. However, the courts will not second guess this entrepreneurial judgment and will not require proof of the relationship between the personnel decision and an actual increase in efficiency. An inefficient employee breaches a duty owed to the employer and gives rise to cause for discharge. Efficient employees may also be removed where the employer seeks greater efficiency or efficiency by different techniques.

Inefficient Decisions

A major element in discharge cases is the judicial recognition of the right of the employer to make basic entrepreneurial decisions that are directed at increasing the efficiency of the business. However, the courts also permit decisions that may go much further. They may permit employer decisions that the courts acknowledge do not promote the efficiency of the enterprise. These "inefficient" decisions are often given the same protection as discharge decisions that are justified on the basis of efficiency.[150] Courts and arbitrators have permitted discharges where the courts and arbitrators themselves have characterized the employer's actions as being arbitrary and malicious,[151] shortsighted and narrowminded,[152] negligent,[153] inhumane,[154] hardhearted,[155] and reprehensible.[156] Basic entrepreneurial decisions will not be subject to second guessing even if they appear to be objectively wrong.

One of the reasons why courts or arbitrators may permit these "inefficient" personnel decisions is that many of them occur in the context of an at will or similarly unrestrained employment relationship. No reason or proof is needed to justify the discharge. Attaching the labels of efficiency or inefficiency becomes legally irrelevant in such a system.

Efficiency may be only one of several different reasons for a discharge. From one perspective, the decision may look "inefficient," but
from another perspective it may not. In an analogous situation, the
Supreme Court has noted that when an employee has been terminated
for a number of reasons, only one of which was unconstitutional, the
challenge of the dismissal may fail if any one of the other reasons for
termination are proper and sufficient.[157] This would seem to state a
general rule that where the employer has several reasons for a discharge, if one reason is valid, the other reasons can be ignored. Usually
employers will argue discharge cases in the alternative: the employee
was at will, but if the employee was not at will, the employer had cause
to discharge, and the employer will include inefficient performance
in the menu of reasons for the action.

A few judicial decisions do not accept employer decisions that lead
to inefficient business results. One court has taken note of the adverse
effect on the overall economic system when efficient employees are
summarily discharged. The court stated that a discharge motivated by
bad faith, malice, or retaliation "is not in the best interests of the
economic system or the public good and constitutes a breach of the
employment contract."[158] Under the "efficiency of the service" standard used in the federal public sector system, a court found that the
efficiency of the service would not be promoted by a certain discharge,
and therefore the arbitrator's reinstatement of the employee was
upheld.[159] Thus there are a few decisions suggesting that if the efficiency argument can be the basis of a justifiable discharge, then a discharge
that does not promote efficiency should not be permitted to go unex-
amined. However, this is a distinctly limited group of cases.

Some courts that permit "inefficient" discharges may point out that
"the marketplace contains a system of rewards and penalties independent of those prescribed by law."[160] The rewards of the market
place may not give much aid to the discharged employee, but the
courts do not decide on that basis: "It is of course true that . . .
(employer) was better able to absorb the loss of an experienced
employee than appellant was able to absorb the unexpected loss of his
job. But a company, no matter how large, can afford only so many
uneconomic decisions."[161] In other words, the courts may not offer any
relief to the discharged employee, but the employer may be seen as
having to pay a marketplace price for discharging an efficient
employee.

Under an at will employment contract, the courts will permit an
employer to give no reason or an arbitrary reason as the basis for the
decision to discharge. The employer may nonetheless offer reasons
such as efficiency. When the challenges to a discharge go beyond the
at will context, the employer's use of makeweight reasons may not be

risk free. Their use may make the employment decision suspect. For example, if the discharged employee charges the employer with discrimination and either no reason or a false reason was given for the discharge, it may help the employee to show that the reason was merely a pretext for discrimination.[162] The court's deference to the employer in the contract at will situation may be reduced when statutory issues are raised.

In summary, a major feature of employer rights is to make decisions that will enhance the efficiency of the business. Efficiency and profitability are touchstones in our method of economic organization. The most fundamental employer right is to quit being in business, and many rights flow from that even while the employer stays in business. Where an employer justifies personnel decisions on the basis of efficiency, courts will rarely require proof to show how efficiency was actually enhanced. The court will not second guess the employer's business judgment. Employees may seek to show that a particular personnel decision actually contributed to inefficiency, but the courts will usually reject the effort to second guess the employer. The employer's judgment, not the employee's, is what is critical to the court, even when the employer might be wrong. Efficiency justifications are frequently used as backup arguments in at will contract situations. A failure to distinguish between cause and at will status adds confusion to the cases. Courts and arbitrators permit employers to be wrong in their judgments about employees. Employee litigation brought for the purpose of obtaining error free personnel decisions fails to understand the essential character of the doctrine of employer rights. However, where the employer is arbitrary or makes an obvious error that infringes upon an employee's statutory rights, the employer's right to take adverse personnel action may be limited.

SPECIAL BUSINESS SITUATIONS

Successor Employers

Many types of special business conditions are recognized that may give the employer greater freedom and prerogatives to make personnel decisions. The new employer may be permitted to have very fluid personnel policies when the new employer is restructuring to meet new conditions and demands.[163] In the face of the currently changing economic environment, this defense is a developing area of law. The Supreme Court has noted the following:

A potential employer may be willing to take over a moribund business only if he can make changes in corporate structure, composition of the labor force, work location, task assignment, and nature of supervision. Saddling such an employer with the terms and conditions of employment contained in the old collective- bargaining contract may make these changes impossible and discourage and inhibit the transfer of capital.[164]

This is undoubtedly another area where the rule for collective bargaining contracts is the same as the rule for individual contracts of employment. The Supreme Court has said: "[a] successor employer is ordinarily free to set initial terms on which it will hire the employees of a predecessor."[165] The collective bargaining agreement generally offers greater job security than individual employment contracts. This "special" collective contract may become unenforceable in some situations where a successor employer takes over the business.[166] If the contract with the most job security (collective bargaining) can be overridden by the new employer, the individual contract will suffer a similar fate.

However, there are limits on successor employers. If the new employer does not substantially change the business, the new employer may be bound, for example to engage in collective bargaining.

[A]ll that is involved is the substitution of one group of workers for another to perform the same task in the same plant under the ultimate control of the same employer. The question of whether the employer may discharge one group of workers and substitute another for them is closely analogous to many other situations within the traditional framework of collective bargaining.[167]

The employees have a stronger claim to their job security interests where there is "substantial continuity of identity in the business enterprise."[168]

Where the new employer makes higher demands of efficiency from the workers and changes the method of operations, the new employer may not be permitted to change things overnight. The employees, one arbitrator stated, should be given an opportunity to adjust.[169] Presumably, a failure to adjust would permit a for cause discharge, even in an other than at will situation. Where the at will relationship exists, the employer could always discharge for an arbitrary reason or for no reason.

In summary, a successor employer may not be bound by all of the terms of the predecessors collective bargaining or individual contracts of employment. Public policies such as the free flow of capital are the justification for the rule. A successor employer will be permitted to discharge employees who cannot meet the successor employer's greater demands of efficiency. In general, an employer gains an element of greater freedom or right to make personnel decisions when the employer is making fundamental changes in the business.

New Organization

An employer is obviously permitted to make major changes in the business even though there may be an adverse impact on the employees.[170] As a general proposition, it appears that the more fundamental the change, the greater the employer right. For example, a merger may cause a reorganization that bumps employees out. "[A]s a result of the merger, the (employer) . . . made a business judgment as to the utilization of personnel . . . among whom was plaintiff who was terminated. This was a legitimate business reason."[171]

New supervisory personnel may be hired. An employee's inability to adjust to and cooperate with a new manager may be grounds for discharge.[172] A nondiscriminatory "get tough" policy enforced by a new manager may result in valid discharges.[173] In one situation, a question was raised concerning the status of employees over the age of 55 who had 20 years with the employer. The argument was that the employer had a discriminatory policy of releasing these older employers. The court, however, noted the changing organization of the employer. The court stated that the statistics "are ambiguous in the context of the indisputable background of a complete change in the nature of the Company's business, accompanied by extensive growth and diversification into new lines that have occurred over the period involved."[174]

During reorganization, the employer's personnel policies may be in flux. Courts may give the employer greater leeway to make decisions under those circumstances. "(The) Hospital was then undergoing the process of consolidation and restructuring following the merger of the two institutions. To expect clear and firmly established personnel policies during such a period is somewhat unrealistic."[175]

An employer undergoing changing circumstances may impose new contact terms on employees. The employees may be deemed to have accepted those terms by continuing to work.

(T)he announcement of the transfer was made in July 1976 at which time the plaintiffs were told that they would be considered resigned if they did not report (to the new location) in April 1977. The plaintiffs continued to work under this policy until April 1977. Regardless of anything that occurred before July 1976, by continuing to work for Bell after that date, the draftsmen bound themselves to the terms as stated in July 1976.[176]

The Supreme Court has listed a number of factors to be considered in determining whether the business has changed sufficiently to warrant the recognition of a new status or whether it is essentially a continuation of the prior organization.

All of the important factors which the Board has used and the courts have approved are present in the instant case: continuation of the same types of product lines, departmental organization, employee identity and job functions. . . . Both Burns and Wackenhut are nationwide organizations; both performed the identical services at the same facility; although Burns used its own supervisors, their functions and responsibilities were similar to those performed by their predecessors; and finally, and perhaps most significantly, Burns commenced performance of the contract with 27 former Wackenhut employees out of its total complement of 42.[177]

The court gives special prominence to such factors as changes, if any, in product, chain of command, old or new hires, location, and supervision.

In summary, where the employer reorganizes the business, the employer can take personnel actions that reflect the new organization. Collective bargaining and individual contracts of employment may be similarly affected. Personnel actions based on the new organization will be found to be based on cause. The new organization may make demands for increased efficiency. New supervisors may impose new standards. Fluid personnel policies may be tolerated in the transition.

Economic Conditions

Changing economic conditions may justify employment decisions by the employer that otherwise might not be permitted. When older workers were cut back due to economic necessity, the fact of the discharges standing alone did not give rise to minimal prima facie case requirement under the ADEA.[178] When the issue was an unfair labor practice concerning the refusal to bargain over the layoff of two employees, the NLRB found economic conditions to be a defense. The NLRB stated in part: "The Respondent's layoff decisions were arrived at on very short notice based on factors outside its control, and were consistent with past business decisions to lay off employees when orders declined substantially."[179]

In a wrongful discharge action, an employee claimed that the employer had discharged the employee in violation of the employer's handbook. The court disagreed with the employee. It found that the employee was discharged as a result of bona fide economic conditions and that the employer's manual had no provisions to cover that situation.[180] The court identified the economic adversity that the employer faced as the basis for a just cause discharge.

Another type of case involves the employee who accepts a new job, quits the prior job, and reports to the new position only to be told that he or she is not needed. One court has held that if the agreement was for at will employment and the employer's reason for the refusal to employ the person is economic, the employee has no grounds for recovery.[181] Of course, if the employment is truly at will, no reason would be required in any circumstance.

A reference to the collective bargaining situation also illustrates the judicial recognition of the effect of changed economic circumstance. Employees who are acknowledged victims of unfair labor practices may not receive a full remedy, such as reinstatement, where changed business conditions make the remedy futile.[182] Both collective and individual contracts may be interpreted in light of how economic conditions impact on the employer.

Small Employer

A recurring question in the case law is whether the small employer is in any different legal position than the larger employer. There is no clear agreement on of how "small" the small employer must be. The short answer is that there probably is little legal difference between large and small employers, outside of specific statutes. Some statutes take account of the smaller employers. For example, Title VII defines employer in terms of one who employs 15 or more persons.[183]

The short answer that there is no general difference between the position of large and small employers, however, may be too short an answer in a few cases. There is occasional recognition of the size of the employer in some cases. One court has noted that the wrongful discharge suits present a special dilemma for the small employer who may not be able to afford extensive litigation.

The more insidious danger . . . is that an employer may justly discharge an employee only at the risk of being compelled to defend a suit for retaliatory discharge. If such a cause of action generally could be maintained, employers, particularly those in small businesses, would be thrust into economic dilemma by every employment decision.[184]

Those who propose a statutory solution to the at will contract issue sometimes exempt the smaller employers from the statute.[185]

Small employers may have less staff flexibility than a large employer. This may mean that employees who, for example, seek leave may be more frequently denied the request because they are more difficult to replace in the small workforce. If the employee then takes the leave without permission, the employee may be subject to discharge.[186] The remedy of reinstatement may be less available to the improperly discharged employee of a small employer because of the frictions that might arise from the much closer employer and employee contact.[187] The argument is that efficiency might be more a critical issue for the small employer because if one person in the small workforce slows down, it has an immediate adverse impact on the ability of all of the others to get their work done.[188]

Another argument that is commonly raised is that an adverse court decision in a given personnel dispute will have a ruinous financial impact on the small employer. Courts routinely reject this argument. One major reason for rejection is that the employers seem unable to back up the claim with facts in the record.[189]

The Supreme Court has given a passing nod to the idea that small employers may sometimes be in a different position than larger employers. "On the other hand, a union may have made concessions to a small or failing employer that it would be unwilling to make to a large or economically successful firm."[190] The discussion Draft Employment Termination Act of the Commissioners on Uniform State Laws defines employers as one who employs 15 or more employees.[191] Smaller employers will not be covered.

In summary, changes in ownership, organization, and economic conditions are likely to expand the employer's flexibility in dealing with employees, so long as the decisions have an economic basis. This result is clearly permitted under collective bargaining contracts and generally applies to individual contracts of employment. The Supreme Court has recognized that collective bargaining contracts have a special status. "It is more than a contract; it is a generalized code to govern a myraid of cases which the draftsmen cannot wholly anticipate."[192] No court has seriously stated that the individual contract of employment is "more than a contract." In situations where employer rights prevail over the collective contract, they must also prevail over the lesser status of the individual contract.

In summary, successor employers will be given great flexibility in the exercise of their employer rights, especially when there are significant changes in organization, production, or other major elements of the business. Similarly, employer rights includes the right to respond to changing economic conditions in a way to attempt to preserve the efficiency and profitability of the business. Changing organization and economic conditions are recognized as constituting cause for discharge, in contact situations where cause is required. Small employers have long argued for recognition of their special status. Outside of specific statutes, this recognition is rarely given.

BALANCING INTERESTS

The thrust of the materials presented to this point is that, in general, employer rights and interests are often weighed more heavily by the common law than whatever interests employees may have. In many areas of the law, it is a common judicial practice to balance and weigh the interests of contending parties to determine who has the paramount interest. Most courts will not use a balancing test for disputes involving individual contracts of employment. This judicial refusal to balance employer and employee interests under the common law is one of the reasons prompting calls legislative reforms. Statutes frequently require balancing employer and employee rights, and they lessen the yoke of judicial restraint.

Courts have discussed use of a balancing process in determining employee and employer rights when it is mandated by statute. In the collective bargaining context under federal law, the Supreme Court has recognized a balancing process. "The objectives of national labor policy, reflected in established principles of federal law, require that the rightful prerogative of owners independently to rearrange their businesses and even eliminate themselves as employers be balanced by some protection to employees from a sudden change in the employment relationship."[193]

In the individual contract area and under the common law or judicial law unaffected by statutes, courts only occasionally talk about a balancing process. One court said, "The employers' interest in conducting their businesses as they see fit must be balanced with the interests of their employees in keeping their jobs."[194] Another said, "As a result, it is now recognized that a proper balance must be maintained among the employer's interest in operating the business efficiently and profitably, the employee's interests in earning a livelihood, and society's interest in seeing its public policies carried out."[195] Another nod toward recognizing the need to balance employee and employer rights is the occasional recognition given to the shock, emotional, and physical distress that a discharged employee might suffer.[196]

Most courts reject such concepts when they simply note that labor relations are often "difficult" and "certain decisions will impact more adversely on one side than the other."[197] A few cases make indirect reference to balancing when they note that the employee usually has little bargaining power with which to negotiate an individual contract.

Employees frequently argue that courts should recognize the extent of the injury suffered by the discharged employee.[198] It is argued that recognition should be given to the employee's claims of injury and the injury should be balanced against the seriousness of the reason for the discharge. The more severe the employee's shortcomings, the less the weight that might be given to the employee's claim of injury. Some arbitrators may acknowledge an injury claim but refuse to give it weight in the particular circumstances. For example, a claim of adverse impact on the employee's family may be given little weight when the employee commits a serious offense like theft.[199] Likewise, a claim of adverse impact on the employee's future job prospects was rejected in the theft situation.[200]

Arbitrators are more likely to acknowledge the impact of a discharge on the employee than are courts. They are likely to recognize that the discharge affects the employee's ability to gain new employment, affects the income of the employee's family, results in the loss of such benefits as hospitalization and medical care, results in the loss of pension benefits, results in the loss of seniority, and involves a stigma of social disapproval.[201] "When termination of employment is in issue, an arbitrator . . . is fully justified in considering the impact of the discipline upon an aggrieved employee."[202]

Courts may attempt to balance the injury and find the balance tips toward the employer.

It is of course true that . . . (the employer) was better able to absorb the loss of an experienced employee than appellant was able to absorb the unexpected loss of his job. But a company, no matter how large, can afford only so many uneconomic decisions and it is well to remember that the marketplace contains a system of rewards and penalties independent of those prescribed by law.[203]

Courts may look at a balancing process through the mutuality doctrine. They refer to the apparent mutuality or balance that results from giving the employer the right to discharge at any time because the employee can quit at any time. A court may also seek a lack of balance adversely affecting the employer. The court may note that the employer will rarely have an effective remedy against an employee who breaches the employment contract because the limited resources of the employee. It is unlikely that the employer could ever collect a judgment against the employee.[204]

Some courts have noted that an employer who issues fair personnel manuals should be bound by them because the employer may benefit from increased loyalty and productivity. They suggest a balance, that where there is benefit, the employer should be bound to follow the manuals.[205] Thus whereas a few cases identify benefits, burdens, injury, and bargaining power, most cases tip whatever balance may exist heavily in favor of employer rights most of the time.

However, there are contradictory approaches in the system. In at least three specific areas, courts are willing to engage in an explicit and detailed balance of employer and employee interests. One area is the free speech, First Amendment rights of public employees. A balance is made to determine "if the interests of the speaker and the community in the speech outweigh the interests of the employer in maintaining an efficient workplace."[206] A second area of explicit balancing is in the arbitration of the off duty conduct of an employee. The employee has a general right not to be disciplined for off duty conduct away from the workplace unless it can be shown to directly impact on the employee's work performance or impact on the employer's reputation or product.[207] The third area is the enforcement of noncompetition agreements that the employee may have been required to sign. The general test is that such an agreement must be reasonable in time and area, necessary to protect the employer's legitimate interest, not harmful to the general public, and not unreasonably burdensome to the employee.[208]

Cases in these three areas show that courts and arbitrators are fully able to make a detailed balance of the various employee and employer interests without unduly second guessing the employer. Apparently, each of these three areas is subject to a balancing test because courts are willing to give recognition of significant interests beyond the employment relationship: First Amendment, personal privacy away from work, and a public policy favoring competition. In the discharge area, however, courts apparently find the employee's economic interests and physical and emotional health interests not important enough to warrant using a general balancing test. In a number of cases where the employee demonstrates significant injury, the courts may still find that the employer has suffered more because of the employee's performance.

A number of parallels between collective bargaining and individual contracts have been identified in these materials. Balancing employer and employee interests is common in statutory collective bargaining analysis. In individual contract analysis, balancing is the exception and not the rule. Where balancing is used, the scales are frequently found to tip in favor of the employer. The general lack of acceptance of the balancing test for individual contracts cannot be based on a perception that the courts are unable to do it. Whether there is a collective contract or a group of individual contracts, a workplace is a workplace. If a balancing test is used in one, it could be used in the other. However, it generally is not used on the individual contract. Employees who argue for a balance will generally lose in court cases. Arbitrators may be more sympathetic toward using balancing tests. Even where a balancing test is used, however, it is important to note that the employer will have weighty interests to put into the balancing process.

ERROR, FAIRNESS, AND EMPLOYER RIGHTS

Implicit or explicit in many of the individual contract cases is the feeling that many plaintiff employees are demanding that employment decisions be shown to be factually correct and error free. If this is the demand, courts state that they are not equal to the task. One court frankly stated that "the moral fairness of the firing is simply beyond our power to review."[209] Probably more important, the doctrine of employer rights is too strong to be overcome by employees who would require an employer to factually justify an employment decision with anything more than the most general facts.

Legislation, legislative proposals, and changing judicial attitudes in some states are all efforts to reform the current status of the individual contract of employment. However, none of these efforts are intended to change the basic nature of the employer rights doctrine, which permits the employer to exercise judgment in making personnel decisions. Where the exercise of judgment is permitted, the decider need not be factually accurate or make error free choices. The most that is expected in the exercise of judgment is a greater effort at fairness and a reasonable consideration of the public's and employee's interests.

Sometimes the employer's decisions will be dictated by economic circumstances beyond the employer's control or reflect employer business judgments made at an earlier point that may have turned out to be wrong. The impact of these situations will fall on the employee regardless of the employee's record of performance and loyalty. The most that reform can here accomplish is to require that the employer's decisions be made in reasonable good faith with a minimum element of arbitrariness.

Sometimes the employer's decisions will be based on the employer's measured judgment about the employee's performance. Subjective elements will necessarily enter into the decision. The most that reform can accomplish here is to require the employer or a third party decider to give good faith and reasonable consideration to the employee's side of the issue.

The plaintiff employee who demands that the employer be able to factually justify each employment decision demands more than the system can offer. Such an employee also is making a demand that the legal system generally does not recognize. The employee who argues for less arbitrary action and more reasonableness and fairness is reaching a broader audience of supporters than ever before. Whatever the level of employee or reformer demand, it is important to note that there is no broad movement toward wholesale modification of the employer rights doctrine. Legislation may require less judicial restraint and more consideration of employee interests, but entrepreneurial control will continue to be the other side of the balance. Legislation must also run through the filter of judicial interpretation that created much of the doctrine of employer rights.

EMPLOYER SUITS AGAINST EMPLOYEES

A small but increasing number of employers are showing little reluctance to sue their employees under individual contracts of employment. Given a system that is based on mutuality, there is no reason in principle why employers cannot sue employees who breach the employment contract. In practice, there may be little incentive for most employers to sue because they have a very broad remedy in the employer's right to discharge. The discharge will probably resolve most problems. Any large judgments against an individual employee might be difficult to collect, especially if the employer has discharged the employee.

There are relatively few employer against employee suits, but there are some. The Supreme Court considered such a suit in the context of a collective bargaining dispute pending before the National Labor Relations Board. In that case, the employer filed suit against a waitress who was attempting to organize a union. The employer claimed that the employee harassed customers, property was blocked, libelous statements were made, and even public safety had been threatened. The Court was concerned with a variety of procedural issues, but the main issue of interest here was the court's examination of whether the employer's suit was based on intentional falsehoods or was knowingly frivolous. The Supreme Court indicated that the suit was not frivolous. There was a reasonable basis for the suit if "there is a general issue of material fact that turns on the credibility of witnesses or on the proper inferences to be drawn from undisputed facts."[210]

Retaliatory motive and lack of reasonable basis are elements to consider.[211] In principle, however, the suit could be maintained.

In another situation, an employer brought an arbitration action against an allegedly "negligent," discharged employee to seek to recover damages. The discharged employee responded with a counterclaim for back pay and lost bonus. The arbitrator ruled in favor of the employee's counterclaim and the employer was out a large sum of money.[212] A suit by one person may invite a countersuit in employment relations as elsewhere.

Plaintiff employer suits are much more common where the employer seeks to enforce a covenant not to compete that the employee was required to sign or where there has been a claim of breach of the duty of loyalty. Actions based on a covenant not to compete will usually seek injunctive relief as well as damages.[213] Lost profits may also be sought.[214] Courts will thoroughly review the covenant to determine its validity. Such an individual contract clause must generally meet standards of reasonableness, protection of the public interest, protection of limited employer interests, and not be unduly burdensome.[215] Depending on the outcome of their examination, courts may enforce, void, or occasionally rewrite such clauses.

The employer suit or action akin to a suit may arise in other ways. The employer may initiate the action, such as in a case where the employer seeks to restrain the former employees from soliciting the employer's customers.[216] The employer suit may arise as a counterclaim to a suit for compensation initiated by the employee.[217] The employer may not directly sue the employee, but may vigorously defend against an employee claim in another forum, for example, for unemployment benefits.[218] Finally, the employer may seek recovery of attorney fees charged to defend the employer when the action brought by the employee was frivolous or unreasonable.[219]

An employer may seek to recover losses caused by employee. Employer self-help against an errant employee, distinguished from a lawsuit, may be limited by state legislation. In one situation, an employer had a signed agreement for payroll deduction against an employee for employer losses due to the misdelivery of merchandise. The agreement was determined to be void under state legislation.[220] In another case a ship owner-employer brought an action for indemnity and contribution against defendant seaman after an action for maintenance and cure asserted by a coseaman. The court held the seaman defendant not liable in the absence of assault.[221] Another court rejected an employer claim against supervisors for indemnity for the employer's liability under the Fair Labor Standards Act.[222] Another court, however, recognized an employer's common law right to sue employees for damage to the employer's property, in this case, a train wreck.[223]

An employee may sue for nonpayment of sales commissions. A common employer reaction is a counterclaim for breach of a noncompetition clause or breach of a duty of loyalty.[224] Patent problems may also result in a suit when the employer seeks to force the employee to sign over patent rights for the employee's work product.[225]

A variety of other employment related activities may result in a suit or claim being brought by an employer. An employer unsuccessfully brought a breach of contract action against an employee who failed to abide by a release of claims that the employee signed at the employer's request. The employee had sued the employer despite having signed a release.[226] Agreements outside of the employment relationship may become intertwined in employment disputes. Wage claims may be set off against rent payments owed the employer.[227] Claims on a promissory note might give rise to a counterclaim based on theft of trade secrets and other claims.[228]

In an interesting arbitration result, an employee bank teller was discharged for cashing a forged check. The union sought arbitration on the issue of just cause. The arbitrator awarded reinstatement with backpay, but required the employee to reimburse the employer for the amount of the bad check from the back pay award. In this manner, an employee challenge to the employer's action resulted in a recovery, in part, for the employer.[229]

Rather than directly suing the employee, the employer may defend against claims made by former employees. This type of employer action typically takes the form of attempting to defeat the former employee's claim for unemployment compensation or other statutory claims.[230]

In summary, employer suits against employees are another expression of employer rights. These suits are mostly likely to arise in the context of covenants not to compete or in the context of a counterclaim to an employee's suit. The number of such suits is not large, but the area seems likely to show relative growth. Existing examples of these types of suits are varied, and the results do not yet define well identified parameters.

CONCLUSION

The employer rights doctrine looks to many sources for its content. Figure 3.1 summarizes some of the sources for employer rights.

The beginning point in the interpretation of any individual employment contract is recognition of the broad range of employer rights.

These employer rights consist of the right to make economic or business judgment decisions, the rights of the employer in special employment relationships, the employee duties owed to the employer, the protected right of the employer to make decisions that enhance efficient operations, and the enhanced employer rights in special business situations. Whereas courts may attempt to balance employer and employee rights in some few specialized situations, in most cases the broad range of employer rights will tip toward the employer, in the absence of specific contractual terms limiting the employer.

There are well-articulated judicial statements of employer rights that are based on the nature of our economic system. There are few corresponding statements about employee rights. Even where statutes articulate employee rights, they are interpreted by courts with an eye toward the importance of accommodating employer rights. Where the issues in employment disputes involve mainly matters of fairness in decision making, some courts may be sympathetic, but the general statement that prevails is that some error is both unavoidable and beyond the power of the courts to remedy.

Within the doctrine of employer rights, several categories can be recognized. One category is absolute rights, such as decisions akin to the decision to quit being in business. These employer rights are matters that are at the heart of entrepreneurial control. Supporting the absolute employer rights is a category of relative employer rights.

Figure 3.1 Employer Rights Summary

```
Inherent Rights:   Entrepreneurial Control
                   Business Judgment, Efficiency
                   Special Business Situations

Contract:          Employee Special Duties
                   Employee General Duties
                   Presumption Of At Will Status
                   Cause And Contract Violation
                   Disclaimed Handbook
                   Oral, Written At Will Terms

Dispute Forum:     Forum Restraint
                   Forum Procedure (e.g., burden of proof)
                   Balance Interests, Great Weight To Employer

Statutes:          Definitions Of Employer, Employee
                   Liability Limitations, Remedies
                   Procedures Benefiting Employer
```

These rights are relative to the status of the employee. The employer has relatively more unilateral authority over higher level employees and employees performing jobs with specialized requirements. Failure of these employees to meet the job requirements result in cause for dismissal.

In addition, the employment contract is two sided. The employer may have an obligation to pay wages and benefits, and the employee has a significant series of implied obligations owed to the employer. Failure of the employee to meet these requirements will result in cause for discharge.

Employers are entitled to exercise a broad range of judgment about the operation of the business. Paramount in this area of judgment is the employer's evaluation of who is efficient and who is not efficient. Courts will rarely examine whether an employer decision based on the efficiency argument really enhances efficient operations.

Courts will rarely perform a balancing of employer and employee rights in the individual contract area, absent a statutory mandate. This enhances the employer's exercise of absolute rights. Where employee arguments are grounded in arguments of fairness or factual error, courts will rarely perform the balance that is implicit in these arguments.

An area of relative inactivity has been suits by the employer against the employee, based on the failure of the employee to uphold that side of the bargain. In part this results from the broad power of the employer to get relief through a discharge. However, as more employees bring suit outside of statutes, employers may respond in kind. Whether this might lead courts to do more balancing is unclear.

The broad scope of employer rights cuts across both individual and collective bargaining contracts of employment. Whereas many treat individual and collective contracts as distinct categories, the contracts share a common element in being subject to the same concepts of employer rights. Doctrines of employer rights established in collective bargaining contract cases are too frequently ignored when considering problems of interpretation of individual contracts of employment. Looking solely at the level of employer rights, it is difficult to justify a doctrinal distinction between individual and collective employment contracts. There are doubtlessly other areas of commonality which should be considered.

The doctrine of employer rights is an important background to keep in mind in construing either actual or proposed legislation that affects individual contracts of employment and job security. Where such statutes seek to do more than alter the nature of the remedies and change the dispute resolution forum, they will have to be very carefully drafted if they are intended to alter any of the basic employer rights. The doctrine of employer rights extends beyond contract interpretation and affects how the courts will interpret statutes.

NOTES

1. Cockels v. Business Expo, 3 Indiv. Empl. Rights 764, 766 (Mich. Ct. App. 1987).

2. Harvey v. I.T.W., Inc., 2 Indiv. Empl. Rights (BNA) 597, 599 (D. Ky. 1987).

3. Cox v. Resilient Flooring, 2 Indiv. Empl. Rights (BNA) 1757, 1766 (D. Cal. 1986).

4. Darlington v. General Electric, 2 Indiv. Empl. Rights (BNA) 1666, 1677 (Pa. Super. Ct. 1986).

5. Furnco Const. Corp. v. Waters, 438 U.S. 567, 578 (1978).

6. Ch. 2, fn. 2–16.

7. First National Maintenance Corp. v. NLRB, 452 U.S. 666, 676–77 (1981).

8. Id. at 678–79.

9. The altered quotation would read: "Management must be free from the constraints of [individual contracts] to the extent essential for the running of a profitable business. It must also have some degree of certainty before hand as to when it may proceed to reach decisions without fear of later evaluations labeling its conduct [a breach of an individual contract]." See also, Linn v. Beneficial Comm. Corp., 3 Indiv. Empl. Rights (BNA) 1557, 1558 (N.J. Super. Ct. 1988).

10. First National Maintenance Corp. v. NLRB, 452 U.S. 666, 688 (1981).

11. Id. at 682–83.

12. Id. at 686.

13. Fibreboard Paper Products Corp. v. NLRB, 379 U.S. 203, 223 (1964) (Justice Stewart, concurring).

14. NLRB v. Burns Int'l Security Services, Inc., 406 U.S. 272, 288 (1972).

15. First National Maintenance Corp. v. NLRB, 452 U.S. 666, 682 (1981).

16. Burk v. K-Mart Corp., 4 Indiv. Empl. Rights (BNA) 182, 183 (Okla. Sup. Ct. 1989).

17. Ch. 7, fn. 45–52 and 133–145.

18. Raysor v. State of N.Y. Dep't of Health, 35 Empl. Prac. Dec. (CCH) 34,870 (D. N.Y. 1984).

19. Civil Rights Act of 1964, 42 U.S.C.A. 2000e-2(a).

20. Raysor v. State of N.Y. Dep't of Health, 35 Empl. Prac. Dec. (CCH) 34,870 (D. N.Y. 1984).

21. Swint v. Volusia Co. Dep't of Public Works, 35 Empl. Prac. Dec. (CCH) 34,734 (D. Fla. 1984) (90 day probationary status extended two times, no discrimination found); Hansome v. Northwestern Cooperage Co., 101 Lab. Cas. (CCH) 55,464 (Mo. Ct. App. 1984) (Fired during probationary period for absenteeism, offer to rehire as probationary when available.)

22. Straton v. Chevrolet Motor Div., 3 Indiv. Empl. Rights (BNA) 418 (Neb. Sup. Ct. 1988); Myrwold v. NCR Corp., 3 Indiv. Empl. Rights (BNA) 1009 (D. Cal.); Kohler v. Ericsson Inc., 3 Indiv. Empl. Rights (BNA) 721 (9th Cir. 1988); Palmer v. Brown, 3 Indiv. Empl. Rights (BNA) 177 (Kan. Sup. Ct. 1988).

23. Ch. 5, fn. 101–115.

24. Stone v. Mission Bay Mortgage Co., 116 L.R.R.M. (BNA) 2917, 2918 (Nev. Sup. Ct. 1983) (per curiam).

25. Fowler v. N.Y.C. Dep't of Sanitation, 4 Indiv. Empl. Rights (BNA) 81, 87 (D. N.Y. 1989).

26. Robertson v. Atlantic Richfield, 2 Indiv. Empl. Rights (BNA) 1433 (Pa. Super. Ct. 1987); Gladden v. Ark. Children's Hospital, 2 Indiv. Empl. Rights (BNA) 506 (Ark. Sup. Ct.); Sennit v. Eastern Rebuilders, 115 L.R.R.M. (BNA) 4444 (N.C. Ct. App. 1981).

27. Dicocco v. Capital Area Comm. Health Plan, 3 Indiv. Empl. Rights (BNA) 446 (N.Y. Sup. Ct. 1988), Freidrichs v. Western Nat'l Mutual Ins. Co., 2 Indiv. Empl. Rights (BNA) 660 (Minn. Ct. App. 1987); Bernstein v. Aetna Life & Casualty, 2 Indiv. Empl. Rights (BNA) 292 (D. Ariz. 1986); Rhoden v. Allstate Insur. Co., 115 L.R.R.M. (BNA) 4808 (D. Mich. 1982).

28. Tautfest v. City of Lincoln, 117 L.R.R.M. (BNA) 2182, 2185 (8th Cir. 1984).

29. Stratton v. Chevrolet Motor Div., 3 Indiv. Empl. Rights (BNA) 1418 (Neb. Sup. Ct. 1988); Myrwold v. N.C.R. Corp., 3 Indiv. Empl. Rights (BNA) 1009 (D. Cal. 1988); Kohler v. Ericsson Inc., 3 Indiv. Empl. Rights (BNA) 721 (9th Cir. 1988); Palmer v. Brown, 3 Indiv. Empl. Rights (BNA) 177, (Kan. Sup. Ct. 1988).

30. Stratton v. Chevrolet Motor Div., 3 Indiv. Empl. Rights (BNA) 1418 (Neb. Sup. Ct. 1988); Myrwold v. N.C.R. Corp., 3 Indiv. Empl. Rights (BNA) 1009 (D. Cal. 1988); Palmer v. Brown, 3 Indiv. Empl. Rights (BNA) 177 (Kan. Sup. Ct. 1988).

31. English v. Whitfield, 3 Indiv. Empl. Rights (BNA) 1357 (4th Cir. 1988).

32. Mont. Code Ann. 39-2-904(2) in Lab. Rel. Rep. Indiv. Empl. Rights Manual (BNA) 567:5 (1989).

33. Duquesne Light Co., 90 Lab. Arb. (BNA) 696 (Probst, Arb. 1988).

34. Transportation Workers Local 234 v. SEPTA, 4 Indiv. Empl. Rights (BNA) 1 (3d Cir. 1988).

35. Duquesne Light Co., 90 Lab. Arb. (BNA) 696, 701 (Probst, Arb. 1988).

36. Bishop v. Wood, 426 U.S. 345, fn. 5 at 354 (1976) (Brennan, J. dissenting).

37. Peters v. MCI Telecommunications Corp., 3 Indiv. Empl. Rights (BNA) 638 (D. N.Y. 1988); Stevenson v. Potlatch Corp., 2 Indiv. Empl. Rights (BNA) 1295 (D. Idaho 1987); Johnston v. Panhandle Co-op Ass'n, 2 Indiv. Empl. Rights (BNA) 1080 (Neb. Sup. Ct. 1987).

38. Johnston v. Panhandle Co-op Ass'n, 2 Indiv. Empl. Rights (BNA) 1080 (Neb. Sup. Ct. 1987).

39. Brewster v. Martin Marietta, 3 Indiv. Empl. Rights (BNA) 1399 (Mich. Ct. App. 1985).

40. Stone v. Mission Bay Mortgage Co., 116 L.R.R.M. (BNA) 2917, 2918 (Nev. Sup. Ct. 1983) (per curiam).

41. BNA Collective Bargaining Negotiations and Contracts, Basic Patterns, Clause Finder, (1983) Hiring-New Employees 55:61.

42. Chism v. Mid-South Milling Co., 3 Indiv. Empl. Rights (BNA) 1846 (Tenn. Sup. Ct. 1988); Golden v. Worldvision Enter. Inc., 2 Indiv. Empl. Rights (BNA) 1468 (N.Y. Sup. Ct. 1987).

43. Chism v. Mid-South Milling Co., 3 Indiv. Empl. Rights (BNA) 1846 (Tenn. Sup. Ct. 1988); Tippit v. Jepco, Inc., 2 Indiv. Empl. Rights (BNA) 959 (Mo. Ct. App. 1987).

44. Abrisz v. Pulley Freight Lines, Inc., 115 L.R.R.M. (BNA) 4777 (Iowa Sup. Ct. 1978).

45. Casillas v. U.S. Navy, 34 Empl. Prac. Dec. (CCH) 34,394 at 33,606 (9th Cir. 1984).

46. Pugh v. See's Candies, Inc., 115 L.R.R.M. (BNA) 4002, 4011 (Cal. Ct. App. 1981).

47. Chamberlain v. Bissell Inc., 115 L.R.R.M. (BNA) 4137 (D. Mich. 1982).

48. Brown v. Dep't of Trans., 116 L.R.R.M. (BNA) 2523 (Fed. Cir. 1984).

49. Kavanagh v. KLM Royal Dutch Airlines, 115 L.R.R.M. (BNA) 4266 (D. Ill. 1983).

50. Brown v. Dep't Of Trans., 116 L.R.R.M. (BNA) 2523 (Fed. Cir. 1984).

51. Parker v. Fed. Nat'l Mortgage Ass'n, 34 Empl. Prac. Dec. (CCH) 34,577 (7th Cir. 1984).

52. Cort v. Bristol-Meyers Co., 115 L.R.R.M. (BNA) 5127 (Mass. Sup. Ct. 1982).

53. Jet Courier Service, Inc. v. Mulei, 771 P.2d 486 (Colo. Sup. Ct. 1989).

54. C. Morris, II *The Developing Labor Law* 1450–1488 (1983).

55. Worth v. Huntington Bancshores, Inc., 540 N.E.2d. 249 (Ohio Sup. Ct. 1989); Royal Crown Co. Inc. v. McMahon, 359 S.E.2d 379 (Geog. Ct. App. 1987).

56. Organization Man's Demise, 3 Empl. Rel. Weekly (BNA) 1573 (Dec. 23, 1985).

57. Haskell v. Kaman Corp., 35 Empl. Prac. Dec. (CCH) 34,613 at 34,717 (2d Cir. 1984).

58. Chamberlain v. Bissell Inc., 115 L.R.R.M. (BNA) 4137, 4148 (D. Mich. 1982).

59. Transportation Management of Tenn., Inc., 82 Lab. Arb. (BNA) 671 (Nicholas, Arb. 1984), Burka v. N.Y.C. Transit Authority, 2 Indiv. Empl. Rights (BNA) 1625 (D. N.Y. 1988).

60. Hoover Universal Inc., 82 Lab. Arb. (BNA) 569, 574 (Cabe, Arb. 1984).

61. Nabisco Foods Co., 82 Lab. Arb. (BNA) 1186, 1192 (Allen, Arb. 1984).

62. Parker v. Federal Nat'l Mortgage Ass'n, 34 Empl. Prac. Dec. (CCH) 34,577 at 34,566 (7th Cir. 1984).

63. Furr's, Inc., 83 Lab. Arb. (BNA) 279, 281 (Daughton, Arb. 1984).

64. Trans. Management of Tenn., Inc., 82 Lab. Arb. (BNA) 671, 674 (Nicholas, Arb. 1984).

65. O'Connor Hospital v. Superior Court, 2 Indiv. Empl. Rights (BNA) 1190 (Cal. Ct. App. 1987).

66. Bulogh v. Charron, 3 Indiv. Empl. Rights (BNA) 82 (D. Mich. 1987).

67. F. Elkouri and E. Elkouri, *How Arbitration Works*, 646 (4th ed. 1985).

68. Minn. Mining & Mfg. Co., 81 Lab. Arb. (BNA) 338, 343 (Boyer, Arb. 1983).

69. Palmer v. Dist. Bd. of Trustees of St. Petersburg Junior College, 35 Empl. Prac. Dec. (CCH) 34,820 (11th Cir. 1984).

70. Chesna v. Int'l Fueling Co., 117 L.R.R.M. (BNA) 2912 (1st Cir. 1984).

71. Model Unif. Employment Termination Act 1(b) (Draft 1989), Lab. Rel. Rep. Indiv. Empl. Rights Manual (BNA) 540:51 (1989).

72. There is an increasing effort to identify implied or common law duties owed by the employer to the employee, for example, in the safety area. E.g., Shimp v. New Jersey Bell Tel. Co., 368 A.2d 408 (N.J. Ch. Div. 1976). It is at least arguable that the rapidly growing list of statutes giving employee rights is recognition that employer rights implied in law are so extensive that there was little room left for implied employee rights.

73. McGraw-Edison, 81 Lab. Arb. (BNA) 403, 407 (Role, Arb. 1983); Todd Pacific Shipyards Corp., 81 Lab. Arb. (BNA) 1095, 1100 (Jones Arb. 1983).

74. Margolis, McTernan, Scope, Sacks & Epstein, 81 Lab. Arb. (BNA) 740, 741 (Richman, Arb. 1983); Legal Aid Society, 81 Lab. Arb. (BNA) 1065, 1075 (Nicolau, Arb. 1983).

75. Fn. 7, Supra.

76. Swint v. Volusia Co. Dep't of Public Works, 35 Empl. Prac. Dec. (CCH) 34,734 (D. Fla. 1984); Coca-Cola Bottling Co., 81 Lab. Arb. (BNA) 56, 58 (Berger, Arb. 1983).

77. Webster Electric Co., Inc., 83 Lab. Arb. (BNA) 141, 146 (Kindig, Arb. 1984).

78. Elwell-Parker Electric Co., 82 Lab. Arb. (BNA) 327, 332 (Dworkin, Arb. 1984).

79. Marion Power Shovel Div., 82 Lab. Arb. (BNA) 1014, 1016 (Kates, Arb. 1984).

80. Challenge Machinery Co., 81 Lab. Arb. (BNA) 865, 869 (Roumell, Arb. 1983).

81. U.S. Army Armor Center & Fort Knox, 82 Lab. Arb. (BNA) 464, 468 (Wren, Arb. 1984).

82. Pierce v. New Process Co., 116 L.R.R.M. (BNA) 3354, 3356 (D. Pa. 1984).

83. Municipality of Anchorage, 81 Lab. Arb. (BNA) 829, 834 (Thomas, Arb. 1983).

84. City of Carrollton, 90 Lab. Arb. (BNA) 281 (Stephens, Arb. 1988).

85. San Diego Gas & Electric Co., 82 Lab. Arb. (BNA) 1039, 1041 (Johnston, Arb. 1983); Monarch Machine Tool Co., 82 Lab. Arb. (BNA) 880, 883 (Schedler, Arb. 1984); Burlington Northern, 90 Lab. Arb. (BNA) 585 (Goldstein, Arb. 1987).

86. Monarch Machine Tool Co., 82 Lab. Arb. (BNA) 880, 883 (Schedler, Arb. 1984); San Diego Gas & Electric Co., 82 Lab. Arb. (BNA) 1039, 1041 (Johnston, Arb. 1983).

87. Crucible, Inc., 81 Lab. Arb. (BNA) 83, 84 (Meiners, Arb. 1983).

88. Tribune-Star Pub. Co., Inc., 82 Lab. Arb. (BNA) 714, 717 (Seidman, Arb. 1984).

89. General Battery Corp., 82 Lab. Arb. (BNA) 751, 754 (Schedler, Arb. 1984).

90. United Trans. Union, 82 Lab. Arb. (BNA) 358, 360 (Draznin, Arb. 1984).

91. Crucible, Inc., 81 Lab. Arb. (BNA) 83, 84 (Meiners, Arb. 1983).

92. Pierce v. New Process Co., 35 Empl. Prac. Dec. (CCH) 34,864 (D. Pa. 1984).

93. Amp Inc. v. Fleischhacker, 3 Indiv. Empl. Rights (BNA) 73 (7th Cir. 1987); Webcraft v. McCaw, 2 Indiv. Empl. Rights (BNA) 1288 (D. N.Y. 1987).

94. Pierce v. Ortho Pharmaceutical Corp., 101 Lab. Cas. (CCH) 55,477 at 76,131 (N.J. Sup. Ct. 1980).

95. Jet Courier Service, Inc. v. Mulei, 771 P.2d 486 (Colo. Sup. Ct. 1989).

96. Potts v. Review Bd. of Indiana Employment Security Div., 475 N.E. 2d 708 (Ind. Ct. App. 1985).

97. Hartford Elevator, Inc. v. Lauer, 289 N.W.2d 280 (Wisc. Sup. Ct. 1980); Jet Courier Service, Inc. v. Mulei, 771 P.2d 486 (Colo. Sup. Ct. 1989).

98. United Board & Carton Corp. v. Britting, 164 A.2d 824 (N.J. Super. Ct. 1959).

99. Jet Courier Service v. Mulei, 771 P.2d 486 (Colo. Sup. Ct. 1989).

100. Id.

101. Legal Aid Society, 81 Lab. Arb. (BNA) 1065, 1074–75 (Nicolau, Arb. 1983).

102. Pierce v. Ortho Pharmaceutical Corp., 101 Lab. Cas. (CCH) 55,477 at 76,130 (N.J. Sup. Ct. 1980).

103. San Diego Gas & Electric, 82 Lab. Arb. (BNA) 1039, 1041 (Johnston, Arb. 1983).

104. Aluminum Foundries, 82 Lab. Arb. (BNA) (Seidman, Arb. 1984); City of Detroit, 82 Lab. Arb. (BNA) 1049, (Roumell, Arb. 1984).

105. Houdaille Indus. Inc., 82 Lab. Arb. (BNA) 366 (Cantor, Arb. 1984).

106. Coca-Cola Bottling Co., 82 Lab. Arb. (BNA) 851 (Belcher, Arb. 1984).

107. Chromally American Corp., 83 Lab. Arb. (BNA) 80, 85 (Taylor, Arb. 1984).

108. Tribune-Star Pub. Co., Inc., 82 Lab. Arb. (BNA) 714 (Seidman, Arb. 1984).

109. Kovarsky and Kovarsky, Economic, Medical and Legal Aspects of the Age Discrimination Laws in Employment, 27 Vand. L. Rev. 839, 848 (1974); C. Edelman & I. Siegler, *Federal Age Discrimination in Employment Law*, 18–22 (1978).

110. Houdaille Industries, Inc., 82 Lab. Arb. (BNA) 366, 371 (Cantor, Arb. 1984).

111. Geary v. U.S. Steel, 115 L.R.R.M. (BNA) 4665 (Pa. Sup. Ct. 1974); Larsen v. Motor Supply Co., 115 L.R.R.M. (BNA) 4298 (Ariz. Ct. App. 1977); Ingram v. Pirelli Cable Corp., 3 Indiv. Empl. Rights (BNA) 1502 (Ark. Sup. Ct. 1988).

112. Geary v. U.S. Steel, 115 L.R.R.M. (BNA) 4665 (Pa. Sup. Ct. 1974).

113. McFarlin v. Rose's Stores, Inc., 35 Empl. Prac. Dec. (CCH) 34,783 (D. S.C. 1984); United Trans. Union, 82 Lab. Arb. (BNA) 358 (Draznin, Arb. 1984).

114. Griffin v. Erickson, 115 L.R.R.M. (BNA) 4300 (Ark. Sup. Ct. 1982).

115. Elwell-Parker Electric Co., 82 Lab. Arb. (BNA) 327, 334 (Dworkin, Arb. 1984).

116. Acme Engineering & Mfg. Corp., 81 Lab. Arb. (BNA) 1057, 1060 (White, Arb. 1983).

117. Star-Kist Foods, Inc., 81 Lab. Arb. (BNA) 577, 579 (Hardbeck, Arb. 1983).

118. Malin, Protecting The Whistleblower From Retaliatory Discharge, 16 J. of Law Reform 277 (1983).

119. Adams v. The Budd Co., 116 L.R.R.M. (BNA) 3158, 3162 (D. Pa. 1984).

120. Tribune-Star Pub. Co., Inc., 82 Lab. Arb. (BNA) 714, 717 (Seidman, Arb. 1984); Chamberlain v. Bissell Inc., 115 L.R.R.M. (BNA) 4137, 4150 (D. Mich. 1982).

121. Purex Corp., 82 Lab. Arb. (BNA) 12 (Fitzsimmons, Arb. 1984); Challenge Machinery Co., 81 Lab. Arb. (BNA) 865, 869 (Roumell, Arb. 1983).

122. Purex Corp., 82 Lab. Arb. (BNA) 12 (Fitzsimmons, Arb. 1984); Lockheed Corp., 83 Lab. Arb. (BNA) 1018 (Taylor, Arb. 1984).

123. Baker Store Equip., Co., 81 Lab. Arb. (BNA) 1077, 1082 (Richard, Arb. 1983); Mitch Murch's Maintenance Mgmt. Co., 81 Lab. Arb. (BNA) 1021, 1024 (Fitzsimmons, Arb. 1983).

124. Gwaltney v. Smithfield, Inc., 81 Lab. Arb. (BNA) 241, 242 (Bernhardt, Arb. 1983).

125. Chamberlain v. Bissell Inc., 115 L.R.R.M. (BNA) 4137 (D. Mich. 1982).

126. Geary v. United States Steel, 115 L.R.R.M. (BNA) 4665 (Pa. Sup. Ct. 1974).

127. Collins v. Walters, 35 Empl. Prac. Dec. (BNA) 34,896 at 35,958 (N.Y. 1984); Challenge Machinery Co., 81 Lab. Arb. (BNA) 865, 869 (Roumell, Arb. 1983).

128. Lockheed Corp., 83 Lab. Arb. (BNA) 1018, 1022 (Taylor, Arb. 1984).

129. Collins v. Walters, 35 Empl. Prac. Dec. (CCH) 34,896 at 35,958 (D. N.Y. 1984).

130. F. Elkouri and E. Elkouri, *How Arbitration Works* 645–46 (4th ed. 1985).

131. Id. at 646.

132. Doscherhol v. Walters, 35 Empl. Prac. Dec. (CCH) 34,685 (D. Minn. 1984).

133. Chamberlain v. Bissell Inc., 115 L.R.R.M. (BNA) 4137, 4151 (D. Mich. 1982).

134. Tribune-Star Publishing Co., Inc., 82 Lab. Arb. (BNA) 714, 717 (Seidman, Arb. 1984); see also Chamberlain v. Bissell Inc., 115 L.R.R.M. (BNA) 4137, 4150 (D. Mich. 1982).

135. Ashland Oil, Inc., 83 Lab. Arb. (BNA) 556, 557 (Gibson, Arb. 1984).

136. C. Morris, I *The Developing Labor Law* 220 (2d ed. 1983).

137. Martin v. Fed. Life Ins. Co., 115 L.R.R.M. (BNA) 4524, 4530 (Ill. App. Ct. 1982).

138. Stokely-Van Camp, Inc., 83 Lab. Arb. (BNA) 838, 841 (Nicholas, Arb. 1984); Formosa Plastics Corp., 83 Lab. Arb. (BNA) 792, 796 (Taylor, Arb. 1984).

139. Whittaker v. Care-More, Inc., 115 L.R.R.M. (BNA) 4599 (Tenn. Ct. App. 1981); Adler v. American Standard Corp., 115 L.R.R.M. (BNA) 4130 (Md. Ct. App. 1981).

140. Kovalesky v. A.M.C. Corp., 115 L.R.R.M. (BNA) 4531, 4534 (D. N.Y. 1982).

141. Oklahoma City Air Logistics Center, 81 Lab. Arb. (BNA) 761, 763 (Dilts, Arb. 1983).

142. Arnett v. Kennedy, 416 U.S. 134 (1974).

143. Staton v. Amax Coal Co., 116 L.R.R.M. (BNA) 2517, 2519 (Ill. App. Ct. 1984).

144. Adler v. Am. Standard Corp., 115 L.R.R.M. (BNA) 4130, 4135 (Md. Ct. App. 1981).

145. Monge v. Beebe Rubber Co., 115 L.R.R.M. (BNA) 4755, 4757 (N.H. Sup. Ct. 1974).

146. Houdaille Indus. Inc., 82 Lab. Arb. (BNA) 366, 371 (Cantor, Arb. 1984).

147. Brown v. Dep't of Transportation, 116 L.R.R.M. (BNA) 2523, 2527 (Fed. Cir. 1984).

148. Mich. Dep't of Mental Health, 82 Lab. Arb. (BNA) 1311, 1315 (Girolamo, Arb. 1984); Kansas City Area Trans. Authority, 82 Lab. Arb. (BNA) 409, 413 (Maniscalco, Arb. 1984).

149. Bishop v. Wood, 426 U.S. 341, 349–50 (1976).

150. Martin v. Platt, 115 L.R.R.M. (BNA) 4782 (Ind. Ct. App. 1979).

151. Snyder v. Wash. Hospital Center, 35 Empl. Prac. Dec. (CCH) 34,786 at 35,428 (D. D.C. 1984).

152. EEOC v. Trans World Airlines, Inc., 30 Empl. Prac. Dec. (CCH) 33,011 at 26,838 (D. N.Y. 1982).

153. Palazon v. KFC Management Co., 29 Empl. Prac. Dec. (CCH) 32,744 at 25,508 (D. Ill. 1981).

154. Pacific Telephone & Telegraph Co., 81 Lab. Arb. (BNA) 259, 264 (Connors, Arb. 1983).

155. Hanlon & Wilson Co. v. NLRB, 101 Lab. Cas. (CCH) 11,093 at 22,431 (3rd Cir. 1984).

156. Mallard v. Boring, 115 L.R.R.M. (BNA) 4750, 4751 (Cal. Ct. App. 1960).

157. Mt. Healthy City Bd. of Educ. v. Doyle, 429 U.S. 274 (1977).

158. Monge v. Beebe Rubber Co., 115 L.R.R.M. (BNA) 4755, 4757 (N.H. Sup. Ct. 1974).

159. Devine v. Sutermeister, 116 L.R.R.M. (BNA) 2495 (Fed. Cir. 1983).

160. Yaindl v. Ingersoll-Rand Co., 115 L.R.R.M. (BNA) 4738, 4746 (Pa. Super. Ct. 1981).

161. Id.

162. Fenton v. Pan American World Airways, Inc., 30 Empl. Prac. Dec. (CCH) 33,185 at 27,688 (D. N.J. 1982).

163. Diamond Int'l Corp., 81 Lab. Arb. (BNA) 797, 801 (Rocha, Arb. 1983).

164. NLRB v. Burns Security Services, 406 U.S. 272, 287–88 (1972).

165. Id. at 294.

166. F. Elkouri and E. Elkouri, *How Arbitration Works* 604–607 (4th ed. 1985).

167. Fibreboard Paper Products Corp. v. NLRB, 379 U.S. 203, 224 (1964) (Stewart, J., concurring).

168. Howard Johnson Co., Inc. v. Detroit Local Joint Executive Board, Hotel and Restaurant Employees and Bartenders, 417 U.S. 249 (1974).

169. Tribune-Star Pub. Co., Inc., 82 Lab. Arb. (BNA) 714, 717 (Seidman, Arb. 1984).

170. Grubb v. W.A. Foote Memorial Hospital, Inc., 35 Empl. Prac. Dec. (CCH) 34,615 (6th Cir. 1984).

171. Stacey v. Allied Stores Corp., 34 Empl. Prac. Dec. (CCH) 34,458 at 33,958 (D. D.C. 1984).

172. Wadeson v. American Family Mutual Ins. Co., 34 Empl. Prac. Dec. (CCH) 34,459 at 33,966–967 (N.D. Sup. Ct. 1984).

173. Injected Rubber Products Corp., 117 L.R.R.M. (BNA) 1291, 1294 (NLRB 1984).

174. Hasken v. Kaman Corp., 35 Empl. Prac. Dec. (CCH) 34,613 at 34,716 (2d Cir. 1984).

175. Grubb v. W.A. Foote Memorial Hospital Inc., 35 Empl. Prac. Dec. (CCH) 34,615 at 34,741 (6th Cir. 1984).

176. Hucks v. Bell Telephone, Inc., 115 L.R.R.M. (BNA) 4501, 4503 (D. N.C. 1981).

177. NLRB v. Burns Security Services, 406 U.S. 272, fn. 4 at 280 (1972).

178. LaGrant v. Gulf & Western Mfg. Co. Inc., 35 Empl. Prac. Dec. (CCH) 34,794 at 35,450 (6th Cir. 1984).

179. Gulf States Manufacturers, 117 L.R.R.M. (BNA) 1015, 1017 (NLRB 1984).

180. Rompf v. Hammons Hotels, 117 L.R.R.M. (BNA) 2185, 2189 (Wy. Sup. Ct. 1984).

181. Bates v. Jim Walter Resources, 115 L.R.R.M. (BNA) 4027 (Ala. Sup. Ct. 1982) (Estoppel was rejected).

182. First National Maintenance Corp. v. NLRB, 452 U.S. 666, 685 (1981).

183. Civil Rights Act of 1964, 42 U.S.C.A. 2000(e)(b).

184. Rozier v. St. Mary's Hospital, 115 L.R.R.M. (BNA) 4391, 4394 (Ill. App. Ct. 1980).

185. E.g., Reforming At-Will Employment Law: A Model Statute, 16 J. of Law Reform 389, 415 (1983).

186. Koehring Southern Plant, 82 Lab. Arb. (BNA) 193, 197 (Alsher, Arb. 1984).

187. Piggly-Wiggly T-212, 81 Lab. Arb. (BNA) 808, 815 (Nelson, Arb. 1983).

188. Majestic Iron Works, 81 Lab. Arb. (BNA) 816, 820 (Fitzsimmons, Arb. 1983).

189. Interior Alterations, Inc. v. NLRB, 101 Lab. Cas. (BNA) 11,100 at 22,470 (10th Cir. 1984).

190. NLRB v. Burns Security Services, 406 U.S. 272, 288 (1972).

191. Model Unif. Employment Termination Act 1(c) (Draft 1989), Lab. Rel. Rep. Indiv. Empl. Rights Manual (BNA) 540:51 (1989).

192. United Steelworkers v. Warrior & Gulf Navigation Co., 363 U.S. 574, 578 (1960).

193. First National Maintenance Corp. v. NLRB, 452 U.S. 666, fn. 16 at 676 (1981).

194. Melnick v. State Farm, 3 Indiv. Empl. Rights (BNA) 730, 735 (N.M. Sup. Ct. 1988).

195. Palmateer v. Int'l Harvester Co., 421 N.E.2d 876, 878 (Ill. Sup. Ct. 1981).

196. Peeler v. Village of Kingston Mines, 3 Indiv. Empl. Rights (BNA) 1794 (7th Cir. 1988); Disario v. Enesco Imports Corp., 2 Indiv. Empl. Rights (BNA) 1570 (Ill. App. Ct. 1987).

197. Malia v. RCA Corp., 3 Indiv. Empl. Rights (BNA) 1510 (D. Pa. 1988); Bohm v. Trans. World Airlines, 2 Indiv. Empl. Rights (BNA) 224 (D. Cal. 1986).

198. Darlington v. General Electric, 2 Indiv. Empl. Rights (BNA) 1666 (Pa. Super. Ct. 1986); K-Mart Corp. v. Ponsock, 2 Indiv. Empl. Rights (BNA) 56 (Nev. Sup. Ct. 1987).

199. Elwell-Parker Elec. Co., 82 Lab. Arb. (BNA) 327, 331 (Dworkin, Arb. 1984).

200. Id. at 332.

201. Washington Scientific Indus., 83 Lab. Arb. (BNA) 824, 828 (Kapsch, Arb. 1984).

202. Elwell-Parker Elec. Co., 82 Lab. Arb. (BNA) 327, 331 (Dworkin, Arb. 1984).

203. Yaindl v. Ingersoll-Rand Co., 115 L.R.R.M. (BNA) 4738, 4746 (Pa. Super. Ct. 1981).

204. Greene v. Oliver Realty, Inc., 2 Indiv. Empl. Rel. (BNA) 1339 (Pa. Super. Ct. 1987).

205. Foley v. Interactive Data Corp., 3 Indiv. Empl. Rights (BNA) 1729 (Cal. Sup. Ct. 1988); St. Yves v. Mid State Bank, 2 Indiv. Empl. Rights (BNA) 1550 (Wash. App. Ct. 1987); Greco v. Halliburton Co., 2 Indiv. Empl. Rights (BNA) 1281 (D. Wyo. 1987).

206. Piver v. Pender Co. Bd. of Educ., 2 Indiv. Empl. Rights (BNA) 1382, 1384 (4th Cir. 1987). See also Rankin v. McPherson, 483 U.S. 378 (1987); Berg v. Hunter, 3 Indiv. Empl. Rights (BNA) 1317 (7th Cir. 1988).

207. Elkouri and Elkouri, *How Arbitration Works* 656–58 (4th ed. 1985); John Morrell & Co., 90 Lab. Arb. (BNA) 38 (Concepcion, Arb. 1987).

208. Modern Telecommunications v. Zimmerman, 3 Indiv. Empl. Rights (BNA) 741 (N.Y. Sup. Ct. 1988); Orkin Exterminating Co. v. Martin, 2 Indiv. Empl. Rights (BNA) 1361 (Fla. Ct. App. 1987).

209. Scott v. Extracorporeal Inc., 3 Indiv. Empl. Rights (BNA) 999, 1005 (Pa. Super Ct. 1988). See also Hill v. Winn-Dixie Stores, 4 Indiv. Empl. Rights (BNA) 1014 (D. Fla. 1989); Weihaupt v. Am. Med. Assoc., 874 F.2d 419 (7th cir. 1989).

210. Bill Johnson's Restaurants, Inc. v. NLRB, 461 U.S. 731, 745 (1983).

211. H.W. Brass Co., Inc., 1989–90 CCH NLRB 15,803 (retaliation found).

212. "Dean Witter Loses In Arbitration Against Bond Chief It Fired, Sued" Wall Street Journal, p. c-1, c.3 (Aug. 15, 1989).

213. Ellis v. James V. Hurson Assoc., Inc., 565 A.2d 615 (D.C. Ct. App. 1989); North American Paper Co., v. Unterberger, 526 N.E. 2d 621 (Ill. Ct. App. 1988).

214. Presto-X-Co. v. Ewing, 442 N.W. 2d 85 (Iowa Sup. Ct. 1989).

215. Ch. 5, fn. 25–29.

216. United Board & Carton Corp., 164 A.2d 824 (N.J. Super. Ct. 1959).

217. Jet Courier Service, Inc. v. Mulei, 771 P.2d 486 (Colo. Sup. Ct. 1989).

218. Potts v. Review Board of Indiana Employment Security Div., 475 N.E.2d 708 (Ind. Ct. App. 1985).

219. Christiansburg Garmet Co. v. EEOC, 434 U.S. 412 (1978).

220. Beckwith v. United Parcel Service, Inc., 889 F.2d 344 (1st Cir. 1989).

221. C.H.B. Foods, Inc. v. Rebelo, 662 F. Supp. 1359 (D. Cal. 1987).

222. LeCompte v. Chrysler Credit Corp., 780 F.2d 1260 (5th Cir. 1986).

223. Sprague v. Boston and Maine Corp., 769 F.2d 26 (1st Cir. 1985).

224. Brunson v. C.B.A., Inc., 376 S.E.2d 706 (Geo. Ct. App. 1989); Windsor - Douglas Assoc., Inc. v. Patterson, 347 S.E. 2d 362 (Geo. Ct. App. 1986); Millwood Mouldings, Inc. v. Wilson, 338 S.E.2d 60 (Geo. Ct. App. 1985).

225. Deere & Co. v. Van Natta, 660 F. Supp. 433 (D. N.C. 1986); Syntex Ophthalmic, Inc. v. Novicky, 795 F.2d 983 (Fed. Cir. 1986).

226. Isaacs v. Caterpillar Inc., 702 F. Supp. 711 (D. Ill. 1988).

227. Demery v. Cook, dba Hasty Shop, 525 So.2d 157 (La. Ct. App. 1988).

228. Gilbert v. Otterson, 550 A.2d 550 (Pa. Super. Ct. 1988); Barrow J. Atco Manuf. Co., 524 N.E.2d 1313 (Ind. Ct. App. 1988).

229. Office and Prof. Employees Int'l Union v. The Trust Co. of N.J., 522 A.2d 22 992 (N.J. Sup. Ct. 1987).

230. Southwest Wyoming Rehabilitation Center v. Employ. Security Comm. of Wyoming, 781 P.2d 918 (Wyo. Sup. Ct. 1989); Farmers Insur. Exchange v. Dept. of Labor, 542 N.E.2d 538 (Ill. App. Ct. 1989).

4

Creating, Modifying, and Ending the Contract

INTRODUCTION

The employment relationship is largely contractual and the individual contract of employment is usually very informal. The U.S. Supreme Court recognized the informal character of many individual contracts in the following rustic comment: "In the context of Title VII, the contract of employment may be written or oral, formal or informal; an informal contract of employment may arise by the simple act of handing a job applicant a shovel and providing a workplace."[1]

In the absence of a written agreement, the existence of a fixed term contract must be ascertained by looking at a variety of different types of evidence. Among them may be statements in personnel handbooks, recruitment promises, the content of job advertisements, the history of employment practices of the employer, and the history of the industry. The focus of this chapter is to look at some of the issues arising in making, modifying, and terminating the individual employment contract. Issues beyond the contract, such as tortious conduct or public policy considerations, are not covered in this discussion on contracts.

Fixed Term and Indefinite Term Contracts

Most employees have little or no power to bargain the terms of their employment contract, and they must accept what the employer offers.[2] The presumption is that what is offered is an indefinite term or at will contract as distinguished from a fixed term contract. An employee who has a written contract with a fixed term can be discharged during the term of the contract only for cause.[3] An employee with an at will (indefinite term) contract, absent statutory considerations, can be discharged for any reason or no reason at any time without breaching the contract.[4] Where the employer can show cause (just cause or good cause), however, it will not matter if there is a fixed or indefinite term contract. A cause based discharge is always permitted.[5]

In a contract based discharge suit, the employee will find it advantageous to allege, if possible, that the discharge occurred during the life of a fixed term contract. If the employee cannot show that a fixed term contract existed, the employer can discharge the employee at will, without showing any cause or without giving a reason. In a trial, the employer will often test whether the contract is at will by presenting a motion to dismiss to the court at the end of the employee's initial presentation. Where only an at will contract has been proved, the court will grant the employer's motion to dismiss the employee's suit because the employer has a right to discharge for any reason.

The employee will have a difficult time proving the existence of a fixed term contract of employment unless there is a writing evidencing the terms of the contract. A variety of legal doctrines are used by courts to determine what type of employment contract exists. These legal doctrines look largely to traditional common law concepts of general contract law. There is usually minimal reference to the characteristics of the employment or to the past practices of the employer or the industry.

The following sections discuss a variety of contract issues arising on the problems of at will (indefinite term) contracts and fixed term or just cause contracts. Figure 4.1 summarizes some of these issues.

CREATING THE EMPLOYMENT CONTRACT

In its more formal aspects, such as a written fixed term contact, the individual employment contract can initially be defined as a mutual agreement negotiated by two or more qualified persons that spells out most or all of the terms and conditions of employment. In its less formal aspects, the at will contract can be created by "handing a job applicant a shovel." There are many elements to making a valid, formal contract. The purpose of this section is to look at some of these elements as they relate to definite term and indefinite term contracts.

Figure 4.1   Contract Issues Summary

```
           SUGGESTING AT WILL                 SUGGESTING FIXED TERM,
                                                      CAUSE

    Advertisements For Job              Constructive Discharge
    Application Form Language           Handbook, No Disclaimers
    At Will Presumption                 Judicial Exception To At Will
    Beyond One Year, No Writing         Mutual Expectations
    Claims After Quit                   Negotiation Environment
    Conflict With Basic Employer        Specific Terms
        Right                           Statutory Protection
    Disclaimed Handbook                 Two Considerations
    Employee Unilateral Expectation     Vested Interest Claim
    Expiration of Fixed Term            Written Contract
    Hiring Agent Without Authority
    Integration Clause
    No Actual Negotiations
    Noncompete Clause Consideration
    Oral Contract
    Parol Evidence Contrary To Writing
    Past, Unwritten Practices
    Quit At Any Time
    Unaware of Handbook
    Unilateral Nature Of Contract
    Unspecified, Long Term Claim
    Vague Terms, Promises
    Waiver In Handbook
    Work As Sole Consideration
    Working After New Policy Issued
```

Oral, Definite Term Contracts

The case law makes it clear that an employee has a very heavy burden of proof when the employee seeks to prove the existence of a fixed term individual contract of employment when there is no written document. Absent a clear writing, the employee is usually able to show only an indefinite term (at will) employment relationship exists. The following discussion looks at some of the types of evidence or lack of evidence that has been identified in the individual contract cases.

A number of individual elements are discussed below. It is likely that in most situations the final determination of the nature of the contract will be made only when a number of these elements can be shown to exist rather than showing that one or two of them exist. Not all of the possible contract issues are discussed here. The choice of factors topics discussed below is based on the frequency with which they appear in the cases.

Presumption of At Will

Most courts begin analysis of individual contract of employment with a presumption that at will status exists where there is no written employment contract that specifies either a definite term or a procedure for determining the term of the employment.[6] The presumption is stated by the courts to be rebuttable,[7] but the rigor of its application by many courts suggests that it takes very powerful evidence to rebut it in many jurisdictions.

Employees will attempt to rebut the presumption of at will status with evidence that shows, for example, fixed term language in employee handbooks, by references to binding oral promises allegedly made, or by showing the giving of a second consideration for the contract. Employers will respond with evidence seeking to refute the employee's evidence and with a variety of contract law defenses such as the lack of the authority of the contracting agent or a violation of the statute of frauds which requires certain contracts to be in writing, among other defenses.

Long Term Is Extraordinary

Both parties must be qualified with adequate authority to enter into a contract. Where a lifetime or other long, fixed term contract is claimed by the employee, courts may find such an agreement to be extraordinary. When making such an extraordinary claim, the employee must be able to show that the employer's agent had a clear authorization to make such an extraordinary agreement.[8] That authorization is rarely found. Where the employer's agent lacked the authority to make a long-term commitment on behalf of the employer, the employment relationship will be found to be at will.

Ambiguity, Specific Terms

When a contract contains no term of definite duration, courts will rely on the evidentiary presumption that the contract is for an indefinite duration or at will. In order for the employee to overcome this presumption, the language claimed to constitute the definite term must be specific and clear.[9] If the language is not specific and clear, an indefinite term contract will be found to exist. Given the informal nature of most individual contracts, clear and specific terms are difficult to find. "Handing a job applicant a shovel" creates only ambiguous terms.

Once sufficient evidence is shown to prove some elements of definite term contract, the contract on its face need not be definite as to all terms. A missing term may be supplied by proof of an implied in fact understanding or by operation of a rule of law.[10]

Courts will carefully scrutinize the language that is put forth as the basis of the definite term contract. To form such a contract, the language must be specific. Talk of a "career situation" or "a job long as" people wish may not be specific enough.[11] Reference to good "growth potential" and the expansion of the area in which the employee will work may be too vague.[12] If the language is too indefinite to enforce or if it relates to optional or discretionary acts by the employer, it is not the language of binding, definite term contracts.[13] The presumption rules.

In summary, much of the language employees rely upon to attempt to show the terms of a definite term contract will be found to be ambiguous. The ambiguity may be because the words are not specific or because they were not spoken in a "negotiation" context. Where the language that the employee relies upon is ambiguous, courts will often find that the presumption of at will status is applicable to the employment relationship. An objective test, not a subjective measure of the employee's expectations is used.

Negotiations

The language must be such that a "reasonable" employee would believe that a contract was being negotiated.[14] An objective standard is used, rather than the standard of what the particular employee may have believed was meant by the words. Discussion about job security in the context of a social gathering may refute the idea that the language was contractual in nature. "The ordinary language of friendship and collegiality should not usually bind the speaker."[15] Where the employee is a sophisticated businessperson, courts may find that the person's sophistication should warn them against relying on casual statements.[16] The courts indicate that experienced, higher level employees are expected to be more on guard than other employees.

An important element in determining whether words constitute a definite term contract is to consider the context in which the language is spoken. Binding agreements are usually evidenced by "protracted employment negotiations."[17] Where the employer shows evidence that the discussion was not conducted in a negotiation environment with employee, that may refute the fixed term claims.[18]

The judicial emphasis on negotiations raises a very practical problem. Most employees are at will employees. If the majority were to individually attempt to negotiate with the employer, the employer could be spending all of his or her time in negotiations. Whereas there is little case law on individual negotiations, there are a few references. In one situation, the employee and employer fruitlessly negotiated a job description for three weeks before the employee gave up and retired.[19]

If individual employees were to seriously negotiate with their employers, a number of them might seek a lawyer's aid or advice. Although there are mixed case results, there is some support for the right of the employer to discharge the employee because the employee sought legal advice.[20]

Judicial emphasis on the need to show negotiations is often contrary to workplace reality. An employer could not realistically negotiate individual contracts with dozens or hundreds of employees if real negotiations were to take place. Many employees could not realistically negotiate without the aid of a lawyer, given the complexities of contract language. If a negotiation standard is to be used, it should reflect actual workplace realties rather than some idealized model existing only in the realm of judicial imagination.

Consideration—One or Two

Consideration is an important element in the creation of a contract. In the usual situation, the work the employee performs is the contractual consideration for the employee's claim for salary or payment. However, the employee's usual work is usually found to be an inadequate contractual consideration for proving the other elements needed for a definite term contract, as distinguished from proving the salary terms. Where a long, definite term contract is claimed to exist, a number of courts require that an extra or second consideration be shown for the additional promise to hire for the definite term.[21] The presumption of at will status becomes more than merely a preliminary consideration.

Beginning of work by itself will not be adequate contractual consideration to show a definite term element of the employment contract. One contractual consideration (working) is not sufficient. Two considerations (working plus something) must be shown to prove that a definite term contract existed. Showing a second consideration (giving of something of value beyond the promise of work) may be one way to help to rebut the presumption of at will status.[22] Actually working for the employer over a long time is not an adequate second

consideration. In the absence of a showing of a second consideration beyond working, one court stated that "the assumption will be
that . . . the parties have in mind merely the ordinary business contract for a continuing employment contract terminable at will."[23]

A variety of other types of additional contractual consideration
(beyond having performed work) have been alleged where the court
requires two considerations to prove the existence of the fixed term in
the contract. The employee may claim that quitting a prior job to come
to work at the request of the new employer is adequate consideration.
This claim is rejected by many courts, some of whom rely on the
inevitable fact that an employee must always quit a prior job to take
the current job.[24] The following examples are sometimes given as
illustrations of valid types of additional, second considerations:
making an investment in the business, resigning from government
service, giving up one's own business, or relinquishing an acknowledged right to recover for injury.[25]

A few courts do not require that additional consideration must be
shown for a definite term element of the contract. One court noted that
because additional consideration need not be shown for terms such as
the right to bonuses, severance pay, or sales commission rates, additional consideration should not be needed for job security
provisions.[26] Courts may treat the two consideration notion as a rule
of convenience and not a rule of law. Where the parties' intent is
otherwise clear, additional consideration may not be required for
long-term job security agreements. Where the intent is not clear,
additional consideration is only one way of determining the real intent
of the parties on the issue of duration.[27]

It is usually the employer who benefits from the two consideration
argument. In one case, an employee unsuccessfully sought to turn the
two consideration argument to the employee's advantage. The
employer in question had modified the working conditions and the
employee objected. The employee claimed that there was no additional consideration for the modification of the contract terms and therefore the modification was invalid. The court disagreed, indicating that
the mutual advantage of the employee's continuing employment was
adequate consideration to support the change.[28] Despite the common
use of the mutuality concept, this illustrates that many legal arguments are not equally available to both parties.

A few courts have avoided the two consideration argument by
recognizing additional consideration that the employer has received
beyond merely having the employee get the work done. For example,
one court found a seniority based layoff provision enforceable because
it was clothed "in the consideration of improved stability of the

workforce and better cooperation between management and the employees."[29]

In summary, many courts require a second form of consideration where a definite term contract of employment is claimed. The second consideration must be something more than performing the job, even though the employee may have satisfactorily performed the job for many, many years. In contrast, employees have been largely unsuccessful in requiring employers to show that the employee received additional contractual consideration when the employer unilaterally alters the terms and conditions of employment.

Employment Application

The employee may attempt to show that the employment application or related papers constitute evidence of a contract of definite duration. One example is the effort to show that the application created a probationary period, which, in turn, might imply a for cause post-probationary status. Courts are reluctant to find contract terms based upon the employment application forms. In one case, the court found that the application was not intended to be a contract. Lack of mutual intent usually means no contract was created. The court further determined that the application form was "completed and signed . . . for informational purposes only."[30] They did not define the informational purpose being served.

The employment application may contain other written statements that the employee may use to attempt to show an intention to create a contract with job security. One employee sought to show that signing a patent assignment agreement in favor of the employer was sufficient second consideration to show a definite term contract. The court found that there was no such intent shown in the particular terms of the agreement.[31] The patent agreement only gave the employee notice of the employee's common law liability on patents. Other documents accompanying the employment agreement might be relied upon. One court indicated that an employee's covenant not to compete might support a claim for cause based discharge, although no such actual finding was made in that particular case.[32]

Another claim of a definite term contract was rejected when the court determined that the employment document in question was only an explanation of application procedures. Even though the document contained references to cause based discharges, the court found that at the time of the receipt of the papers the person was not yet an employee. At the time of acceptance of the job, no further mention was made of the document in question.[33] Apparently, the court found that the employee did not actually rely on the language of cause at the time of acceptance.

In summary, employee efforts to use application forms as the basis of the claim for a definite term contract are usually rejected. Among the common reasons given for this rejection is the court's determination of the employer's lack of contractual intent in using the application forms, or by finding that the employee did not rely on the forms as an expression of contract terms when they were actually signed, or that the forms were only for "informational purposes."

Expectations and Reliance

Definite term bilateral contracts cannot be created on the basis of the subjective expectations of one party, the employee alone. Where the employee's expectations are deemed to be subjective and not shared by the employer, there is not the mutual meeting of the minds necessary for a long-term contract.[34] Outward manifestations of intent, not uncommunicated subjective beliefs, are what matter.[35]

Employees frequently testify about their subjective expectations. The subjective expectations may be based on the history of the company. This is not sufficient for a contract. For example, no long-term contract was found in circumstances where the employer was shown to have the following characteristics: a family operation, low salaries, virtually no employee turnover, and the employer usually continued to pay employees who were absent because of illness.[36] The general atmosphere may have been one in which the employee could have the expectation that the employer took care of the employees, but the one sided expectation was found to have no contractual effect in the discharge situation.

In a few situations, courts may find sufficient evidence to demonstrate that the employee had a reasonable, not merely subjective, expectation of a definite term contract. In such a case, the employee will have the benefit of a definite term contract requiring cause for discharge. The following factors are among those identified as being important in determining whether some courts will find the expectations to be mutual and reasonable: independent (second) consideration, past employer policies and practices, longevity of service, actions or communications by the employer reflecting assurances of continued employment, and the practices of the industry reflecting job security concerns.[37] Just one of these elements standing alone is not likely to be sufficient. The finding of a long-term contract will usually require that more than one of these evidentiary elements be present.

An employee's job security expectations may be reasonable or unreasonable. Obviously, if the expectations are unreasonable, the employer has no contractual obligation to the employee. If the employee's expectations are reasonably based upon the employer's actions, policies, and statements, some courts may find that there is a contractual obligation. Where there is a reasonable expectation, but that expectation clashes with a fundamental employer right,[38] no contractual obligation is likely to exist. Just as reasonable employee expectations are not always protected under the collective bargaining requirements of the National Labor Relations Act, they are not likely to be always protected under individual contracts.[39]

In summary, employees frequently present extensive evidence about their expectations for the job. However sincerely the expectations may be held, courts usually will not find a definite term contract solely on the basis of the employee's subjective expectations. Courts require that the expectations be reasonably held by both parties. Both the employer and employee must share the same expectation about the employment relationship.

Mutuality

Mutuality has been said to be the legal underpinning for the at will contract doctrine.[40] A contract suggests a mutual exchange of promises and obligations. However, many employment contracts are not of this nature. They are unilateral contracts. The employer offers employment and employee accepts, not by exchanging promises but by performing services.[41] Despite the unilateral character of most employment contracts, courts explicitly or implicitly put great stock in the mutuality doctrine. A basic tenet of the mutuality doctrine, in effect, says that if the employee can quit at any time, for any reason, the employer should be able to discharge the employee at any time for any reason. An extension of the argument suggests that if the employer has no effective remedy against a defaulting employee, the employee should not be able to hold the discharging employer responsible.[42]

Where employees state at trial that they felt that the employees could leave the employer at any time, many courts are likely to find that the employer could discharge the employees at any time. Unless there is a mutual obligation, the employer is not bound to a cause requirement for discharge.[43] If the employee is not bound to work, the employer is not bound to keep the employee. Even when the employee has worked for the employer for many years, the performance of long term service seems to be evidence of acceptable mutuality only for salary claims, not for job security claims. Long term service provides no additional element in the doctrine of mutuality.

Whereas mutuality suggests that many legal doctrines should be equally applicable to either the employee or employer, in practice many of the legal doctrines offer more protection to employers than to employees. For example, employees may have to show special consideration was given for protective contract terms, but employers do not have to give special consideration to modify the terms and conditions of employment by issuing a new handbook.

Parol Evidence

It is folklore knowledge to say that an obligation may not be binding unless it is in writing. As a practical matter, it is obvious that a writing is more definite and complete evidence than a recollection of oral statements made at some much earlier time. Where the proof requirements are stringent, as they are in the employment area, the failure to obtain a writing usually means that the employee cannot prove the existence of a definite term contract.

The parol evidence rule limits the use of oral evidence to establish the terms of a contract. In this context, one of the more common summaries of the rule is that when a written contract sets forth the terms of the agreement, evidence of prior, inconsistent negotiations or terms cannot be considered.[44] There cannot be a valid express (written) contract and a contradictory implied contract embracing the same subject matter.[45] If a writing evidences an at will contract, the employee cannot use mere oral promises to overcome the writing and show a definite term contract.

There are some situations, however, in which oral evidence of some terms of the employment contract can be used. Where there is a written contract, but it does not contain the entire agreement, parol evidence can be used to explain the intended meaning of the unwritten elements.[46] Such information might provide a method to determine the duration of a contract where it was found to intend some definite duration. Parol evidence can be used to show terms where the written contract is incomplete on one point and the oral evidence is not inconsistent with the written terms.[47] In each of these situations, however, there must be enough of a writing to show the existence of a basic contract. The basic terms must be shown in the writing and can be supplemented by the parol evidence. Where a five year contract was never fully written out, an employee who worked for two and one-half years under the initial letter of agreement was found to have a valid contract.[48]

The U.S. Supreme Court has recognized that not all terms in a contract must be in writing. In a comprehensive summary, they stated:

> A written contract with an explicit tenure provision clearly is evidence of a formal understanding that supports a teacher's claim of entitlement to continued employment unless sufficient "cause" is shown. Yet absence of such an explicit contractual provision may not always foreclose the possibility that a teacher has a "property" interest in re-employment. For example, the law of contracts in most, if not all, jurisdictions long has employed a process by which agreement, though not formalized in writing, may be "implied." Explicit contractual provisions may be supplemented by other agreements implied from "the promisor's words and conduct in the light of the surrounding circumstances." And, "[t]he meaning of [the promisor's] words and acts is found by relating them to the usage of the past."[49]

In summary, the rule precluding the use of parol evidence in many circumstances will prevent the employee from using oral statements to show a fixed term contract. Another of the more common applications of the parol evidence rule is where the employee seeks to use parol evidence to show a modification of the terms of a written at will agreement.

Integration Clause

Another device that may be used to limit the use of oral or parol evidence is the integration clause that is commonly used at the end of contracts. Such a clause generally states that the written agreement evidences the entire agreement and that the written agreement supersedes all prior agreements or statements that were made to the employee. In the absence of fraud, accident, or mistake, the integration clause will preclude the use of oral evidence of earlier prior statements to expand or explain the contract.[50] The integration clause will frequently arise as an issue where the employee has been recruited by employer representatives who orally promise a prosperous and long-term future. When the employee later accepts the job, a written contract with an integration clause, but without a written version of the earlier promises may cut off the legal effect of the oral promises.[51] The general effect of an integration may cause something of a dilemma for some employers. Employer handbooks may contain language that permits the employer to change the terms at any time. It has also been suggested that where the contract itself provides that its terms can be changed at any time, it cannot be an integrated contract.[52] If it cannot be an integrated contract, then the employee may attempt to show that subsequent employer statements modified the handbook contract and the modification is permissible under the nonintegration language used in the handbook. If it is not an integrated contract, the handbook will also not preclude the employee from making contract claims based on agreements made outside of the handbook.

In summary, an employee attempting to prove a definite term contract usually needs a writing of some type. The informal, unilateral nature of most employment contracts usually means there is no writing, unless the employer issues an employee handbook. Where the employee has a written employment contract, it may include an integration clause that cuts off reference to any prior promises about the nature of the employment.

Statute of Frauds—A Writing

The statute of frauds generally requires that to be enforceable, a contact that is not to be completed within a year must be evidenced in writing. Employees frequently contend that they have a long-term contract, one that is longer than a year in duration. If the agreement is not in writing, the contract of employment for a term of more than a year is not enforceable and the employee is at will. A contract for employment for a definite term that extends beyond one year is covered by this requirement of writing.[53] Where there is no writing as required by the statute, the employee who claims to have an oral contract of employment for more than a year will be treated as an at will relationship.

An at will agreement is capable of being performed within one year, because the employee could be fired or could quit at any time. Because it could be completed within a year, the oral at will contract is not limited by the statute of frauds. The effect of the statute of frauds is that employers are usually "protected from an entirely oral agreement for a definite term in excess of one year."[54]

An employee might die or might resign from employment within the first year of work. Because of these possibilities, employees will claim that the statute of frauds has been satisfied even though the unwritten contract extends for more than the statutory one year. Most courts do not agree that this potential method of completing the contract within a year will take the claim of a longer term employment agreement outside of the statute of frauds.[55] If the statute applies, an oral contract for permanent or lifetime employment would clearly not be enforceable and the employee is at will.[56] One court, however, has optimistically stated that "courts and commentators have consistently accepted the view that indefinite permanent employment contracts . . . fall outside the statute because they are capable of full performance within one year."[57]

The benefits of strict application of the statute of frauds are seen as reducing fraud and problems of proof.[58] Some courts indicate that this rationale for the statute of frauds actually benefits both employees and employers. However, in practice the statute is most often used by employers to defeat employee claims of long-term contracts and not to give any protection to employees.

The statute of frauds may also play a role in the renewal of employment contracts. An employee may have a valid written employment contract for a period of more than one year. After its expiration, a renewal of that multiyear contract may not be enforceable without a writing.[59] An oral renewal agreement that would extend beyond one year would not be enforceable if the court applies the statute of frauds. Similarly, merely continuing to work would be viewed by the statute of frauds as an at will relationship.

Where a contract contains a probationary period, the employee can be fired at will during that time. Such a probationary termination usually would occur within the year. Where the employee survived the probationary period, one court held that the remainder of the contract was not within the statute of frauds because the contract might have been completed within the year, that is, during the probationary period.[60] This is not a commonly accepted view, but it is one that might be tested in various jurisdictions.

Whether or not the statute of frauds is applicable, it is clear that it is in the best interests of clarity to have a writing covering the terms of the employment. A writing may also be in the best interests of the employer at times. With a writing, there is less likelihood of a misunderstanding and less likelihood of subsequent litigation. However, few employees are in a position to demand a writing, and few employers offer them.

In summary, the statute of frauds requires that a contract is to be in writing if it cannot be completed within a year. Where employees claim to have a definite contract, they usually claim one longer than a year. Without a writing, the long-term claim is defeated by the statute of frauds and the employee becomes an at will employee. A few courts say that the employee's death or resignation could occur within a year of the employment. These courts do not find the statute of frauds to be a barrier to the employee's long-term employment claim.

Many Elements, Not One

A single example of any one aspect of the types of evidence mentioned above is rarely as convincing as multiple pieces of evidence all pointing in the same direction. This is particularly true of the employment contract. Where there is only an employee's personal expectation that is being used for the basis of a claim of a fixed term contract, the employee has a difficult case to prove. Where there are several elements, the case for the employee becomes stronger. Employer statements concerning job security, definite contract term statements made by authorized employer agents, statements made in the context of actual negotiations, or other combinations of evidence make a much stronger case than one item alone.

An example of multiple types of evidence occurs when the employee shows that there were actual negotiations. Employer statements made in the context of actual bilateral negotiations are likely to be binding. In one such case, the employee was insistent upon a permanent contract and quit her prior job only after receiving clear assurances.[61] The court found that the statements were made in the context of actual bilateral negotiations, and not statements made unilaterally by the employer.

Another court listed, in the negative, many elements that might be shown to show other than at will status when the court said:

> Plaintiff (employee) testified that he never signed an employment contract ... that he does not recall ever discussing (employer's) ... policies with regard to job security, tenure, layoff or discharge; that he does not recall that any promises were made to him with regard to these areas; that he never received any documents or written versions of company policies on job security or discharge; that he had no understanding with the company about his term of employment; and that he was never informed during his tenure ... that he had any protection against layoff .... (W)e cannot excuse plaintiff's failure to come forward with evidence showing the existence of genuine issue for trial.[62]

If the employee has some evidence on several of the aforementioned topics, the employee might be able to prove the existence of a definite term contract.

In summary, the employee who attempts to show the existence of a definite term contract beyond one year faces many obstacles. In the usual case where the employee has no writing, the statute of frauds may defeat the claim. Where the employee has a writing evidencing at will status, the parol evidence rule or an integration clause may defeat the claim for a fixed term contract. In the effort to show a writing, reliance on application documents will usually be unsuccessful. Where the oral or written statements are ambiguous, courts will reject claims to long-term job security. The presumption of at will is likely to be the determining factor where the evidence is otherwise uncertain.

Some courts are moving away from the strict application of many of these traditional contract rules. Where the employee can amass a variety of different types of evidence, courts may find the presumption of at will status has been overcome. Some form of a writing, clear oral statements, and evidence of more consideration than mere satisfactory job performance may tip the scales in the employee's direction.

Where courts strictly apply traditional law contract doctrines of the types mentioned above, employees will usually be found to be at will. Where courts are willing to recognize that the typical employment situation has characteristics that distinguish it from the traditional contract environment, the employee's expectations are more likely to be found to be reasonable. For example, where there is evidence of actual negotiations, then the employer's statements are more likely to be binding. The judicial requirements for finding a fixed term contract may make sense in the world of traditional, commercial contract. They make little practical sense in the world of employment. If every employee tried to seriously negotiate with his or her employer over the every employment contract, workplace efficiency would drop to unheard of lows. This type of negotiation, however, seems to be the judicial message implicit in the presumption of at will status. The reluctance of courts to find fixed term contracts might also indicate that many courts treat the presumption of at will status as more than a presumption. It is treated as a rule of law in the workplace.

Most of the litigated cases involve employees who are attempting to show a long-term or for cause discharge type of contract. The same rationales used by courts to find that the employee has no binding contract have, in a few situations, been used by the employee to show that the employer has no binding contract obligation on the employee. In one situation, the employer sought to show the employee had certain obligations under a conflict of interests policy promulgated by the employer. The court held the language too vague to do more than restate the general duty of loyalty. There was no contractual obligation.[63] Where employers sue employees, the employee must consider the same contract arguments that employers do in the opposite situations.

EMPLOYEE HANDBOOKS

Unilateral Promulgation

Increasingly, one of the most litigated topics in individual employment area is the contractual nature, if any, of the employer's unilaterally promulgated employee handbook. The handbooks may cover diverse topics, including the employer's philosophy, benefits, vacations, expectations, discipline, and discharge.[64] Handbooks often speak optimistically about the company's and employees' long-term future and role of the employees in that future. They may have a tone that suggests that the workplace is a "big happy family" where everyone takes care of everyone else, implying that discharge will occur only for cause. The effect of the statements is that many employees feel that the employer is saying that as long as the employee performs satisfactorily, the employee has a long duration job. However, if this handbook language is found not to be a contract, the employment is merely at will. That is the usual situation.

Because they are often the only writing evidencing the terms of employment relationship, employees will rely on handbooks as evidence of a definite term contract. The rules of interpretation of the handbook are not dissimilar from the rules of contract creation identified in the preceding section. However, the volume of litigation on handbooks warrants this separate discussion.

Specific Terms

Many courts treat the statements on job security in personnel manuals as a "mere" gratuity. They say the manual is a document intended to be used for informational purposes only. Courts often declare that there is no mutual intention to be bound, that is, the employer did not intend the statements in the handbook to be binding.[65] What the employer did intend by the statements is not made clear. The presumption of at will status continues to apply.

Frequently, the job related statements in the manual are made in very broad and general terms, and reliance upon such ambiguous statements to create a contract is found to be misplaced. Without specific language or without specifically identified procedures, the handbook will not be deemed to be evidence of a long-term discharge for cause contract.[66] Where the language of the handbook is phrased in terms of "guidelines" and is couched in permissive or vague language, it will not be binding by its very terms.[67] Even the use of the word "should" in the handbook may be deemed to be discretionary.[68]

One court cites the need for "great clarity" in the handbook language to overcome the presumption of at will status.[69] An employee can "reasonably" believe that an offer to contract has been made only when it is specific.[70]

The use of specific examples of workplace situations may add to the needed specificity to suggest a contract.[71] Most cases, however, treat handbook examples as illustrative and not as being specific, contractual limitations on the employer. For example, where the handbook contains six examples of discharge for cause, the six examples do not mean that there are no other grounds for discharge or that the employees have lost their at will status.[72]

Outside sources may help give handbook language specific meaning. Employers are often bound by law to not discriminate and to accommodate handicapped persons. These nondiscrimination, accommodation policies may be spelled out in a handbook. The language of these provisions may be general, but it may take on specific meaning when read against the enormous quantity of agency rules and case law behind the provisions. One court found such a handbook provision on handicap accommodation to be a binding contract where the employee claimed that the employer had failed in the employer's duty to accommodate.[73]

In summary, the claimed handbook contract is like any other contract. The terms must be specific and unambiguous. There must be a mutual intention to create a contract. The presumption of at will status continues to play its paramount role. Unless these terms are met, the handbook will be treated as an informational document and not a contract.

Disclaimers

Employers are now commonly using disclaimer statements in handbooks. An employer can be protected against definite term contract liability based on the personnel manual by including appropriate disclaimers on the face of the manual.[74]

The disclaimers must be obvious. Some courts have even suggested what typesetting formats should be used. The disclaimers should "contrast" in type, color, size, or borders from the remainder of the handbook.[75] The disclaimer must be conspicuous.[76]

The disclaimers may be of several types.[77] They should state that the employees are at will regardless of what other language the handbook contains. The disclaimer should reserve the employer's right to modify the handbook at any time.[78] In addition, a history of actually having changed policies helps. The disclaimer might state that the handbook is a statement of intent, but not a contract.[79] An employer may have the employees sign and return the cover page of the manual to evidence their receipt and understanding of the contents.[80] The signature and return are frequently in the nature of a release or waiver of rights to anything other than an at will contract relationship.

Where disclaimers are found not to exist or not to be effective, a court may find that the handbook terms constitute a contract for fixed term employment, which means that discharge during the life of the contract can only be for cause. An employer is not required to issue a handbook, and if an undisclaimed handbook is issued and reasonably relied upon, the employer may be contractually required to follow its terms.[81] The contractual consideration the employer receives is "an orderly, cooperative and loyal workforce" as a result of the statements.[82] In other words, these courts find the level of consideration or a mutuality of obligation necessary for a binding contract. If the employer expects the employees to abide by the terms of the handbook, then the employer has created an atmosphere in which the employees can justifiably rely on the statements in the handbook.[83] In other words, if the employer expects the employees to abide by the handbook then the employees can expect the employer to abide by the handbook.

Appropriate disclaimers may prevent the handbook from being treated as a contract. In this situation, the employer cannot use the handbook as a defense if the employee seems to prove the existence of a fixed term contract based on considerations outside of the handbook.

Employee Reliance

Where a handbook has reasonably been relied upon by an employee, it may form the basis of a definite term, for cause contract. An obvious example of reasonable reliance is where the handbook became one of the subjects of actual negotiations when determining the terms and conditions of employment. Such a handbook may be incorporated into the contract of employment.

Where an employee negotiates an actual written, individual employment contract, and the individual employment contract incorporates the terms of the employer's personnel handbook, those terms of the incorporated handbook will be found to be binding.[84] The rule in collective bargaining is similar. Cross references between the personnel manual and the collective bargaining contract may show the binding nature of the personnel manual.[85] In the absence of such incorporation and cross references, a grievance arbitrator may give little weight to the employer's policy manual.[86]

If the employee did not know about the terms of the handbook at the time when the job was accepted, the employee cannot claim to have relied on the handbook as a part of the contract.[87] If the employee was aware of the handbook at the time of hiring, the employee may be able to show justifiable reliance on any long-term or for cause employment statements. If there is a written contract of employment establishing at will employment that does not incorporate a handbook, any statements in the unincorporated handbook suggesting other than at will are not likely to be binding.[88] Where the employer has specifically reviewed the handbook with the employee, it is some evidence of reliance and mutuality for a contract.[89]

One court, trying to escape from finding that there was a binding handbook, held that if the handbook was to be binding on the employer, it must be shown to have been both read and understood by the employee. If the employee did not understand the terms of the handbook, the employee could not have relied on it. This court denied that this was a return to a variation of the "fallacious" mutuality argument, but its statements makes the denial unclear.[90]

In summary, where a handbook exists at the time of the hiring, the employee will often show that there was reliance on the handbook. The employee's best evidence is to show that the handbook was actually incorporated into the contract. At a minimum, the employee will have to show awareness of the handbook in order to show reliance on it.

Timing and Reliance

The timing of the issuance of the manual may be an important consideration. A court may find that a manual issued after employment status is established is less likely to be binding than one issued prior to the establishment of the employment status.[91]

History of Changes

Related to this is the question of whether there is a history of unilateral changes in the handbook policies by the employer. If there have been changes in the past, it may be additional evidence of the noncontractual character of the policies because the employee is put on notice of future unilateral changes.[92] Where there is a history of changes, however, the employer may not be able to use the handbook to prove the existence of at will status where the employee can prove terms of a contract by statements outside of the handbook.

Distribution

Another important factor on the question of whether an employee handbook can be considered to be an employment contract is the extent of distribution of the handbook. There are at least two types of distributions mentioned in the cases. One type is distribution generally to all employees. This handbook is the one that is the more likely of the two to be found to be a contract under appropriate circumstances. The second type of handbook contains extensive personnel policies, but is given limited distribution. The distribution of this type of handbook is limited to a few supervisors or those similarly situated. Where the distribution is limited to supervisors, the nonsupervisory employees are unlikely to be aware of its contents and therefore could not show reliance on it as terms of their contract.[93] However, where distribution is limited to supervisors, but it is the intent and practice of the employer that the employees be made aware of the contents of the handbook, then the binding nature of the terms remains an open question.[94]

Employer Reliance

The question of reliance on the handbook can also be raised in the context of employer reliance. The question can be put in the context of a discharge where the handbook becomes the cited source for the reason of discharge. If the employer has cited the handbook in the discharge action, can the employee require that the discharged employer then abide by the other handbook terms, such as following a grievance mechanism? One court has suggested that the answer is yes; however, most courts have not discussed the issue.[95] Where the employee has been determined to be at will, the employer needs no reason to discharge and the handbook reference may be superfluous. At some point, however, continued employer reference to and reliance on handbook provisions may overcome the disclaimers the employer has put into the handbook.

In summary, an employee who bases a long-term employment claim on a handbook is required to show that employee actually relied on it. Factors suggesting reliance include negotiations which referenced the handbook, knowledge of the existence and content of the handbook at the time of hire, and distribution of the handbook to the entire workforce. Factors suggesting no reliance include the limited circulation of the handbook, issuance after negotiations are over, and lack of knowledge of the contents of the handbook.

Unwritten Practices

Somewhat related to the handbook question is the question of whether unwritten employer policies that are provable as past practices can constitute a contract. One such claim was rejected because unwritten customary practices could not meet the test used for handbooks, namely, specific language that the employee was specifically aware of the language (practice) and proof that the employee worked in reliance on it.[96] Another court said that a past practice does not constitute an intentional surrender of the employer's at will rights.[97] In arbitration under a collective bargaining contract, properly qualified customs and past practices may be enforceable if they meet certain criteria. Common requirements are that the practice be unequivocal, be clearly enunciated and acted upon, be of reasonable duration, and have been accepted by both parties.[98]

Handbooks: Good or Bad

The judicial interpretation of employee handbooks has led to conflicting conclusions. Many employers want to use them, but they do not want to be bound. Employees are being mislead when the handbooks are later found to be not binding. One case summed up the matter in this way: "Springs contends that employers will stop providing handbooks, bulletins, and similar materials if they are bound by them. If company policies are not worth the paper on which they are printed, then it would be better not to mislead employees by distributing them."[99] Another court said that "the attempt to regularize personnel practices through the use of handbooks is commendable," but went on to say that to construe "any imperfection" against the employer would "inhibit the attempt."[100] Other courts have noted that employers can benefit from the use of handbooks. Employers may get "an orderly, cooperative and loyal workforce."[101] Both employees and employers stand to benefit.[102] Handbooks may inspire "loyalty and productivity."[103] Handbooks can "remove an element of arbitrariness."[104]

However favorably courts may view about the use of handbooks, most courts are reluctant to find them binding. A finding that the handbooks are binding might "discourage the preparation"[105] or "discourage employers from adopting such worth-while policies."[106] If the courts want to encourage only nonbinding handbooks, the courts are, in effect saying that the presumption of at will status will not be overcome. If the employees cannot rely on the job security implications of the language of the handbooks, they should be advised to ignore them. If employees should ignore nonbinding handbooks, it creates confusion when courts talk about handbooks as worthwhile policies.

Statutes and Handbooks

Statutes may impact on the employer's use of handbooks. The Montana Wrongful Discharge legislation states that if the employer has written internal procedures under which an employee may appeal a discharge, then the employee must exhaust those procedures, so long as they can be completed within 90 days.[107] This could mean that the use of a binding handbook may save some employers a trip to court. The discussion draft of the Commissioners on Uniform State Laws provides that due [substantial] deference shall be given to the resolution of the dispute in the employer's internal procedures, again suggesting the avoidance of a trial.[108] Under Title VII equal employment legislation, the Supreme Court has suggested that an internal grievance mechanism (handbook) may be a matter courts will consider as part of the employer's defense in sexual harassment cases.[109] Whereas these statutory and judicial references to handbook grievance mechanisms may not mean that the employer can use the handbook as a complete defense, the employer with an adequate internal grievance mechanism is likely to be better off than the employer who has no such handbook provision. In other words, these statutes and proposals, as well as the statements of the Supreme Court suggest the importance of having an employee handbook. However, nonbinding handbooks are not likely to meet these statutory or judicial objectives. The employer may be faced with some difficult decisions to make about handbooks.

MODIFYING THE CONTRACT, HANDBOOK TERMS

Modification of a written contract usually involves a mutual renegotiation of the contract. What was mutually agreed upon must be changed by mutual agreement. Questions about the modification of an oral, unilateral contract, such as the usual at will contract, or modification of a first handbook by issuance of a second handbook are more difficult issues. Part of the problem is the question of whether the presumption of at will status that permits arbitrary discharges also permits arbitrary changes in other terms and conditions of the employment relationship. Courts that have seriously addressed the issue are uncertain, but few courts have given it serious attention.

Modification issues often involve an employee handbook. In the modification situation, the employer may want to argue that the handbook is a binding contract. The employer may want it to be a binding contract because the later handbook is clearly disclaimed and makes all employees at will. Earlier handbook statements may not have been so clearly at will. One scenario involves an employer that has hired a number of employees and, after their employment, issues an employee handbook. The subsequently issued handbook is some-what less likely to be binding than one issued before the hire. How-ever, in appropriate circumstances, the subsequently issued handbook may be found to be binding.[110] Another scenario involves the employer who has issued a first handbook and then issues a second or third handbook modifying the earlier ones. For example, an employer may issue a second handbook replete with disclaimers, seeking to avoid any notion that the earlier handbook without dis-claimers was a fixed term or for cause contract.[111]

Continuing to Work as Acceptance

The most commonly stated handbook modification rule is that the second or later handbook is binding if it contains specific language, is adequately communicated to the employees, and is accepted by the employees by their continuing to work after being aware of the hand-book offer, that is, the issuance of the later handbook.[112] In other words, the modification becomes the terms of any claim of any con-tract. A variation on this theme is to require that the employee be aware of the handbook, that the employee understood its terms, and that the employee continued to work according to the new terms.[113]

A major problem in the foregoing analysis lies in the third step, namely, the employee continues to work under the new terms. Clearly the later handbook is binding where the employee actively agreed to accept its new terms.[114] Some courts, however, are saying that merely continuing to work after the issuance of the handbook is adequate acceptance.[115] Apparently, the employee would have to quit to show nonacceptance of the new handbook! If continuing to work after issuance of the new terms is all that is required, it is tantamount to saying the mere issuance of the handbook makes it binding. Few employees have alternatives immediately available that permit them to quit merely to show rejection of the terms of a new handbook. Of course, quitting does much more than reject the new handbook.

It is easy to find that starting to work for the first time is acceptance of the employer's general working conditions. However, continuing to work is different. The new handbook often seeks not only to impose new conditions, but also to waive or release all prior, specific conditions of employment. If a court says continuing to work is acceptance, it has to add that it is also a waiver. A waiver should be more difficult to find, particularly if it is a waiver of such a critical term as job security. What many courts are saying is that silence (continuing to work) is acceptance of the terms of a new contract, including a release or waiver of rights. Such a rule of law on acceptance seems to be unique to the field of individual contracts of employment.

A secondary question becomes one of how the employee can continue to work and express rejection of the new handbook or policy, thus continuing the terms of the earlier handbook or policy. The reasoned case law is unclear and most courts use the silence as an acceptance approach. One case rejected the view that such an employee would have to give specific notice of rejection because silence (continuing to work) is not usually considered to be acceptance.[116] Another case required that the employee must know of the changes and have time to consider them.[117] Silence and additional circumstances might mean acceptance.[118] In one unusual case an employee did not remain silent, but specifically rejected the offer.[119] However, the general rule seems to be that acceptance of new handbook terms is shown by merely continuing to work.

The issue presents practical difficulties. One desirable purpose of the handbook from the employer's perspective, in part, is to establish uniform personnel policies. If the law tells each employee that they can preserve earlier rights by announcing specific rejection of each new handbook, that desirable uniformity will be lost and the employer could be engaged in endless individual negotiations. In contrast, if the employee is already an at will employee, the employer can simply discharge the at will employee who refuses to accept the new handbook terms. It seems likely that most courts are, in fact, using a silence (continuing to work) as acceptance. This is, however, saying that the normal rules of contract do not apply to individual employment contracts, a doctrine that many courts will not specifically acknowledge.[120] Where a court adopts a silence as acceptance doctrine, it also appears to give the employer the power to change all of the terms and conditions of employment at will, whether or not they relate to discharge. The doctrine seems really to be saying that an at will contract can have no binding terms of any kind. Not only is discharge at will, but all terms are at will. It is a reaffirmation of the overriding power of the employer rights doctrine.

Promulgation

The method of promulgating a handbook may affect the modification process. Where the first handbook was distributed in a special meeting with elaborate explanations, an attempted modification by a second handbook may require an equally detailed meeting.[121] The many possible variations that can arise when a later handbook is issued may have led the ground breaking Michigan court to the position that the issuance of a second handbook does not necessarily mean that all prior contracts or implied in fact contracts are automatically modified. They found, for example, that a prior "express promise of the employer *apart* from the employment manual may create a jury-submissible issue," even after a later handbook has been issued.[122] The point seems to be that some contracts may have been made or confirmed separate and apart from any handbook. The issuance of a later manual does not automatically affect them. Each individual contract must be viewed on its own facts, which, of course, is implicit in the very notion of individual, not collective, contracts. However, many courts refuse to do this.

Future or Vested

The employer's attempted modification might be intended to relate only to future terms of employment or the employer might intend to attempt to modify the entire, past and future, employment relationship. Accrued or vested rights may not be subject to the modification, even if the employee is an at will employee and continues to work.[123] The loss of accrued rights, such as vacation or severance pay, is not favored.[124] Accumulated sick leave earned prior to the promulgation of new policy may be protected.[125] The new handbook may modify the job security status and all future working conditions, but vested benefits will not be changed. Apparently, long service alone does not usually result in any vested right in being given more consideration than an inexperienced newly hired employee.

By way of comparison, modification of a collective bargaining contract requires that the parties renegotiate the contract. The individual employee under a collective bargaining contract cannot enter into an individual contract with the employer that would modify any of the terms of the collective bargaining contract that apply to the employee.[126] An employer can unilaterally promulgate and impose changed terms and conditions of employment only if the contract has expired and only after meeting the employer's obligation to bargain in good faith. Promulgation plus employees who continue to work do not meet the statutory duty to bargain about the contract in good faith in collective bargaining.

Modifying "Privileges"

The effect of statutes must be considered when individual contract working terms and conditions are modified. The Supreme Court, in the related context of determining whether a due process property (e.g. contract) interest might exist, has recognized that there can be a "common law" of employment established by the policies and statements of an employer. "Just as this Court has found there to be a 'common law of a particular industry or of a particular plant' that may supplement a collective-bargaining agreement, so there may be an unwritten common law in a particular university that certain employees shall have the equivalent of tenure."[127] The Supreme Court has cast great doubt on the proposition that employer statements in a personnel manual can be considered "mere gratuities" when a Title VII employment discrimination charge is raised. The Court stated:

> An employer may provide its employees with many benefits that it is under no obligation to furnish by any express or implied contract. Such a benefit, though not a contractual right of employment, may qualify as a "privilege" of employment under Title VII. A benefit that is part and parcel of the employment relationship may not be doled out in a discriminatory fashion, even if the employer would be free under the employment contract simply not to provide the benefit at all. Those benefits that comprise the "incidents of employment," . . . or that form "an aspect of the relationship between the employer and employees," . . . may not be afforded in a manner contrary to Title VII.[128]

Otherwise nonbinding (noncontractual) statements made in manuals or during recruitment might be viewed as a privilege under Title VII. The employer will be bound to apply such privileges or policies in a nondiscriminatory manner. In such a suit, the employer who retracts such statements (privileges) may be required to come forward with a nondiscriminatory reason once the employee has established the prima facie case.[129] This doctrine seems to make it easier to establish a privilege than it is to establish a contract.

In summary, many employees who seek to prove the existence of a definite term (discharge based on cause) contract look to the language of any written handbooks that the employer may have distributed. As is the case with oral statements, a handbook will not be found to be binding where the language is ambiguous and nonspecific. The handbook will not be binding where the employee cannot show reliance on its terms. Courts permit the employer to disclaim the contractual nature of the handbook if it is done in a conspicuous fashion. Employers can doubtlessly disclaim their oral statements, too, although the effect of injecting disclaimers into ordinary conversation would be somewhat hilarious. Unwritten past practices are usually rejected in individual contract disputes, but may be allowed under certain circumstances where there are collective bargaining contracts. The reason for the distinction is not obvious.

Handbooks seem to put courts in a dilemma. They apparently want to encourage their use, but the courts are reluctant to find them binding. It is not clear why a nonbinding handbook has any utility, as it is not likely to further the goals of uniformity, loyalty, production, and cooperation.

One of the most difficult problems is to explain the effect of the issuance of a later handbook on whatever rights may have been granted in the earlier handbook. The most common rule is the simplistic approach of saying that the employee accepts the second handbook unless the employee quits, with the possible exception of some accrued or vested rights. This rule makes all facets of working conditions subject to an at will status that goes far beyond what is necessary to protect the employer's entrepreneurial rights.

As is true throughout much of the area of individual contracts of employment, what the judicial at will doctrine encourages the employer to do with employee handbooks may be contrary to the employer's best interests when viewed from other perspectives. For example, actual or proposed wrongful discharge legislation and antidiscrimination legislation may look with significant favor on the employer who has a handbook with a binding grievance mechanism, while the at will doctrine encourages arbitrary personnel policies.

ENDING THE CONTRACT

The individual employment contract may be ended in a variety of ways. The indefinite term employee may quit or be discharged. The definite term employee may reach the end of the term and not be renewed. Within this basic outline, many complications can arise. The purpose of this section is to summarize some of the relevant considerations about ending the individual contract of employment.

Quit

The contract may end by the employee quitting. Part of the mutuality of the at will doctrine is that the employee can quit at any time for any reason. A quit normally terminates all contractual obligations. However, as discussed below, an employee who quits may have some continuing obligations to the employer under a valid covenant not to compete, or similar agreements.[130] A voluntary quit must be distinguished from a constructive discharge, which has been discussed above.[131] Vested rights may still be owing after a quit.

Discharge

It is common to summarize the status of at will employees by saying that, as a matter of contract law, they are subject to discharge for any reason or no reason. This quick summary must be understood to include the restriction that the at will employee cannot be discharged for an illegitimate reason.[132] The list of illegitimate reasons is not very long nor very clear, but it is expanding. The easiest example of illegitimate reasons is found in projections offered in other statutes, such as the list of protected classes under antidiscrimination legislation.[133] Individual rights under a valid affirmative action plan may also be included in the contract of an indefinite term employee.[134]

Additional limitations on the at will discharge may be found outside of the contract, such as when the reason for the discharge violates a public policy defined by legislation or recognized by the courts. One of the most common examples of a violation of public policy is a discharge resulting from the employees having been absent because the employee served on a jury.[135] The judicial self-interest is obvious. There are continuing attempts to expand the range of public policies that might cover the at will employee, but most of the claims are not successful in most jurisdictions.

Where contractual discharge procedures are in place, they must be followed. For example, notice may be required[136] or an in house appeals system may be in place.[137]

Fixed Term, Nonrenewal

For the employee with a fixed term contract, discharge should be distinguished from nonrenewal. Discharge is an action that occurs during the life of the contract and is intended to terminate the contract relationship. Cause is normally required for a discharge during the term of a fixed term agreement. Nonrenewal is a failure to renegotiate a new employment contract after the contract has expired by its own terms. Once the fixed term contract has been completed, the employer is permitted to refuse to renew the contract at will. One court stated that the nonrenewal of an at will contract cannot give rise to a claim of tortious interference with a contract because nonrenewal does not involve a breach of contract.[138] There is no discernible movement to change the "at will" nature of the fixed term contract renewal question, although there may be disputes over whether certain acts or words constitute a renewal.

The expiration of a fixed term contract does not necessarily mean that the fixed term employee stops working. If the contract is renewed, of course, the employee continues under the renewal terms. If the contract is not renewed and the employee continues working, the employee is probably an at will employee, with the nondurational terms of the expired contract still applicable.[139] However, one court has stated that at the end of a fixed term contract, a rebuttable presumption arises that the employee continues under a renewed contract for a "like" term.[140]

Cause

As discussed below,[141] both a definite or indefinite term employee can always be discharged for cause. From the cause perspective, there is no difference between the indefinite term, at will employee, and the definite term employee. For this reason, when litigation over the termination of the employment arises and there is uncertainty over the nature of the contract, the employer's best defense is to attempt to show a cause basis for the discharge, if the facts can support the claim. Ultimately, cause is likely to provide the basis for more protection for the employer's rights than the protection offered by at will status.

Third Party Interference

An at will employee may be subject to discharge by the employer for arbitrary reasons or no reasons. The fact that the employer can be arbitrary in discharge does not permit third parties to arbitrarily interfere with the employment relationship. The employee may have an action against third parties who cause a discharge by their interference in the employment relationship, even if it involves an at will relationship. Courts have stated that enforceability of the underlying contract is not required in an action for malicious interference against a third person.[142] Thus it is not material that the at will employee could be discharged by the employer at any time. However, the employer or the authorized employer's agent who had a lawful right to discharge the employee cannot be found to be a conspirator in an action by the employee against a third party.[143]

In a limited number of situations, an employee may have an action against an agent of the employer for improperly discharging the employee. If the employer's agent does not have the authority to fire an employee but does proceed to fire the employee in an improper manner, the agent may be construed to be a third party tortfeasor in an action for tortious interference in the employment contract.[144] However, the employer's agent has a wide range of immunity so long as the agent is working in the legitimate interests of the employer.[145] A parent corporation may also be held liable for interference in some situations.[146]

GENERAL OR SPECIAL CONTRACT RULES

A useful question to ask about the individual contract of employment is whether it is subject to the same rules of interpretation as other contracts or whether the employment area has special legal rules of contracting. One court has stated that it "discern(s) no basis from departing from otherwise applicable general contract principles."[147] Many courts will talk about rules of contract consideration, statute of frauds, and other contract interpretative devices as though the employment relationship were the same as any other contract situation. However, given the importance of employer rights and other special considerations,[148] it seems more accurate to say, as one court has, the law of individual employment contracts "has developed contrary to all of the standard modern contract principles. . . ."[149] Certainly the rigor with which general contract principles are applied to individual contracts amounts to virtually a special method of contract interpretation. It seems likely that what courts are attempting to do is to use traditional contract doctrine to give great deference to the employer's entrepreneurial control rights. If that is true, it would be preferable to simply acknowledge that fact and find that the employer's right to discharge at will can be overcome only in the unusual case. This would acknowledge that individual employment contracts are subject to special rules, based on the court's view of a paramount public policy protecting employers.

The next question becomes whether individual employment contracts should be treated any differently than other contracts. By analogy, a collective bargaining contract is "more than a contract; it is a generalized code to govern a myriad of cases. . . ."[150] Does this "more than a contract" status arise because of the policies underlying the institution of collective bargaining or does the status arise because of the nature of the workplace? The answer may lie in the nature of collective bargaining, but that is unlikely. Collective bargaining per se is not the goal; rather, the goal is to provide opportunity for the necessary employment for individuals and to provide a peaceful workplace condition that is conducive to the efficient production of goods and services that the nation needs and desires. The individual employee and the noncollective bargaining employer are no different in this regard. The protection of management rights deemed essential to the nature of our capitalist economy and the protection of employee rights essential to individual survival and the pursuit of happiness can better be balanced by recognition that neither the collective bargaining contract nor the individual contract of employment are "mere" contracts. The individual contract shares more commonality with the collective contract than it shares with the purchase of a piece of real estate or an automobile. Nonetheless, policy considerations lead to great disparity between the treatment of individual and collective contracts of employment, even though both may deal with identical problems arising under identical working conditions. Uniformity of treatment may have some value where there is uniformity of conditions and national goals.

BEYOND THE CONTRACT

As indicated the U.S. Supreme Court has identified for nondiscrimination Title VII purposes an area of protected employment relationships that seem to exist outside of the employment contract. This is the area of employment "privileges."[151] Privileges are "benefits that it (the employer) is under no obligation to furnish by any express or implied contract."[152] These privileges cannot be extended or withheld on a discriminatory basis, even though the employer is under no contractual obligation to provide the privileges.

There is limited litigation concerning this concept. In one case, the degree of supervisory responsibilities extended to a supervisory employee was found to be within the privilege protection of Title VII. A black supervisor could not be given less responsibility than a white supervisor if the allocation of responsibility was based on race.[153] Denial of hospital staff privileges based on protected status,[154] denial of a written contract to a black newsperson when white newspersons were given written contracts,[155] and denial of partnership status based on protected status[156] have been identified as areas of protected privilege.

Where there is a nondiscriminatory basis for the differential treatment of privileges, Title VII has not been violated. Thus where predominantly black union employees were denied severance pay but predominantly white employees were given severance pay, the difference between collective bargaining employees and noncollective bargaining employees was found to be an adequate nondiscriminatory reason.[157]

The National Labor Relations Board has also identified an area of the collective bargaining employment relationship that may not be covered by the contract and that is beyond the requirements of statutory good faith bargaining. It is variously described as "merely gifts," or expressions of good feelings between the employer and the employees, or as merely a bonus. The specific subject matter often relates to such matters as giving a Christmas turkey or similar other bonus or gift to the employees. Such gifts may be unilaterally discontinued by the employer without bargaining.[158] These gifts might, however, qualify as Title VII privileges.

Presumably there are similar topics in individual employment relationships, such as gifts, which are within the unilateral authority of the employer and outside of the indefinite or definite term contract. Some of these may qualify as privileges under Title VII and be protected against discriminatory action regardless of whether the contract is at will or not. Given the general judicial reluctance to find the existence of any binding individual contract rights, gifts given over a long time are likely to remain as gifts and not become contract rights.

What the NLRB has identified as being initially a gift outside of the contract, however, may be brought within the contract or within the bargaining obligation under the National Labor Relations Act. For example, if the amount of bonus is determined by an objective formula, it begins to look more like salary or benefits. If it is given over a long period of time, it looks more like an employee right than an employer gift.[159]

In summary, the employment relationship is generally viewed as one based on contract. However, there seem to be a few terms and conditions attached to employment that are beyond the contract. Assuming such items exist, employer action may eventually make them contractual in nature. If such items do exist outside of the contract, it is a doctrine that can only contribute to confusion. As suggested above, the individual contract of employment often contains more implied than express terms. For example, the duties owed by the employees are usually implied, not express. Careful analysis should precede any attempt to create an area of noncontractual privileges or bonuses. A contractual analysis could lead to the same results.

CONCLUSION

The individual contract of employment is commonly described as being either a definite or indefinite term contract. Either description has historically focused on whether the employer can discharge only for cause or discharge for any or no reason. The law recognizes an initial presumption that an employee is at will and can be discharged for arbitrary reasons. The employee can overcome the presumption by showing that a definite term contract exists. Most courts apply traditional contract dogma with great rigor when the employee seeks to show an individual, definite term contract exists. The terms of a definite term contract must be shown with great clarity, and usually by a writing. Because an employee is always permitted to quit, courts find it unfair to require the employer to show cause for a discharge through the device of adopting a rigorous application of the mutuality doctrine. One upshot of these judicial requirements is that the employee who seeks protection through the contract approach to a discharge dispute is often unsuccessful. The employee inevitably begins looking at a tort based approach, with its potential for greater doctrinal flexibility and punitive damages. If the contract approach to the discharge dispute were less rigorous, the specter of tort punitive damages, which are often not available as a contract remedy, might recede.

The requirement of clear proof of a contract is best shown by a writing. Given the informal nature of the individual employment contract, the most available writing is usually an employee handbook, if one exists. Courts also take a rigorous approach to examining employer handbooks to determine whether they can be read as a binding contract. The courts frequently find themselves in the anomalous position of attempting to encourage the promulgation of handbooks but denying that they have any contractual character. The most difficult questions concern the efforts to modify whatever rights may have been granted in an initial handbook or policy by issuing a second handbook that disclaims any contractual character. The most common rule is that the employee accepts the terms of the later handbook by merely continuing to work. This overkill approach apparently permits the employer to treat every term and condition of employment as though it were "at will," that is, to arbitrarily eliminate every right except accrued rights.

The individual contract can be ended in a variety of ways, by discharge, quit, or nonrenewal, for example. The arbitrary nonrenewal of a definite term contract has attracted little judicial attention to date. One likely reason is that so few definite term contracts are found to exist.

It is at least arguable that a discharge system that focused primarily on an employee's performance (cause based discharges) rather than on the nature of the original hire (at will or not) would be more conducive to efficiency and production than the current emphasis on the at will presumption. The concept of cause has always included significant protection of entrepreneurial control and rights to meet changing economic conditions. The current emphasis on protection of the right to arbitrarily discharge, regardless of performance, seems misplaced in the era of a highly competitive global economy. However, that seems to be the inevitable result of a legal system that puts all of its emphasis on the conditions of the creation of the employment contract instead of emphasizing the conditions under which the employment contract should be ended.

Implicit in the notion of individual contracts of employment is the ability of the employment relationship to take on many shades of obligation. Courts generally reject an analysis that each individual contract must be viewed in the light of its particular terms. Instead the courts use wholesale approaches that treat most individual contracts as if they were identical. The use of stringent presumption of at will status effectively denies many employees the right to have the particular details of their individual contract considered. The end result is that the bulk of the individual contracts are given a more uniform meaning than is given to individual contracts coexisting with collective bargaining contracts.

Collective bargaining contracts and individual contracts both cover similar situations in similar workplaces. The two probably can never be treated the same for all purposes, but a greater effort at uniform interpretation might be in the interests of both employers and employees, as well as the national interest. Competitiveness and efficiency are not solely the concern of employers, despite what current judicial policy suggests.

Courts use an overkill doctrine on handbooks. They usually treat the handbook as a totality, where job security, economic benefits, and all other terms are equal. Obviously that cannot be accurate. However, effective the disclaimers may be, they do not disclaim the employees rights to economic benefits or disclaim the employees obligations to the employer.

NOTES

1. Hishon v. King & Spalding, 467 U.S. 69, 74 (1984).
2. Magnan v. Anaconda Industries, Inc., 101 Lab. Cas. (CCH) 55,485 at 76,182 (Conn. Sup. Ct. 1984).

3. Perry v. Sinderman, 408 U.S. 593, 601–02 (1972); Alpern v. Hurwitz, 115 L.R.R.M. (BNA) 5102 (2d Cir. 1981); Toussaint v. Blue Cross & Blue Shield, 115 L.R.R.M. (BNA) 4708 (Mich. Sup. Ct. 1980); Pine River State Bank v. Mettille, 115 L.R.R.M. (BNA) 4493 (Minn. Sup. Ct. 1983).

4. Foley v. Interactive Data Corp., 3 Indiv. Empl. Rights (BNA) 1729 (Cal. Sup. Ct. 1988).

5. Lowenstein v. Harvard College, 115 L.R.R.M. (BNA) 4753 (D. Mass. 1970).

6. Ruch v. Strawbridge & Clothier, Inc., 101 Lab. Cas. (CCH) 55,465 at 76,073 (D. Pa. 1983).

7. Martin v. Federal Life Insurance Co., 115 L.R.R.M. (BNA) 4524, 4527 (Ill. App. Ct. 1982).

8. Boleman v. Congdon and Carpenter Co., 115 L.R.R.M. (BNA) 4892 (1st Cir. 1981).

9. Pine River State Bank v. Mettille, 115 L.R.R.M. (BNA) 4493, 4496 (Minn. Sup. Ct. 1983).

10. McKinney v. National Dairy Council, 115 L.R.R.M. (BNA) 4861, 4862 (D. Mass. 1980).

11. Hardie v. Cotter & Co., 109 Lab. Cas. (CCH) 55,933 at 77,954 (8th Cir. 1988).

12. Chaiton v. Frito-Lay, Inc., 2 Indiv. Empl. Rights (BNA) 1679, 1681 (D. Pa. 1987).

13. Stewart v. Chevron Chemical Co., 3 Indiv. Empl. Rights (BNA) 1552, 1553 (Wash. Sup. Ct. 1988).

14. Moore v. Illinois Bell Tel. Co., 2 Indiv. Empl. Rights (BNA) 1568 (Ill. App. Ct. 1987); Engstrom v. Nuveen & Co., 2 Indiv. Empl. Rights (BNA) 1205 (D. Pa. 1987).

15. Clay v. Advanced Computer Applications, 2 Indiv. Empl. Rights (BNA) 1657, 1663 (Pa. Super. Ct. 1988).

16. Engstrom v. Nuveen Co., 2 Indiv. Empl. Rights (BNA) 1205 (D. Pa. 1987).

17. Shah v. General Electric Co., 3 Indiv. Empl. Rights (BNA) 312 (D. Ky. 1988).

18. Jackson v. ABCD, 3 Indiv. Empl. Rights (BNA) 1102 (Mass. Sup. Ct. 1988).

19. Duerksen v. Transamerica Title Ins. Co., 234 Cal. Rptr. 521 (Cal. Ct. App. 1987).

20. Putlik v. Professional Resources, 887 F.2d 1371 (10th Cir. 1989); Johnston v. Del Mar Distrib., 776 S.W.2d 768 (Tex. Ct. App. 1989).

21. Littell v. Evening Star Newspaper Co., 115 L.R.R.M. (BNA) 4511 (D.C. Cir. 1941).

22. Id.

23. Id. at 4512–13.

24. Page v. Carolina Coach Co., 115 L.R.R.M. (BNA) 4128 (4th Cir. 1982).

25. Littell v. Evening Star Newspaper Co., 115 L.R.R.M. (BNA) 4511, 4512 (D.C. Cir. 1941). Settlement of a claim as consideration for a just cause requirement, Speckman v. City of Indianapolis, 4 Indiv. Empl. Rights (BNA) 936 (Ind. Sup. Ct. 1989).

26. Pine River State Bank v. Mettille, 115 L.R.R.M. (BNA) 4493, 4498 (Minn. Sup. Ct. 1983).

27. Martin v. Federal Life Ins. Co., 115 L.R.R.M. (BNA) 4524, 4527 (Ill. App. Ct. 1982).

28. Hauser v. Watson, 115 L.R.R.M. (BNA) 4509, 4511 (D.C. Muni. Ct. App. 1948). See also, Leong, 3 Indiv. Empl. Rights (BNA) 983 (D. Haw. 1988).

29. Williams v. Maremont Corp., 109 Lab. Cas. (CCH) 55,919 at 77,907 (Tenn. Ct. App. 1988).

30. Stone v. Mission Bay Mortgage Co., 116 L.R.R.M. (BNA) 2917, 2919 (Nev. Sup. Ct. 1983) (per curiam).

31. Thompson v. St. Regis Paper Co., 116 L.R.R.M. (BNA) 3142, 3145 (Wash. Sup. Ct. 1984).

32. Wiley v. Mo. Pacific R.R. Co., 115 L.R.R.M. (BNA) 5170, 5173 (La. Ct. App. 1982).

33. Terrebonne v. La. Assoc. of Educators, 115 L.R.R.M. (BNA) 5191, 5195 (La. Ct. App. 1983).

34. Johnson v. Panhandle Co-op Assoc., 2 Indiv. Empl. Rights (BNA) 1080 (Neb. Sup. Ct. 1987).

35. Hardie v. Cotter and Co., 3 Indiv. Empl. Rights (BNA) 556 (8th Cir. 1988); Hoffman-LaRoche v. Campbell, 2 Indiv. Empl. Rights (BNA) 739 (Ala. Sup. Ct. 1987).

36. Schwartz v. Michigan Sugar Co., 115 L.R.R.M. (BNA) 4535 (Mich. Ct. App. 1981).

37. Pugh v. See's Candies, Inc., 115 L.R.R.M. (BNA) 4002, 4009 (Cal. Ct. App. 1981).

38. Ch. 3, fn. 7.

39. NLRB v. Burns Int'l Security Services, 406 U.S. 272, 304 (1972) (Rehnquist, J., concurring and dissenting).

40. Bartinikas v. Clarklift of Chicago North, 115 L.R.R.M. (BNA) 4912, fn. 2 at 4913 (D. Ill. 1981).

41. Langdon v. Saga Corp., 115 L.R.R.M. (BNA) 4975, 4976 (Okla. Ct. App. 1976).

42. Greene v. Oliver Realty, Inc., 2 Indiv. Empl. Rights (BNA) 1333 (Pa. Super. Ct. 1987).

43. Ch. 5, fn. 146.

44. Harrison v. Fred S. James, P.A., Inc., 115 L.R.R.M. (BNA) 4052, 4054 (D. Pa. 1983).

45. Crain v. Burroughs Corp., 115 L.R.R.M. (BNA) 5008 (D. Cal. 1983).

46. Hansrote v. Amer. Indus. Technologies, 116 L.R.R.M. (BNA) 3286, 3287 (D. Pa. 1984); Harden v. Warner Amex Cable Communic. Inc., 642 F. Supp. 1080 (D. N.Y. 1986).

47. Bussard v. College of St. Thomas, 115 L.R.R.M. (BNA) 4586, 4590 (Minn. Sup. Ct. 1972).

48. Walker v. Goodson Farms, Inc., 369 S.E.2d 122 (N.C. Ct. App. 1988).

49. Perry v. Sindermann, 408 U.S. 593, 601–02 (1972).

50. Aluminum & Chemical, 2 Indiv. Empl. Rights (BNA) 180 (Cal. Ct. App. 1986). Harrison v. Fred S. James, P.A., Inc., 115 L.R.R.M. (BNA) 4052, 4054 (D. Pa. 1983).

51. Malstrom v. Kaiser Aluminum & Chemical, 2 Indiv. Empl. Rights (BNA) 180 (Cal. Ct. App. 1986).

52. McLain v. Great American Ins., 4 Indiv. Empl. Rights (BNA) 501 (Cal. App. Ct. 1989).

53. Toussaint v. Blue Cross & Blue Shield, 115 L.R.R.M. (BNA) 4708, fn. 24 at 4715 (Mich. Sup. Ct. 1980).

54. Toussaint v. Blue Cross & Blue Shield, 115 L.R.R.M. (BNA) 4708, fn. 24 at 4715 (Mich. Sup. Ct. 1980); DeMinico v. Monarch Wine Co., 2 Indiv. Empl. Rights (BNA) 171 (D. Cal. 1986).

55. Compare, Brudnicki v. General Electric Co., 115 L.R.R.M. (BNA) 4919, 4920 (D. Ill. 1982) and Martin v. Federal Life Ins. Co., 115 L.R.R.M. (BNA) 4524 (Ill. App. Ct. 1982).

56. Savodnik v. Korvettes, Inc., 115 L.R.R.M. (BNA) 4601 (D. N.Y. 1980).

57. Hodge v. Evans Financial Corp., 2 Indiv. Empl. Rights (BNA) 395, 399 (D.C. Cir. 1987).

58. DeMinico v. Monarch Wine Co., 2 Indiv. Empl. Rights (BNA) 171 (D. Cal. 1986).

59. Gonzales v. United Southwest Nat'l Bank, 115 L.R.R.M. (BNA) 4853 (N.M. Sup. Ct. 1979).

60. Stone v. Mission Bay Mortgage Co., 116 L.R.R.M. (BNA) 2917, 2919 (Nev. Sup. Ct. 1983) (per curiam).

61. Rabago - Alvarez v. Dart Indus., 115 L.R.R.M. (BNA) 4704 (Cal. Ct. App. 1976).

62. Wickes v. Olympic Airways, 117 L.R.R.M. (BNA) 2667, 2671–72 (6th Cir. 1984).

63. Radio TV Reports, Inc. v. Ingersoll, 4 Indiv. Empl. Rights (BNA) 1218 (D. D.C. 1989).

64. Reilly V. Stroehmann v. Brothers Co., 2 Indiv. Empl. Rights (BNA) 1244 (Pa. Super. Ct. 1987).

65. Fn. 34–39, supra.

66. Leong v. Hilton Hotels, 3 Indiv. Empl. Rights (BNA) 983 (D. Haw. 1988).

67. Mursch v. Van Dorn Co., 3 Indiv. Empl. Rights (BNA) 893 (7th Cir. 1988).

68. Stewart v. Chevron Chemical Co., 3 Indiv. Empl. Rights (BNA) 1552 (Wash. Sup. Ct. 1988).

69. Scott v. Extracorporeal Inc., 3 Indiv. Empl. Rights (BNA) 999, 1002 (Pa. Super. Ct. 1988).

70. Morgan v. Harris Trust & Savings Bank, 2 Indiv. Empl. Rights (BNA) 577 (D. Ill. 1987).

71. Duder v. Donaldson, Lufkin & Jenrelle Futures, Inc., 3 Indiv. Empl. Rights (BNA) 97 (D. Minn. 1986).

72. Hinson v. Cameron, 4 Indiv. Empl. Rights (BNA) 266 (Okla. Sup. Ct. 1987); Fink v. Revco Discount Drug Centers, 3 Indiv. Empl. Rights (BNA) 115 (D. Mo. 1987); Johnston v. Panhandle Co-op Ass'n, 2 Indiv. Empl. Rights (BNA) 1080 (Neb. Sup. Ct. 1987); Gladden v. Ark. Children's Hospital, 2 Indiv. Empl. Rights (BNA) 560 (Ark. Sup. Ct. 1987); Drake v. Scott, 2 Indiv. Empl. Rights (BNA) 559 (8th Cir. 1987).

73. Skirpan v. United Airlines, 4 Indiv. Empl. Rights (BNA) 924 (D. Ill. 1988).

74. Leikvold v. Valley View Hospital, 116 L.R.R.M. (BNA) 2193, 2195 (Ariz. Sup. Ct. 1984).

75. Jiminez v. Colo. Interstate Gas Co., 3 Indiv. Empl. Rights (BNA) 1646 (D. Wyo. 1988); Nettles v. Techplan Corp., 3 Indiv. Empl. Rights (BNA) 1261 (D. S.C. 1988).

76. Nettles v. Techplan Corp., 3 Indiv. Empl. Rights (BNA) 1261 (D. S.C. 1988).

77. E.g., Chambers v. Valley Nat'l Bank, 3 Indiv. Empl. Rights (BNA) 1476 (D. Ariz. 1988).

78. Johnson v. McDonnell Douglas Corp., 2 Indiv. Empl. Rights (BNA) 1799 (Mo. Sup. Ct. 1988); Lee v. Sperry Corp., 2 Indiv. Empl. Rights (BNA) 1108 (D. Minn. 1987).

79. Moore v. Ill. Bell Tel. Co., 2 Indiv. Empl. Rights (BNA) 1568 (Ill. App. Ct. 1987).

80. Pratt v. Brown Machine Co., 3 Indiv. Empl. Rights (BNA) 1121 (6th Cir. 1988).

81. Nettles v. Techplan Corp., 3 Indiv. Empl. Rights (BNA) 1261 (D. S.C. 1988).

82. Toussaint v. Blue Cross & Blue Shield, 115 L.R.R.M. (BNA) 4708, 4716 (Mich. Sup. Ct. 1980).

83. Thompson v. St. Regis Paper Co., 116 L.R.R.M. (BNA) 3142, 3147 (Wash. Sup. Ct. 1984).

84. Enis v. Continental Ill. Nat. Bank, 116 L.R.R.M. (BNA) 2047, 2050 (D. Ill. 1984).

85. Hayssen Manuf. Co. and UAW Local 1432, 84–1 Lab. Arb. Awards (CCH) 8150 (Flaten, Arb. 1984).

86. City of Evansdale, Iowa, 81 Lab. Arb. (BNA) 1188, 1191 (McClimon, Arb. 1983).

87. Blair v. CBS Inc., 2 Indiv. Empl. Rights (BNA) 478 (D.N.Y. 1987); Bernstein v. Aetna Life & Casualty, 2 Indiv. Empl. Rights (BNA) 292 (D. Ariz. 1986).

88. Reilly v. Stroehmann Bros. Co. 2 Indiv. Empl. Rights (BNA) 1244 (Pa. Super Ct. 1987).

89. Pundt v. Millikin Univ., 2 Indiv. Empl. Rights (BNA) 235 (Ill. App. Ct. 1986).

90. Darlington v. General Electric, 2 Indiv. Empl. Rights (BNA) 1666 (Pa. Super. Ct. 1988).

91. Caster v. Hennessey, 100 Lab. Cas. (CCH) 55,451 (11th Cir. 1984).

92. Richardson v. Charles Cole Memorial Hospital, 99 Lab. Cas. (CCH) 55,428 (Pa. Super. Ct. 1983).

93. Stevenson v. Potlatch, 2 Indiv. Empl. Rights (BNA) 1295 (D. Idaho 1987); Skramstad v. Otter Tail Co., 2 Indiv. Empl. Rights (BNA) 1463 (Minn. Ct. App. 1987); Owens v. American Nat'l Red Cross, 2 Indiv. Empl. Rights (BNA) 1145 (D. Conn. 1987); Marsh v. Digital Equip. Corp., 2 Indiv. Empl. Rights (BNA) 791 (D. Ariz. 1987); Morgan v. Harris Trust & Savings Bank, 2 Indiv. Empl. Rights (BNA) 577 (D. Ill. 1987); Sabetay v. Sterling Drug Inc., 2 Indiv. Empl. Rights (BNA) 150 (N.Y. Ct. App. 1987).

94. Thompson v. Kings Entertainment Co., 2 Indiv. Empl. Rights (BNA) 1592 (D. Va. 1987); Morris v. Coleman Co., 2 Indiv. Empl. Rights (BNA) 844 (Kan. Sup. Ct. 1987).

95. DeRubis v. Broadmoor Hotel Inc., 4 Indiv. Empl. Rights (BNA) 831 (Colo. Ct. App. 1989).

96. Walton v. St. Anne's Hospital, 3 Indiv. Empl. Rights (BNA) 1594 (D. Ill. 1987).

97. Bruno v. Plateau Mining Co., 2 Indiv. Empl. Rights (BNA) 1653 (Utah Ct. App. 1987); but see Ross v. State Farm Ins. Co., 2 Indiv. Empl. Rights (BNA) 1545 (D. Mich. 1988).

98. F. Elkouri and E. Elkouri, *How Arbitration Works* 437 (4th ed. 1985).

99. Small v. Spring Industries, Inc., 2 Indiv. Empl. Rights (BNA) 266, 268 (S.C. Sup. Ct. 1987).

100. Fink v. Revco Discount Drug Centers, 3 Indiv. Empl. Rights (BNA) 115, 117 (D. Mo. 1987).

101. Greco v. Halliburton Co., 2 Indiv. Empl. Rights (BNA) 1281, 1282 (D. Wyo. 1987).

102. St. Yves v. Mid State Bank, 2 Indiv. Empl. Rights (BNA) 1550 (Wash. Ct. App. 1987).

103. Foley v. Interactive Data Corp., 3 Indiv. Empl. Rights (BNA) 1729, 1740 (Cal. Sup. Ct. 1988).

104. Nork v. Fetter Printing Co., 3 Indiv. Empl. Rights (BNA) 667, 670 (Ky. Ct. App. 1987).

105. Fink v. Revco Discount Drug Centers, 3 Indiv. Empl. Rights (BNA) 115 (D. Mo. 1987).

106. Darlington v. General Electric, 2 Indiv. Empl. Rights (BNA) 1666, 1671 (Pa. Super. Ct. 1986).

107. Mont. Code Ann. 39–2–911, in Lab. Rel. Rep. Indiv. Empl. Rights Manual (BNA) 567:6 (1989).

108. Model Unif. Employment Termination Act 4(b) (Draft 1989) (Lab. Rel. Rep. Indiv. Empl. Rights Manual (BNA) 540:54 (1989).

109. Meritor Savings Bank, FSB v. Vinson, 477 U.S. 57 (1986).

110. Greco v. Halliburton Co., 2 Indiv. Empl. Rights (BNA) 1281, 1282 (D. Wyo. 1987); Small v. Springs Indus., Inc., 2 Indiv. Empl. Rights (BNA) 266 (S.C. Sup. Ct. 1987); Pundt v. Millikin Univ., 2 Indiv. Empl. Rights (BNA) 235, 236 (Ill. App. Ct. 1986).

111. Chambers v. Valley Nat'l Bank, 3 Indiv. Empl. Rights (BNA) 1476 (D. Ariz. 1988).

112. Hoffman - LaRoche v. Campbell, 2 Indiv. Empl. Rights (BNA) 739, 745–46 (Ala. Sup. Ct. 1987); Morgan v. Harris Trust & Savings Bank, 2 Indiv. Empl. Rights (BNA) 577 (D. Ill. 1987).

113. Jiminez v. Colorado Interstate Gas Co., 3 Indiv. Empl. Rights (BNA) 1646, 1649 (D. Wyo. 1988); Thompson v. Kings Entertainment Co., 2 Indiv. Empl. Rights (BNA) 1592 (D. Va. 1987).

114. Shaver v. F.W. Woolworth Co., 2 Indiv. Empl. Rights (BNA) 534 (D. Wis. 1986).

115. Texas Employment Comm. v. Hughes, 3 Indiv. Empl. Rights (BNA) 451 (Tex. Ct. App. 1988); Johnston v. Panhandle Co-op Ass'n, 2 Indiv. Empl. Rights (BNA) 1080 (Neb. Sup. Ct. 1987).

116. Thompson v. Kings Entertainment Co., 2 Indiv. Empl. Rights (BNA) 1592 (D. Va. 1987).

117. Nat. Rifle Assoc. v. Ailes, 94 Lab. Cas. (CCH) 55,357 at 75,516 (D.C. Cir. 1981).

118. Bartinikas v. Clarklift of Chicago North, 115 L.R.R.M. (BNA) 4912, 4913 (D. Ill. 1981).

119. Id.

120. Fn. 147, infra.

121. Preston v. Claridge Hotel & Casino, 4 Indiv. Empl. Rights (BNA) 493 (N.J. Super. Ct. 1989).

122. Bullock v. Automobile Club of Michigan, 4 Indiv. Empl. Rights (BNA) 684, 687 (Mich. Sup. Ct. 1989).

123. Langdon v. Saga Corp., 115 L.R.R.M. (BNA) 4975 (Okla. Ct. App. 1977).

124. Id.

125. Gilman v. County of Cheshire, 493 A.2d 485 (N.H. Sup. Ct. 1985).

126. Musicians Union of Las Vegas, Local 369 v. Del E. Webb Corp., 101 Lab. Cas. (CCH) 11,111 at 22,531 (9th Cir. 1984).

127. Perry v. Sindermann, 408 U.S. 593, 602 (1972).

128. Hishon v. King & Spalding, 467 U.S. 69, 75–76 (1984).

129. Furnco Const. Corp. v. Waters, 438 U.S. 567 (1978).

130. Ch. 5, fn. 25–29.

131. Ch. 1, fn. 32–48. See also Patterson v. Portch, 853 F.2d 1399 (7th cir. 1988).

132. Lekich v. IBM, 115 L.R.R.M. (BNA) 4678 (D. Pa. 1979).

133. Civil Rights Act of 1964, 42 U.S.C. 2000(e)(2).

134. Goodman v. Board of Trustees of Comm. College Dist., 29 EPD 32,798 (D. Ill. 1981).

135. Nees v. Hocks, 272 Or. 210 (1975).

136. Ch. 5, fn. 5.

137. Ch. 2, fn. 47–62.

138. Bernhard v. Dutchess Comm. College, 28 Empl. Prac. Dec. (CCH) 32,540 at 24,400 (D. N.Y. 1982).

139. Sablosky v. Edward S. Gordon Inc., 3 Indiv. Empl. Rights (BNA) 1021 (N.Y. Sup. Ct. App. Div. 1988).

140. Miller v. Sevamp, Inc., 2 Indiv. Empl. Rights (BNA) 1202, 1204 (Va. Sup. Ct. 1987).

141. Ch. 6.

142. Haupt v. Int'l Harvester Co., 117 L.R.R.M. (BNA) 2309, 2312 (D. Ill. 1984); Aberman v. Malden Mills, 2 Indiv. Empl. Rights (BNA) 1430 (Minn. Ct. App. 1987); Sterner v. Marathon Oil Co., 4 Indiv. Empl. Rights (BNA) 592 (Tex. Sup. Ct. 1989). The U.S. government can be such a third person. Merritt v. Mackey, 827 F.2d 1368 (9th Cir. 1987); Chernin v. Lyng, 874 F.2d 501 (8th Cir. 1989).

143. Nelson v. M & M Products Co., 115 L.R.R.M. (BNA) 4965, 4966 (Ga. Ct. App. 1983); Aberman v. Malden Mills, 2 Indiv. Empl. Rights (BNA) 1430 (Minn. Ct. App. 1987).

144. Cummings v. Walsh Constr. Co., 115 L.R.R.M. (BNA) 4070, 4077 (D. Ga. 1983); Arco Alaska v. Akers, 3 Indiv. Empl. Rights (BNA) 809 (Alaska Sup. Ct. 1988).

145. Feaheny v. Caldwell, 4 Indiv. Empl. Rights (BNA) 432 (Mich. Ct. App. 1989); Payne v. Kathryn Beich & Nestle, 2 Indiv. Empl. Rights (BNA) 1528 (D. N.Y. 1988); Davenport v. Epperly, 2 Indiv. Empl. Rights (BNA) 1456 (Wyo. Sup.

Ct. 1987); Sorrells v. Garfinkel's, 2 Indiv. Empl. Rights (BNA) 618 (D.C. Super. Ct. 1987); Nietert v. Overby, 2 Indiv. Empl. Rights (BNA) 89 (10th Cir. 1987).

146. Keenan v. Artintype Inc., 546 N.Y.S. 2d 741 (N.Y. Sup. Ct. 1989).

147. Foley v. Interactive Data Corp., 3 Indiv. Empl. Rights (BNA) 1729, 1738 (Cal. Sup. Ct. 1988).

148. Ch. 3, fn. 7.

149. Greene v. Oliver Realty, Inc., 2 Indiv. Empl. Rights (BNA) 1333, 1336 (Pa. Super. Ct. 1987).

150. United Steelworkers v. Warrior & Gulf Navigation Co., 363 U.S. 574 (1960).

151. Trans World Airlines, Inc. v. Thurston, 469 U.S. III (1985); Hishon v. King & Spalding, 467 U.S. 69 (1984).

152. Judie v. Hamilton, 872 F.2d 919, (9th Cir. 1989).

153. Judie v. Hamilton, 872 F.2d 919 (9th Cir. 1989).

154. Mallare v. St. Luke's Hospital of Bethlehem, 699 F. Supp. 1127 (D. Pa. 1988).

155. Lowery v. WARC-TV 658 F. Supp. 1240 (D. Tenn. 1987).

156. Hishon v. King & Spalding, 467 U.S. 69 (1984).

157. Marshall v. Western Grain Co., Inc., 838 F.2d 1165 (11th Cir. 1988).

158. Benchmark Industries and Textile Workers, 1983–84 CCH NLRB 16,237 (1984).

159. Freedom WLNE-TV, Inc., 1986–87 CCH NLRB 18,255; Jacobsen Mfg. Co., 80–1 CCH Arb. 8236 (Williams, Arb. 1980).

5

Individual Contract Clauses

INTRODUCTION

The preceding chapter deals in general terms with the creation, modification, and termination of the individual employment contract. This chapter discusses some of the specific clauses and language that might be found in the individual contract, especially in the at will contract.[1] No attempt is made to catalogue all of the possible clauses. Rather the chapter focuses on some of the more common clauses that have been the subject of recent litigation. They include, among others, job security provisions, noncompetition provisions, waiver clauses, last chance agreements, and employee assistance plans.

In addition, this chapter looks at some of the essentially individual contract clauses that also occur when there is a collective bargaining contract.

OTHER THAN DISCHARGE TERMS IN AT WILL CONTRACT

Some courts seem unwilling to accept that some job security provisions can exist within the at will or indefinite term contract. In other courts, however, job security provisions and a variety of other clauses can be included and enforced even though the discharge or durational clause is at will.[2] One court has explained the at will status in the following terms: "Construing the employee's continued employment with Defendant as at will whereby either party could terminate the relationship, it is still evident that until termination the parties had a contractual relationship."[3] In a public sector case, the

U.S. Supreme Court has noted that job security related provisions, such as specified termination procedures, can coexist with an at will employment. "[T]he ordinance may also be construed as granting no right to continued employment but merely condition an employee's removal on compliance with certain specified procedures."[4] These examples show that many courts are willing to recognize that an at will contract is still a contract that can contain terms beyond the at will or durational clause. A variety of other clauses might be used.

Notice

One type of job security provision that may be included in the at will contract is a notice requirement. The indefinite term contract can include a requirement that the employer give seven or more days notice, for example.[5]

Severance Pay

Another type of clause that has been suggested provides for severance pay when the at will employee is discharged.[6]

Benefits

Contractually due vacation time can be collected at dismissal time.[7] An at will employee may be permitted to use accumulated sick leave without being discharged.[8] The at will term does not override vested benefits.

Grievance Mechanism

A grievance mechanism can coexist with at will status. Under such a mechanism, an employee can argue that there is a procedural restriction on the right of discharge, even though the discharge need not be based on cause. The restriction is the grievance mechanism, which may require that certain procedures be followed before the discharge is valid.[9] For example, the employer may have an "open door" policy that permits investigation before the discharge becomes effective.[10] One court has described such a situation as follows:

> The trial court acknowledged the rule that the employment agreement was terminable at will. . . . Thus it reasoned that plaintiff's continued job status, including demotion, was likewise determinable at the will of the defendant.

Plaintiff agrees that a contract of employment which states no definite term is considered to be . . . at . . . will. . . . However, he contends that defendant is contractually bound to follow the disciplinary provisions of its personnel manual.

We conclude that plaintiff's allegation of breach of contract because he was demoted in violation of the defendant's policy and procedure manual is sufficient to survive defendant's motion to dismiss.[11]

Another court recognized the right to negotiate job security provisions in an at will contract in the following terms:

There is . . . no public policy against providing job security or prohibiting an employer from agreeing not to discharge except for good or just cause. That being the case, we can see no reason why such a provision in a contract having no definite term of employment with a single employee should necessarily be unenforceable and regarded, in effect, as against public policy.[12]

Where job security provisions are included in an at will contract, the agreement does not necessarily lose its discharge at will character. The presence of a specified, contractual procedure for termination does not necessarily turn the at will, no cause contract into a for cause discharge contract.[13] In other words, the presumptive no cause discharge clause can coexist with other job security clauses.

Restoration to Unit

Supervisors do not have a protected right to engage in collective bargaining under the National Labor Relations Act. They are likely to have individual at will contracts. Generally, they cannot be covered by the rank and file collective bargaining agreement. However, many supervisors are promoted out of the rank and file. When a collective bargaining unit employee is promoted, the employee as supervisor will lose the protection of the cause discharge requirements that are usually found in the collective bargaining contract. Such an employee may bargain an individual agreement to protect the employee in case the promotion is not successful. In one such case, the employer sought to discharge the employee as an at will supervisory employee. The employee successfully argued that there was an agreement that the employee would be returned to the bargaining unit if the supervisory job did not work out. The court found that there was such an agreement and found that the employer was bound to restore the employee to the prior position and could not summarily discharge the employee under the at will doctrine.[14] The supervisory position may have been an at will position, but the court said the employee had a valid job security provision covering how that supervisory position must be terminated.

Another case described a clause in an at will contract involving a form of job security and severance pay in the following terms:

> [Employee] . . . contends that although he was an at will employee with no written contract of employment, [employer] . . . had a contractual obligation to grant him redundancy status and provide him with severance pay. Because the company declined to do so, plaintiff declares it has breached the agreement.

> [P]laintiff had a contractual right to have his redundancy application considered in a non-arbitrary manner.[15]

Vested Rights and Compensation

The discharge of an at will employee does not mean that the employee's vested rights are lost. Dismissed at will employees have been permitted to exercise stock option rights under the employment contract.[16] Similarly, an at will employee is entitled to contractually deferred compensation, in the same way that the at will employee has an obvious claim to wages for hours worked.[17] Unlike the usual approach where courts find that the vague terms of duration lead to the finding of an indefinite term contract, courts are willing to find that terms on compensation and fringe benefits are usually sufficiently specific and can be ascertained objectively.[18] The at will employee may be subject to an arbitrary discharge for any reason or no reason, but the at will employee cannot be arbitrarily denied vested rights for any reason or no reason. The arbitrary decision-making process is protected only on the issue of duration of employment.

An at will employee may have paid into a pension plan. Upon discharge, the at will employee is still entitled to the employee's full share of pension benefits paid into the program up to the date of the termination.[19] A strong statement on protecting the vesting of pension plans was given by a New York court:

> To allow an employer to avoid the vesting of rights in a pension plan after thirteen years of service by a model employee, under the guise of the employment at will doctrine does not sit well with

this Court. Such behavior not only suggests the employer never fully intended to comport with the spirit of the Plan, but also that it sought to avoid its obligations thereunder by systematically terminating its employees at will prior to the vesting of their rights under the Plan. Accepting plaintiff's allegations as true . . . defendant here has clearly violated New York's policy favoring the integrity of pension plans to protect the interest of the participants in such plans. If ever there was a case to invoke the doctrine of abusive discharge, this is it.[20]

Many courts permit an employer to unilaterally modify the future terms and conditions of employment for the at will employee.[21] However, the employee may have a right to any accrued benefits up to the time of the unilateral change.[22] Some courts may find a breach of covenant of good faith in a situation where the employer seeks to eliminate vested benefits by a unilateral change of policy: "As currently applied in Massachusetts . . . a breach of good faith implies an overreaching upon the part of the employer by taking advantage of its superior bargaining power and depriving the employee of 'compensation that is clearly identifiable and is related to the employee's past service.'"[23]

A common litigation situation involves an at will salesperson who is paid on commission and discharged shortly after the salesperson has made a large sale. The employer will not be permitted to withhold the commissions that were earned on the sales made prior to the discharge. One court described the following situation:

We think that the evidence and the reasonable inferences to be drawn therefrom support a jury verdict that the termination of Fortune's twenty-five years of employment as a salesman with NCR the next business day after NCR obtained a $5,000,000 order . . . was motivated by a desire to pay Fortune as little of the bonus credited as it could.[24]

In summary, the at will element of an employment contract goes to the discharge clause. It does not infect the entire contract in a way that permits the employer to summarily extinguish other rights in the same way the employer can summarily end the employment right. Job security provisions can be included that might, for example, require the employer to give notice or make severance payments when the at will discharge option is exercised. Inhouse grievance mechanisms may coexist with the employer's right to discharge at will. Vested rights are not lost as the result of an at will discharge. Sales commissions that have come due are still owed after the at will sales person has been discharged. Whereas many courts are unwilling to scrutinize the contract beyond the presumption of at will status, the courts are willing to recognize that there can be more to the employment relationship than the right to discharge.

NONCOMPETITION CLAUSES

Some employers may require a newly hired employee to sign a noncompetition agreement that will apply in the event that the employee leaves. These agreements seek, for example, to limit the ex-employee's contacts with the employer's customers or limit the ex-employee's use of patents or inventions developed while working for the employer. The scope of the clauses range from the protection of common law employer rights to clauses that nearly make the former employee unemployable.

Balancing Interests

When reviewing the enforceability of such clauses, courts express no difficulty in balancing the employer's interest in protecting the employer's right to the exclusive use of certain information and balancing the public's and former employee's interests in free competition. Courts carefully scrutinize such agreements and balance employee and employer interests, unlike their approach to most individual contract employment issues. In other words, the traditional rules of individual employment contract interpretation of the discharge clause involving presumptive employer rights do not apply to this clause in the contract of employment.[25] The noncompetition clause may be strictly construed against the drafter of the clause, the employer, as part of the balance.[26] Several items are put into the balance in these cases. They include a limitation on the scope of the clause to legitimate employer interests, the clause must be limited in time and scope as to the employee, the clause must not injure the public, and some may require that the employer provide special consideration in exchange for the limitation.[27]

When a restrictive clause is found to be excessive after the interests are balanced, the court may do one of several things. It may refuse to enforce any aspect of the clause, or it may delete the onerous terms leaving the remainder of the clause, or it may otherwise alter the agreement so long as it was a good faith agreement.[28]

One unique contract clause provided that the terminated employee would receive one-half of his former salary for the period of noncompetition. The court indicated that this was an important element to balance in favor of the employer in looking at the various interests.[29] Whereas many courts may tolerate the harshness of the presumption of at will, they may also give the employer credit for generosity when looking at other clauses.

PLACEMENT EFFORTS

Some employers promise to assist their discharged employees in their attempts to find a new job. This is more likely when it is a discharged long-term employee. Such promises may speak in terms of assisting in finding jobs of similar content or similar grade, or finding a "suitable placement."[30] These agreements are not generally read to require that the former employer actually locate a new job, but rather, they are read to require that the employer provide some assistance.[31] There may be a contractual time limit, such as 30 days.[32] Providing an external placement service[33] or a secretary and telephone[34] may be sufficient. Because these promises are often vague, they may create no contractual liability whatsoever.[35]

INDIVIDUAL CLAUSES AND COLLECTIVE BARGAINING

In general, the workplace can be divided into two overall contract categories. One is that of collective bargaining contracts and the other is that of individual contracts. However, the two categories are not mutually exclusive. In professional sports, there may be a combination of individual contracts and a collective contract.[36] Some contract issues, such as individual waivers, releases, and consents, cut across both categories. These essentially individual clauses can be found in the collective bargaining environment as readily as the individual contract environment.

The U.S. Supreme Court has stated that individual contracts cannot be used to subvert the collective contract, but individual contracts can coexist with collective bargaining contracts.[37] Courts permit an individual contract to give additional rights to employees that are not found under a concurrent collective bargaining agreement.[38] A fairly common situation involves employees who are promoted from a collective bargaining position to a supervisory, noncollective bargaining position. This often means moving from a discharge for cause position to an at will position. Employees may seek individual agreements protecting them from discharge if the supervisory position does not work out.[39] The U.S. Supreme Court said: "Thus, individual employment contracts are not inevitably superseded by any subsequent collective agreement covering an individual employee, and claims based on them may arise under state law.... [A] plaintiff covered by a collective-bargaining agreement is permitted to assert legal rights independent of that agreement.... "[40] A voluntary individual termination plan with possible eligibility for rehiring can coexist with a collective bargaining contract.[41] Many of the clauses discussed in the following sections can be found in both individual and collective contract environments. Figure 5.1 summarizes some areas of arguable overlap and distinction between individual and collective contracts.

TESTING, RELEASES, AND OTHER DOCUMENTS

In both the union and nonunion workplace there are a number of situations in which the employer will impose special contract clauses on employees, often in a take it or leave it manner. The employee can accept the special working conditions and continue to be employed, or the employee can reject the conditions and quit or be fired. Some examples include medical testing, releasing medical records, releases, and settlements tailored to the individual employee. The employee may or may not have any bargaining power in these situations. Where a union is involved, the union may also be a party to the agreement.

Figure 5.1 Individual-Collective Contracts

INDIVIDUAL	POSSIBLE OVERLAP	COLLECTIVE
At Will Presumption	Bilateral	Arbitration
Claim Lifetime	Cause	Bilateral
Claim Permanent	Discriminaiton Legis.	Fixed Term
Common Law Rules	Employee Duties	Individual Clauses
Cover Any Employee	Employer Rights	Limited Coverage
Montana Type Legis.	Fixed Term	Mandatory Topics
Noncompetition Clauses	Greivance Mechanism	NLRA .
Oral	Judicial Restraint	Permissive Topics
Unilateral	Nonretaliation Legis.	Special Status
	Probationary Status	Progressive
	Settlement Clauses	Discipline
	Testing Clauses	
	Waiver Clauses	
	Whistleblower Legis.	
	Working Conditions	

For these purposes, these agreements are considered to be individual contract clauses whether or not a union is also involved.

If there is a collective contract that covers the requested individual contract clause, its terms must be followed. If there is a collective contract that does not cover the topic and it is a mandatory topic of bargaining that has not been waived, the employer may be under a duty to bargain the topic before proceeding.[42]

Constitutional or statutory rights as well as contract rights may also be involved. For example, in the drug testing situation, constitutional, statutory, and contractual issues all may be raised. The courts have created a broad area of permissible testing of employees.[43] Statutes may prohibit or limit certain types of testing, especially those involving the polygraph.[44] The rights of the employer to test are still developing and it is always necessary to consult the latest decisions in the relevant jurisdiction. It is not the purpose here to explore the circumstances under which conducting the test may be constitutionally legal or illegal. The purpose here is to look at some of the employer demands on testing and releases that may have contract overtones.

A number of common situations have been identified that are the subjects of individual contract coverage. The following give some examples of the variety of the agreements: consent to polygraph examination[45]; consent to use the results of drug tests in a criminal prosecution[46]; consent to employer's use without charge of employee's patented device[47]; consent to make disclosures of accusations against employee to prospective employers[48]; consent to drug test[49]; waive right to Title VII discrimination complaint[50]; disclosure of personal information under privacy legislation[51]; consent to court enforcement of agreement and consent to jurisdiction of specified court[52]; consent to general settlement[53]; consent to union dues check-off[54]; contract not to compete[55]; acknowledgment of receipt of employee handbook[56]; and signing untrue statement about overtime pay[57] or other statements of "fact."

Other situations involve consenting to testing as a pre-employment condition. Another common situation involves agreeing or refusing to agree to provide access to medical records. The employer may request release of existing medical records, the employee may be required to be examined by a physician selected by the employer.

A variety of issues may be raised by the request to sign a document. The document that the employer wants signed may be false. It may be a waiver of a statutory right. Common statutes for which employers may seek releases are worker compensation and civil rights legislation. The waiver or release can involve several degrees. The release might purport to involve a total and absolute waiver of all past and future rights to bring an action against the employer. A more limited waiver might involve a period of contractual limitations after which the employee agrees not to sue the employer. The employee may sign a severance agreement that the employer later claims to be a total release that goes beyond termination. Finally, the employee and employer may have signed a dispute settlement agreement that the employee later challenges.

In summary, there are a variety of situations where the employer requests the employee to agree to something or to sign something. These situations arise in both collective and individual employment contract situations. In either situation, the essence of the contract relationship is that of an individual contract. The following sections discuss some of these situations in greater detail.

The case law on testing, releases, and other documents is treated here as contractual aspects of the individual's working conditions. The cases used come from a variety of jurisdictions. When the cases are mixed together, the results often have elements of contradiction and confusion. In part, the lack of clarity in these areas is evidence of the lack of certainty and agreement that inevitably arises while the subject matter is still evolving. The effort here is not directed toward distilling the best possible set of rules that should be used but to illustrate some of the contractual elements of the disputes.

Often the courts or arbitrators do not talk the language of contracts, although it seems clear that contractual releases, waivers, settlement clauses, or other consents are involved. Frequently the context is "take it or leave it," without reference to the element of negotiation that is almost inherent in the contractual relationship. It is useful to look at the terms of the individual contract of employment, however mixed the various results in individual cases might be. Part of the utility lies in demonstrating how courts treat different clauses in the individual contract in highly disparate ways. In addition, this is one of several areas where there is great overlap between the individual contract and the collective contract.

Testing

One line of cases involves testing for drug and alcohol use, or other medical conditions. Testing may be a condition of employment and discharge can be the penalty for refusal.[58] General testing procedures may be permitted, but conducting the tests in an outrageous manner may nonetheless lead to employer liability.[59] In addition to "consenting" to the testing, the employee may be required to sign a release.

Many complications arise. In one situation, a grievant taking a prescription cough syrup with a high alcohol content refused to be tested for alcohol use. The employee was discharged and grieved under the collective contract. The arbitrator suggested the better approach for the employee was the traditional arbitration rule of "work (test) now, grieve later," but mitigated the discharge to a two week suspension.[60] The question of the appropriateness of this traditional work now approach to a situation involving fundamental liberties as opposed to the usual contract rights situation was not discussed. The work (test) now rule used by the arbitrator is tantamount to an immediate waiver of whatever privacy right may be involved, but waiver was not discussed in the opinion. Once privacy is waived, it cannot be reclaimed, unlike many traditional grievances such as pay which can be made up. New applicants may have to qualify for a job by agreeing to undergo a physical examination, including various drug and alcohol tests. This seems to be commonly accepted.[61] Again, the employee has had to contractually waive significant interests.

Medical Records

An employer conditioned an employee's return after a leave on either signing a medical records release or submitting to testing by another doctor. The employee refused the options and the arbitrator upheld the employer's discharge.[62] The requirement of providing medical statements was justified on several broad grounds of employer needs, including the need to justify absences, to provide the employer with an understanding of the employee's condition, and to provide a warning of future absences.[63] Counterbalancing employee interests were not mentioned.

Signing Documents

Failure to sign a consent form to take a polygraph test may lead to discharge even if the employee is willing to be tested.[64] The alternative of losing the job is often seen as insufficient duress to invalidate the consent.[65] However, some judicial response is more responsive to employee interests where employees fail to sign such waivers.[66] Similarly, there is mixed judicial response to requests to sign waivers by current employees, compared to applicants, involving searches of personal property and consents to drug testing.[67]

An employee who refused to sign a statement indicating that a carpal tunnel syndrome problem was not work related may, however, present a retaliation claim under a worker compensation statute.[68] The invocation of the compensation statute raised a strong public policy issue. Other courts may view the discharge threat as within the employer's rights. Where the employee is terminable at will, one court found that the only "coercion" was the threat to exercise its legal right to discharge at will.[69] The court almost seemed to be relying on a traditional at will rule that an at will contract can have no job security or public policy clause other than a discharge clause. The refusal to sign or approve false or possibly illegal documents has also lead to a valid discharge. An attorney was discharged for failure to approve possibly illegal documents.[70] An employee was discharged for refusing to sign a false statement concerning the discharge of another employee.[71] However, an employee had grounds to challenge a discharge resulting from her refusal to testify falsely.[72]

Courts seem to show reluctance where employees are asked to forfeit broad general rights in the workplace. Where there is a specific antiretaliation provision in a statute, courts proceed more cautiously. These decisions reflect traditional judicial restraint and protection of employer rights until a legislative body has spoken.

Releases and Settlements

Releases are commonly considered to be an intentional relinquishment of a known right. That may or may not be the situation in the workplace. In a situation where discharged employees accepted a termination payment, the employer claimed that they had also waived their right to contest the discharges at a subsequent time. One court disagreed by looking at traditional contract dogma. It said that there was no reasonable mutual expectation that acceptance of the payment would also be a total waiver of all possible claims.[73] Settlements and waivers are contract clauses, just as the at will or fixed term elements of the employment contract. However, courts do not usually give the same scrutiny to employee waivers that they give to employee claims of a for cause discharge right.

When these documents are viewed as contracts, they should be required to meet the usual requirements of a contract. They should be specific, may require additional consideration, are more likely to be valid if it can be shown that they are the product of negotiations, may need to be written, and must meet the requirements of mutuality and mutual expectations. These are the same elements discussed in the creation of the individual employment contract. These documents differ from the traditional job security clause in the employment contract when the settlement or waiver is seen as having a public policy overtone arising from a specific statutory protection extended to the employee. The usual public policy issues that courts recognize as arising in the traditional individual employment contract are those of employer rights.

In addition to the public policy protection of the statutory rights of the employee, there is usually a statutory public policy generally favoring private settlement over public litigation.[74] The circumstances surrounding the settlement or waiver agreement must be balanced with the general policy favoring private settlement. A settlement signed in the light of pending charges against an employer may be more likely to be valid than a broadly phrased waiver of undefined future charges.[75] As in the consideration of definite or indefinite term contracts, courts give little attention to general claims but may give closer scrutiny to specific claims. Specific claims are more likely to be found in statutes. Significant changes in the contractual employee-employer relationship are thus more likely to come from legislatures than courts.

The employer drafted settlement or waiver cannot contain terms that would conflict with other basic public policies. Where the employee signed an individual settlement of certain claims in the context of collective bargaining, a court ruled that the individual waiver did not waive the union's right to seek arbitration of the claims under the contract.[76] A settlement under the age discrimination legislation should not contain terms that punish signatories if they "counsel or assist" prosecution of age discrimination claims. That clause would conflict with the no reprisal provisions of the statute.[77]

In another situation, an employee signed a general waiver several months after beginning work. Citing the contract rule that no consideration was given by the employer for waiver, the court refused to enforce it.[78] Other courts seem to find few problems where employees are required to sign waivers, some of which relinquish their right to sue the employer after, for example, six months, even though legislation may provide a longer period of limitations.[79] Where traditional contract principles are applied, a broadly drawn release may be found to be too vague and too broad and be deemed to be unreasonable.[80]

Voluntarily taking a drug test may be deemed to be consenting to it.[81] Refusal to sign a polygraph examiner's consent forms may be cause for discharge.[82] A signed release may protect the employer from liability for a polygraph test.[83] Employees may be left with few choices where refusal to take the test or refusal to sign a consent to the test may lead to discharge, and where signing the consent effectively terminates the employer's liability resulting from testing. The employer must, however, conduct the testing in good faith.[84] If many of these employer created statements were tested by traditional strict contract analysis, the results might be less favorable to employers.

Waivers of rights granted by civil rights legislation have attracted considerable recent judicial attention. At one extreme, a blanket waiver involving no contractual consideration signed by an uninformed employee under coercion is of doubtful validity. At the other extreme, a negotiated settlement involving the relinquishment of known claims is likely to be favored.[85] The knowledge of the person making the waiver is an important factor. When the corporate labor lawyer signs a release, it may be valid.[86] Some courts may make the blanket statement that waiver of the right to file under a civil rights statute is against public policy, but other courts have indicated that an employee may waive the right to personal recovery but not waive the right to file a charge to inform the agency of the situation.[87] Invalidity may result from overreaching or exploitation.[88] However, threats involving discharge for failure to agree may not be sufficient overreaching.[89]

In an unusual employee handbook case, employees were required to sign and acknowledge adherence to the employer's handbook rules, which included an employer policy of opposition to unions. The National Labor Relations Board found a violation of the employee's Section 7 rights under the National Labor Relations Act.[90] The requirement that the employees abide by the handbook policies was found to be an unlawful waiver of the employee's Section 7 rights. The case is interesting because it clearly recognized that the handbook was an attempted waiver. It also refused to accept a broadly worded clause in the face of a statute conferring specific rights.

Balancing

A variety of factors may be looked at by the courts to determine whether the individual contract terms of the release or settlement are valid. They may look at the role of the employee in negotiating any terms, the specificity of the terms, and whether new consideration was received for the waiver.[91] Courts have identified a number of other elements to determine if the employee has voluntarily and knowingly released potential claims against the employer. The following are among the elements that courts have identified: clarity and lack of ambiguity of agreement, employee's education and business experience, and whether legal counsel was used[92]; training in the army[93]; amount of time for deliberation, whether employee knew or should have known employee rights, whether there was opportunity for negotiation, and whether consideration was given by employer[94]; education of employee's spouse[95]; whether employee's job involved careful attention to detail in complex matters[96]; whether agreement was presented without explanation and without warning[97]; and the presence or absence of fraud or duress.[98]

A review of the elements of voluntariness is useful for several reasons. Such a list identifies elements that each party should consider when signing or proposing a waiver or release. It illustrates the disparate ways in which courts approach different clauses in the individual contract of employment. On the durational term, some courts are unwilling to look at evidence beyond the presumption of at will status. On a claimed release, some courts are willing to look at an extensive list of elements and balance the evidence on each side of the dispute.

The Supreme Court has recently invoked the doctrine of implied waiver of a fundamental employee right, without attempting to balance the interests. The Court found a general implied consent to "significant restrictions" in the employee's freedom of movement while on the job and then extended the implied consent to taking compelled drug tests in certain situations.[99] The employee's general duty to perform the job adequately may easily be seen as an agreement to remain in place to perform the work for which the employee is being paid. However, it is a different matter to extend the duty to perform work to cover an implied consent to testing, which involves a fundamental individual interest. The Court's implied consent approach seems to be akin to the implied consent of accepting the terms of a new contract or handbook merely by remaining on the job. There is no suggestion that the employee could do anything to revoke the implied consent, which suggests that it may really be an irrebuttable presumption of consent, much like the at will doctrine. This again illustrates the diverse judicial approaches to various elements of the contract. Some will be scrutinized and some will not, without any judicial guidance on the distinctions. The employee's short answer to the implied consent to a drug test would be to quit after the incident triggering the test, but before the test. If consent is implied from the continuation of employment, then ending the employment would seemingly end the implied consent. However, the nonutility of this response is obvious.

Hopefully, the Court's implied consent statements will not be generalized to the point of saying that so long as the employment relationship continues and the employer proposes new terms or conditions to the employment contract, the employee's continuing to work will imply consent.

A review of the cases involving individual contracts of employment conditions involving releases, testing, and other consents makes a useful comparison to cases involving at will termination. In the termination cases, the court's often give little weight to the employee's offers of contradicting evidence and give maximum protection to the employer's rights under the at will doctrine. In cases involving clauses other than the discharge issue, courts are often faced with statutory issues of public policy that must be considered. Some courts continue to treat these cases as though the arbitrary powers available to the employer under at will discharge doctrine extended to these other aspects of the contractual relationship. Other courts will attempt to balance the various statutory (public), employee, union, and employer interests. The conflicting approaches illustrate a basic problem in employment law. The problem is what is the character of the employment contract. The courts, at various times, are saying that it is a contract governed by a strong at will presumption of strong employer rights. At other times, it seems to be a contract governed by the general rules of private contracts, such as intention of the parties, mutuality, and consideration. At yet other times, it seems to be a contract with public policy overtones involving the interests of the employer, the employee, the union, and a broader public policy interest. The collective bargaining contract does not usually face this schizophrenic approach. It is more likely to be interpreted in terms of production, efficiency, and other concerns of the workplace. If the employer's paramount concern is efficiency, product, and profit, then employment decisions should reflect factual analysis of those concerns.

Going back to specific topics, the law is still developing on the topics of releases and waivers. The public's interest in some statutes is found by some courts to be too strong to permit waivers, but other courts disagree. Courts will accept good faith settlements of actual disputes. Courts are more willing to balance employer, employee, and the public interest here than they are when dealing with at will or cause discharge clauses in contracts. They are most willing to make a balance when the employee claims specific statutory rights as compared to broad claims of general rights. Waivers may be found in many situations, including statements in employee handbooks, consents to testing, continuing to work, and in specific documents so denoted. Some courts adhere rigidly to the at will doctrine as the overriding public policy and employment term. They permit waivers to be based on threats to discharge an at will employee. Various other tests may also be used, including ordinary contract principles and totality of the circumstances.[100]

EMPLOYEE ASSISTANCE PROGRAM AGREEMENTS

Employee Assistance Programs (EAPs) are increasingly being used by employers in the effort to rehabilitate employees who abuse drugs or alcohol. These agreements are used in both union and nonunion environments. Case law and arbitration law are in the early stages of development and there will doubtlessly be many interesting changes before major trends are clear.

Terms of the Agreement

The general tenor of the employee assistance programs is that the identified employee is required to undertake the therapy or rehabilitation program or face discharge. Other than exercising the at will right to quit or be fired, the identified employee has few choices. Courts and arbitrators treat the terms of an EAP in the main as a contractual matter, but it is a contract that primarily burdens the employee.

One arbitrator found that the employer has no duty to warn employees to use the program, despite the fact that the employer spelled out the program in elaborate detail.[101] This is consistent with court decisions that do not generally require the giving of warnings, such as the rule that an employer has no duty to warn an employee about substandard work performance.[102] Similarly, the EAP does not give the employee a choice of electing to use the EAP where the employer has already decided on discharge.[103] When the employee seeks to use a therapy program not sponsored by the employer and bypass the employer's program, the employee may be treated as though the employee has refused to participate in the employer's plan.[104] The employee may have sought to bypass an employer's plan because the employee will usually be put on unpaid leave during the treatment period. Similarly, it will usually do the employee little good to go through a nonemployer treatment program after discharge and then try to regain the job. Post-discharge rehabilitation may not be treated as a mitigating factor in a grievance disputing the discharge.[105]

Employees may be required to enter the program as a preventive action. The employer need not necessarily wait to use the program until the employee has evidenced job impairment by having an accident.[106] However, one arbitrator denied the right of an employer to send an employee directly into the treatment program without going through the diagnosis step.[107] Once an employee has entered one of these programs, they may have created a record tagging them as a substance abuser. A one time effort at rehabilitation through the treatment program is probably all that is required, and the employer may discharge rather than having to recycle the employee through the treatment several times.[108] The decision to put an employee into a rehabilitation plan is a very serious one, with unclear future implications. The goal of the EAP is rehabilitation, but courts and some arbitrators seem more inclined to make decisions based on the prerogatives of the employer than on the rehabilitation goals. The terms of the EAP are often not given a strict contract analysis.

Effect On At Will Status

The treatment programs are usually set up so that if the employee successfully completes the program and continues to be drug or alcohol free for a specified period of time (e.g., 18 months), the employee can regain regular employee status. Failure to complete the program can lead to discharge.[109] Courts are mixed on whether the employee who has failed the program must be considered for "accommodation" of a handicap where the substance abuse qualifies as a handicap.[110]

The next issue after successful participation or successful completion of the program is whether the terms of the EAP limit the employer's right to discharge the employee at will or for other reasons. The issue is raised, in part, because the programs usually have various phases with various rewards spelled out in specified time periods. The general rule is developing that even though specified time periods are mentioned, a prior at will status is not changed. In other words, successful ongoing participation or successful completion does not mean that the employee can be discharged only for cause. A promise to re-employ after completion of treatment may not be binding.[111] Designating the term of the program as 18 months does not necessarily constitute a contract of employment for 18 months.[112] Many of the programs are explained in vague or general language that is not found to be specific enough to constitute a contract.[113] Participation in the program does not preclude disciplinary actions for events that occurred prior to or after the program.[114] The employer's administration of the program, however, may be required to evidence good faith.[115] Again, these cases are often not given a strict contract analysis.

OTHER INDIVIDUAL CLAUSES

There are other types of individual contracts also found in the collective bargaining context. Where there is a conflict between the individual agreements and the collective agreement, the individual agreements must give way.[116] However, employee may have nonconflicting individual agreements that will be valid under the collective agreement.

Locker Assignments

The assignment of lockers to collective bargaining employees may include signing an individual agreement consenting to inspections and waiving 4th Amendment rights.[117]

Permanent Strike Replacements

Permanent strike replacements who are subsequently discharged may have an individual employment contract right enforceable in state courts.[118]

Signing False Agreements

An arbitrator permitted a grievance to go forward where the employer required the individual employees to sign a statement acknowledging the receipt of safety training. The employees signed and then grieved, following the basic arbitration rule of "work now, grieve later." The employees were grieving because they did not feel that they had in fact received adequate training, despite the signed acknowledgment.[119] It has been suggested that a discharge for refusal to sign a false statement may be improper where the employer knew of the untruthfulness or was unconcerned with its truthfulness.[120]

Buy Backs

In another situation, an employer was permitted to engage in individual buy backs of union negotiated seniority and other rights.[121]

Settlements in Arbitration

Another type of agreement is more difficult to classify as being either fully individual or fully collective bargaining. These agreements are the settlements of grievances awarded by arbitrators under a collective bargaining contract. The employee's personal consent to the award may not be needed in the strict sense, but where the employee does consent, it is significant.[122] At a minimum, the award constitutes a special contractlike action that sets the terms and conditions for an individual employee.[123] Once the settlement has been reached, the union will withdraw the grievance.[124]

Last Chance Agreements

A common type of arbitration award may reinstate an employee at the final warning level, which means that, for example, the employee's next absence will be the last and will not be treated like that of any other employee (i.e., cannot be grieved).[125] These "last chance" agreements are increasingly being used in the case of employees with personal problems or drug or alcohol abuse problems, and are related to EAPs. They are also commonly used in many other areas, such as for employees with high tardiness or absentee records. If the employee meets the conditions of the last chance agreement they continue to be employed, if not, they are discharged.[126] Such agreements will be strictly construed and arbitral mitigation will not generally be used in construing the last chance agreement.[127] The last chance agreements usually include a waiver of the right to appeal a discharge based on a violation of the agreement. One court found a waiver to be overly broad when it attempted to cover all forums. Under the rehabilitation legislation, a waiver might violate the public policy of the legislation, especially given the state of mind of the alcoholic employee involved.[128] The last chance agreement is not available to all employees who violate the work rules. Drug users, but not drug distributors, may have access to the program.[129]

One arbitrator left the terms of the last chance agreement to "the thinking" of the employee, the union, and various employer representatives.[130] The actual role of the employee was not defined, but the award indicated that the individual employee was to play some role in determining the terms of this special contract. The last chance agreement might contain language that is rather vague, such as using a standard of "earnest effort at improved productivity within 2 months."[131]

Another type of related arbitration award may set very specific conditions for an individual employee. One such award provided that if an employee were to pass a qualifying exam, he would have a 40 day probationary period on a new job position, and if he failed meeting the standards of the job, he would return to his prior position.[132]

These examples highlight the commonly recognized fact that individual employees have little bargaining power with an employer regardless of whether the issue is at will status or some other topic. This fact has never been given much weight by the courts under the at will contract doctrine and these cases seem to be a continuation of that approach. Whereas the courts explicitly or implicitly suggest that the employee who wants more than at will can negotiate other terms, the reality is frequently to the contrary. This seems to be another acknowledgement of judicial reluctance to become significantly involved in the employment relationship, and an acknowledgment that special contract rules are in play. Perhaps there is another unannounced doctrine at play, namely that employers do not have to negotiate fundamental employer rights.

In summary, even in a collective bargaining context there are ample opportunities for individual contracts to coexist with the collective contract. These include explicit contracts and terms included in the arbitrator's awards. It can be disputed whether, for example, an arbitrator's award can be characterized as a true individual contract, but the individual employee may be involved in developing its terms and there can be no question that the awards set special terms and conditions for the individual employee. Beyond arbitrator's awards, individual contracts may be used in a variety of situations, including locker assignments and in determining rights in the event that a promotion to a noncollective bargaining position is not successful.

Although the amount of case law involving individual-collective contract combinations is not large, what it does suggest, however, is that these individual-collective contracts may not be read with quite the same rigor as individual contracts in the noncollective bargaining workplace. This conclusion is still quite tenuous, but it does indicate a need for careful watching of the matter. Case law has just begun to develop on waivers of employee rights and the related subject of EAPs, and firm conclusions are not possible at this point.

Testing waivers, medical releases, and waiving the right to sue are part of EAPs and last chance agreements. They raise significant public policy statutory issues, not the least of which are constitutional questions. Once it is determined that employer contract demands do not necessarily violate public policy, courts tend to construe them with an eye toward employer rights. Arbitrators more frequently relate them to concerns of workplace efficiency and discipline, which also have a high element of employer rights. Employee assistance programs to date are generally treated as not creating enforceable rights for employees. Whereas failure to participate in EAPs may lead to discharge, successful participation or completion does little to alter the basic at will status of most employees, despite the inclusion of explicit durational terms. Employer drafted documents do not usually receive the same amount of scrutiny that is given to employee claims of an individual definite term contract.

COVENANT OF GOOD FAITH

Implied or Express Term

In addition to express terms, an individual employment contract may contain implied terms. The covenant of good faith and fair dealing may be one of the implied terms recognized in some jurisdictions. Not all states recognize the covenant.[133] It basically requires that the employer act in good faith. This may mean that in some situations the employer is bound by the employer's actions or statements to discharge only for cause. The commonly stated prerequisites for the application of the covenant are long-term service and express actions or policies by the employer implying job security or the fair adjudication of grievances.[134]

Fairness in Application

The covenant has been described as one to protect the express terms of the contract and not to protect some general public interest not directly related to the contract's purpose.[135] The fairness notion relates to whatever terms are found in the contract and not in broader societal notions of fairness or public policy. The covenant that might otherwise be implied may be overcome by an express clause to the contrary.[136] In some situations, the covenant's duty of fairness may be found in the express terms of an employee handbook. In one case the court found the covenant when the handbook stated that the policies would be "applied fairly."[137] Whereas arbitrators do not often speak in terms of a covenant of good faith, their decisions more frequently require good faith than do court decisions. The exercise of arbitrator's power to mitigate discipline is an example of this.

Remedies

As of the time of this publication, the leading discussion of remedies for breach of the covenant is found in the California case, *Foley v. Interactive Data Corp.*[138] The the California Supreme Court held that tort damages were not available for breach of the implied covenant.

The employee is entitled only to contract damages if breach of the covenant is proved.

In summary, the covenant of good faith and fair dealing is a powerful clause favoring the employee in jurisdictions that recognize it. Application of the covenant may mean enforcement of the terms of duration found in handbooks or terms stated in conversations not conducted in an environment of negotiation. The covenant is most likely to apply to long-term employees. The status of the covenant should be monitored in the relevant jurisdiction because this is a rapidly changing area of employment law.

TERMS OF DURATION

An employee can gain job security by negotiating a written, long-term employment contract. That is not an easy task. Courts rigorously apply contract doctrine in the interpretation of the employment relationship. The use of general language involving commonly used words that suggest a fixed or long-term duration might appear to offer job security protection. This is often not the situation. The judicial presumption of an at will relationship is one of the most pervasively used tools in interpreting alleged long-term employment contracts. To avoid its application, the employee must use the most careful language in drafting a fixed term or for cause contract. Only a few employees with significant bargaining power will be able to negotiate such terms.

The purpose of this section is to consider some of the language of duration commonly found in individual contracts. Much of the language is from cases where the employee sought to establish a fixed term or long-term contract. In many of the examples, the courts have found that the language was inadequate. In a few cases, the courts found that the language was sufficient to create a fixed term contract. The beginning point is to look at some contract language that clearly created an at will relationship. Emphasis then shifts to the use of more problematical language.

At Will Contract Language

The mere fact that employees have an individual written contract of employment or a collective bargaining agreement does not necessarily protect them from being discharged at will. The written contract may contain language that specifically gives the employer the common law right to discharge at will. The contract may provide that the employer has the sole and exclusive right to discharge and may provide no provision for a grievance procedure for disputes. Under such a contract, the employer has the contractual right to discharge at will.[139]

The following very strong language is an example of a clause in an individual contract providing for at will employment. The language is particularly useful to illustrate the effort by the employer to overcome any employee expectations based upon statements made by lower company officials which might appear to modify the at will language of the main part of the agreement:

My employment and compensation can be terminated, with or without cause, and with or without notice, at any time, at the option of either the company or myself. I understand that no store manager or representative of . . . (the employer) other than the president or vice president of the Company has any authority to enter into any agreement for employment for any specified period of time, or to make any agreement contrary to the foregoing.[140]

At will language can also be evidenced by combining some of the following concepts: either party could cancel or terminate the agreement at any time, no oral agreements or understandings were made that affect the contract, no alteration or variation can be made unless made in writing and signed by both parties, the present contract supersedes and annuls all other contracts, the employer has sole discretion to determine the duration of employment, the personnel manual is for informational purposes only, the personnel manual provisions are not conditions of employment, the personnel manual provisions may be modified or revoked at any time with or without notice, and the personnel manual is not intended to create a contract.[141] Disclaimers that might also be part of an employee handbook have been discussed above.[142]

Conflicting Terms

Sometimes an employee will have a contract or handbook that indicates in one place that the employee is at will and indicates in another place that cause is the basis of discharge. When faced with such a contradiction, the court might let it be resolved by a jury,[143] or compare a contract with a handbook to determine intent,[144] or follow the more specific of the two conflicting clauses.[145] The presumption of at will status will play its usual role.

Employee Admits Freedom to Leave

In litigation over contract employment duration, an employee is frequently asked if the employee could leave the employer at any time. The employee frequently must answer affirmatively. It is a very damaging admission in those courts that rely heavily on the mutuality of obligation argument to support the at will doctrine. Under that doctrine, if the employee could leave at any time, the employer should be able to discharge the employee at any time.[146]

However, where the employee has negotiated a valid permanent contract with the employer, the fact that the employee can quit at any time should not necessarily trigger the mutuality argument permitting the employer to discharge at any time. In one such case, the court noted that the employee had paid valuable consideration in exchange for the right to a cause based discharge.[147]

Lifetime

In litigation, a frequent claim is that the contract was intended to last for the lifetime of the employee. Courts rarely recognize a contract of such duration. Such contracts are found to be extraordinary or unusual, which means that the employee must have unusually strong proof.[148] A lifetime contract must be expressed in clear and unequivocal terms before an employer will be bound by such a "weighty obligation."[149] A lifetime contract may require a second, independent, and substantial consideration.[150] Unless there is a second consideration given, courts may not recognize a lifetime contract.[151] Courts may examine the independent consideration, for it must be of "substantial value."[152] One suggested example of such valuable consideration would be the giving up of a personal claim against the employer.[153]

One employee's claim of a lifetime contract was defeated when the contract was shown to contain a renewal clause. The court noted that a "lifetime" contract would not need to be renewed.[154] One court has stated that in order to create a lifetime contract, the employee need not promise to work for a lifetime. Exact mutuality need not be shown.[155] Other courts have indicated that if the employee is free to leave at any time, the employer is free to discharge at any time.[156] An advertised offer of "lifetime opportunity, permanent and stable business" was not found by one court to mean that a cause standard will be used at discharge. The offer was for an at will relationship, the court said, not a lifetime relationship.[157]

Assume that an actual lifetime contract has been made. The duration of such an agreement must still be considered. One court has indicated that a lifetime contract would last only as long as the employer had need for the employee's services.[158] It is not clear whether "need" would be measured by the employer's subjective determination, which would be the usual at will approach, or whether need would be measured by an objective or cause standard. If the employer could unilaterally declare that the need was over, the contract would really be an at will relationship.

In another case where a lifetime contract was found to exist and where the employer had breached it, the court awarded damages, and not specific performance.[159] Remedies present some difficult issues, but where reinstatement is denied, the lifetime contract may have little meaning, absent substantial front pay. In another case, the court found a binding employment for "the rest of her life." The court found that it meant employment for a definite term, that is, until normal retirement age.[160]

Not to Exceed

A contract provided that the term was "not to exceed" three years. The court held that the period was the maximum, and not a minimum. The employment was at will.[161]

Permanent

A permanent contract is much like a lifetime contract. It is very difficult to prove, and it is viewed as being extraordinary in nature. Where the hiring employer advertised for a "permanent member of the staff," employment was found to be indefinite term and was not permanent.[162] Even a hiring that is "permanent until retirement" may be found to result in an at will status.[163] Proof of actual negotiations is the type of strong evidence that may overcome the at will presumption. In one such example, a prospective employee was shown to be very hesitant about giving up an existing job unless the new employer offered a permanent position. The employee agreed to accept the job only after authorized representatives of the employer promised her that she would be given a permanent position and that she could be discharged only for cause. The court held that a valid, permanent position was offered, given the specific nature of the negotiations.[164]

The presence of additional consideration beyond the performance of services is also important evidence in determining whether a permanent arrangement was agreed to. One lenient court has indicated that the second consideration could consist of such items as the willingness to move to another city.[165] Many courts will not find that moving is adequate consideration, especially because moving is often required in any job change.

In one case, an employee argued that a permanent contract was contemplated. The court found that the contract contained a probationary period. The court ruled that the existence of a probationary period negated the notion of a permanent contract.[166] The court did not explain why a probationary period would be needed in an at will relationship.

An employee handbook may distinguish between a "permanent" and a "temporary" employee. The court may find that the words do not relate to duration, or if they do, it will still be at will employment.[167] What appears to the employee as a permanent contract is frequently found to be an at will contract by the court.[168]

In courts that are willing to find permanent contracts, the question remains as to the duration of a contract that is found to be permanent. Permanent employment may be equated with employment until cause for discharge is shown. Thus permanent does not mean permanent. It means the same thing as any definite term contract, that termination can always occur upon a showing of cause.[169] Another definition of permanent is that it means employment so long as the employer is in business, has work for the employee, and the employee performs that work in a satisfactory manner.[170] Again, the question remains as to the standard for determining whether there is work to be done. The choices for the standard are the employer's subjective determination or the court's more objective determination.

Courts have stated that "permanent" can mean "steady" as opposed to "temporary or part-time employment, when there was no clear meeting of the minds."[171] The distinction itself was not made clearer. Another court states that permanent means "until one or the other of the parties shall desire to terminate the connection."[172]

One court has suggested that the general rule that a contract for permanent employment will be construed to be terminable at will is arguably "too mechanical" an answer.[173] They did not, however, elaborate on the less mechanical alternatives. Another court was unwilling to automatically equate permanent with terminable at will. It would require the parties to go forward with their evidence (deny the motion to dismiss). The evidence and not the imposition of a definition as a matter of law would control the duration of the contract.[174] Another court suggested that permanent meant until the employee died.[175]

Probationary Period, Seniority Terms

All of the terms of the contract should be scrutinized to determine if any of the clauses suggest or negate the basis of at will status. The existence of a probationary period in the contract is usually read to overcome other expectations for long-term or permanent employment.[176] The probationary employee can be fired at any time, which is inconsistent with the argument that a long-term contract was intended. A seniority clause, in contrast, may suggest something other than at will status.[177] One common purpose of a seniority clause is to limit the employer's power over the more senior employees, as compared to the more junior employees.

Reasonable Time

A lifetime or permanent position is rarely construed to last a lifetime or to be permanent. More frequently, they are deemed to be at will. The argument has been raised that there should be a middle ground between at will and permanent. Whereas the parties may not have clearly intended a literal lifetime or permanent duration, neither did they intend the words to be meaningless. The middle ground is that the contract should be construed to last for a "reasonable" period of time.

The at will presumption can be overcome by showing the "intent of the parties that the contract last for some . . . reasonable time."[178] The case law on "reasonable" duration contracts is mixed. A golf coach sought to show that the established past practice was for coaches to stay a long time, and that he was hired to develop the program, which would take time. The court held that the circumstances were insufficient to show a definite time contract and the coach could be fired at will.[179] Another employee showed that he had agreed to work in the company security division for two years in exchange for a promise to transfer him to management. The court said that it would be appropriate to find that the duration of the management period was for a reasonable time.[180] In another case, that court indicated that the sacrifice of other employment opportunities might constitute consideration that would extend the period of employment to a reasonable period of time.[181]

Assume that the parties agreed to a contract with a "reasonable" period of time duration. The next question is how long is a reasonable period of time? Time to recoup the employee's expenses made in furtherance of the employer's interests may be one measure. Where an employee purchased a truck and office equipment to do the employer's work, the court said that a reasonable period of time ran from 1969 to 1975.[182] The reasonable period of time for another employee who incurred expenses (i.e., contractual consideration beyond the providing of services) on behalf of the employer would be that period of time necessary to recoup those expenses.[183] Another court reached a similar result by saying that the reasonable time "should be commensurate with the hardship the employee has endured or the benefit he has bestowed."[184]

By way of specific numbers, one employee argued that his 15 years of employment was not yet a reasonable time. The court disagreed.[185] Another employee was hired earlier, but relied on statements made in 1969. He was dismissed in 1985. The court found that the 16-year period was a reasonable period of time.[186]

One court has noted an anomaly in the reasonable period of time argument. Where an implied contract for a reasonable period of time existed, the contract might offer relief to the employee who was fired after two months, but it would not seem to offer relief to the faithful employee who had worked for 40 years, well beyond a "reasonable" time.[187] The long-term employee might have already worked for a "reasonable" period of time when the discharge occurs. The court worried that the result of a reasonable period interpretation might be to help the short-term employee but not help the long-term employee. This need not necessarily be a concern. The longer the employee is employed, the longer the reasonable expectation for future employment might become.

Until Retirement

A contract until retirement has been found to be a definite term contract by some courts, but it has been found to be too indefinite by other courts. Where a definite term contract until retirement exists, the employee can be discharged only for cause. Some courts will read the contract to mean an employee's normal retirement age.[188]

One employer sought to defeat a claimed contract until retirement by raising questions about the effect of the death of the employee or the employer going out of business prior to the retirement of the employee. The employer's argument was basically that if all of the essential terms of the contract were not definite, an at will contract existed. The court did not find an explicit agreement to employ until retirement, but it found a violation of covenant of good faith and fair dealing in terminating a 60-year-old employee after 19 years of service.[189] Other decisions are to the contrary. "Until retirement" is too indefinite to overcome the presumption of at will status in some courts.[190]

Salary Period

A common employee argument is to attempt to equate the duration of the contract with the period of salary. Thus an employee paid by the year should be found to be hired for a definite term of a year. Courts usually reject this argument and find that the salary period cannot be extended beyond the salary topic.[191] Equating job duration and salary term has, however, been adopted by legislation in one state.[192] The time table for accumulating vacation time is also not a durational term.[193]

Satisfaction

A contract for "so long as the service is satisfactory" is usually found to be an at will contract.[194] Under the at will doctrine, satisfaction means the employer's subjective satisfaction. One reason given for using the employer's subjective determination of satisfaction is that the courts are reluctant to substitute their judgment for that of the employer as to what is satisfactory.[195] The same rule was applied where the employee's job was contingent upon the satisfactory completion of a medical examination and the employee was found to have diabetes.[196] Satisfaction will be determined by the employer's subjective judgment and not by a just cause standard.[197] The statement of dissatisfaction must be made in good faith.[198] Where an employer uses "satisfactory" as a standard, and where that employer couples its use with the existence of an appraisal system, the employer's personal satisfaction may no longer be the test. Rather, the test may be satisfaction as determined by the appraisal system.[199]

So Long As

A common provision is that the employment will continue "so long as" some other circumstance exists. These contracts are usually found to be at will contracts. Thus an agreement for so long as the territory was producing was found to be at will.[200] A contract for "so long as the employee did a good job" was found to be an at will agreement.[201] A contract for "so long as the manager operated the railroad successfully, profitably, and efficiently" did not provide sufficient contractual guidelines and was an at will relationship.[202]

A contract for "so long as it was satisfactory to both" was found to be at will.[203] The court said that either person could independently terminate the contract. It did not require the agreement of both to terminate.

Someone Who

An employer may advertise for "someone who intends to stay." Courts find these contracts to be at will agreements. Where the employer wanted "someone who would not run in and out," the employer could still discharge at will.[204] Where another employer wanted "someone who intends to stay," the court found it too vague a representation to constitute a binding agreement for a definite term.[205]

Project Life

Employment on a long-term project does not necessarily mean employment for the life of the project.[206] Vague terms will be treated as an at will contract. A hiring in the context of a five-year operational plan was not found to be a five-year contract.[207]

Month to Month

Where a contract is month to month, the renewal is an "at will" decision. Under such a contract, an employee can be nonrenewed (discharged) without cause at the end of the month, but not during the month unless cause existed.[208]

In summary, many courts use the presumption of at will status to overcome the common meaning of any terms of duration in common use in the workplace. Absent a clear writing, the giving of second consideration, evidence of adversarial negotiations, or other evidence, words such as "permanent," "lifetime," "yearly salary," and "until retirement" are interpreted to mean at will. Where such terms are given their obvious and common meanings, they give rise to just cause for a discharge employment relationship. The safest terms of duration seem to be specifically a day, month, and year in a written agreement. Some courts are willing to find a middle duration between at will and lifetime. The willingness to recognize a reasonable time duration of employment allows the court to look at the circumstances of the employee and employer, rather than looking only at formal contract doctrine.

CONCLUSION

Where an at will contract exists, courts split on the question of whether the at will durational term permits the existence of other enforceable (not at will) clauses. The better reasoning allows such terms and recognizes that at will is only a durational clause, and other clauses, even other job security clauses not involving duration, are enforceable.

Noncompetition clauses are an example of an individual contract clause that is treated as an unusual element in the employment contract because they are one of the few clauses where courts will examine the exact language and make a balance between the interests of the employer, the employee, and the public.

With the increasing recognition given to alcohol and drug use in the workplace, courts and arbitrators are having to look at employer drafted contract clauses involving the waiver of employee rights, especially in testing and searches, and at the employer's obligations under an EAP. To date the limited case law reads employee waivers and consents broadly and reads employer obligations under EAPs in a restricted manner. There will be a great deal more activity in these areas.

The interface between individual contracts and collective bargaining contracts is not new, and it should receive much greater scrutiny. At least two facets are involved. One is the traditional question of the role of the individual contract in collective bargaining. Consents, waivers, last chance agreements, and EAPs are a major focus here. The second facet is the degree of symmetry between the rules of contract interpretation of individual and collective contracts. The traditional approach seems to treat them as distinct classifications, but closer analysis indicates that there is no doctrinal reason why a contract is not a contract, so to speak. Both contracts exist in the common environment of the workplace. Rules of reason and the "law" of the shop are more likely to be more conducive to the common goal of efficiency than are attempts to impose the fully adversarial notions of common law contract doctrine.

When courts review alleged terms of duration, especially those involving long periods of time ("permanent," "lifetime"), the common meaning of words are usually lost in the application of the presumption of at will status. Courts seem very reluctant to recognize a contract that extends beyond the moment (at will), even though the employer is always protected by the right to discharge for cause. The reluctance to recognize longer term contracts is further manifested in judicial efforts to provide remedies, such as employment for a "reasonable" time or to provide anything beyond back pay. As an ironic generalization, a rule of thumb might be stated that says the longer the duration of the claimed contract, the more likely it becomes that the court will find an at will contract.

One way to view the process of interpreting individual contract of employment clauses is to break them into three categories: 1. The arbitrary power granted the employer under the presumption of at will status governs both the discharge clause and most other terms of the contract. 2. The contract will be subject to strict scrutiny under traditional contract doctrine, including mutuality, statute of frauds, requirements of clarity, giving of consideration, and similar rules. 3. The contract will be reviewed with an effort to balance employee and employer interests, as well as the public interest. Where a court is the interpreting forum, categories one and two are commonly used. When arbitration is the interpreting forum, categories two and three are commonly used. Category one does not usually look to the day to day experiences in the workplace, whereas category three usually takes account of the practices in the workplace. Category two can be used to ignore the workplace and look to the strict rules of formal law or to consider the common rules of the workplace. Individual contracts are more likely to fall into categories one and two, whereas collective bargaining contracts are more likely to fall into categories two and three.

In the field of collective bargaining, the subjects of the contract are frequently described as being either mandatory or permissive topics. The employer is obligated to bargain in good faith over mandatory topics, but the employer need not but may voluntarily bargain in good faith over permissive topics. In the field of individual contracts courts do not use the dichotomy. Little actual bargaining is found in the "negotiation" of individual contracts, even where the individual terms arise in the context of collective bargaining. If an analogy to two-fold breakdown in collective bargaining were to be used in individual contracts, the two individual contract categories might be those clauses that are essentially not negotiable (termination at will) and permissive topics. The good faith requirement plays little role outside of jurisdictions that recognize the covenant of good faith.

The individual-collective contract distinction can be rationalized to some extent by noting that one is largely the product of the common law and the other is the product of statutes. This distinction may belie, however, the most important common point, namely that both spring from a common environment, the workplace. The basic question for a dispute resolution forum then becomes the question of whether the forum will emphasize the differences between the two contracts or the common environment. The latter would seem to be the better choice, because it focuses on the real world of production and efficiency, which lie at the heart of the relationship.

The case law presents another major dichotomy in contract analysis. When the employee seeks to prove the terms of a contract, the employee will be held to a very high standard of proof, usually under traditional contract doctrine that has no reference to the workplace. When the employer seeks to prove the terms of a contract, especially waivers and settlement, the employer is not held to such a high standard of proof in most cases. The employer will be held to a higher standard of proof where specific statutory rights are involved. In the absence of specific statutory rights, the employer may benefit from evidentiary presumptions and implied consents. Perhaps what is at work is not really a question of contract analysis, but a question of judicial restraint and the pervasive impact of employer rights. Some courts frequently recite the rule that if a change in judicial doctrine is needed, it is a matter for the legislature, not the courts. This rule probably states a more basic truth about the workplace in general than many have been willing to recognize. Statutes are the major way of requiring courts to lessen judicial restraint and diminish the presumption of at will status.

NOTES

1. Portions of this chapter originally appeared in Brodie, Individual Contracts of Employment (Part 1), 39 Labor L.J. 585 (1988) and Part II, 39 Labor L. J. 663 (1988). The cooperation of the Labor Law Journal is greatly appreciated.

2. Morris v. Lutheran Medical Center, 115 L.R.R.M. (BNA) 4966 (Neb. S. Ct. 1983); Lewis v. Or. Beauty Supply Co., 2 Indiv. Empl. Rights (BNA) 1135; (Or. Sup. Ct. 1987); Johnston v. Panhandle Co-op Ass'n, 2 Indiv. Empl. Rights (BNA) 1080 (Neb. Sup. Ct. 1987).

3. Langdon v. Saga Corp., 115 L.R.R.M. 4975, 4977 (Okla. Ct. App. 1977). See also, Williams v. Maremont Corp., 109 Lab. Cas. (BNA) 55,919 (Tenn. Ct. App. 1988).

4. Bishop v. Wood, 426 U.S. 341, 345 (1976).

5. Todd v. S.C. Farm Bureau Mut. Ins. Co., 115 L.R.R.M. (BNA) 4899, 4901 (S.C. Sup. Ct. 1981); Reilly v. Stroehmann Brothers Co., 2 Indiv. Empl. Rights (BNA) 1244 (Pa. Super. Ct. 1986); Keneally v. Orgain, 115 L.R.R.M. 4576, 4577 (Mont. Sup. Ct. 1980); Cox v. Radiology Consulting Assoc., Inc., 2 Indiv. Empl. Rights (BNA) 233 (D. Pa. 1987); Clutterham v. Coachmen Industries, Inc., 2 Indiv. Empl. Rights (BNA) 164 (Cal. Ct. App. 1985); Fuselier, Ott & McKee v. Moeller,

3 Indiv. Empl. Rights (BNA) 197 (Miss. Sup. Ct. 1987); Huber v. Standard Ins. Co., 3 Indiv. Empl. Rights (BNA) 1 (9th Cir. 1988).

6. Ariganello v. Scott Paper Co., 117 L.R.R.M. (BNA) 2064 (D. Mich. 1982); McGregor v. Board of Commissioners, 3 Indiv. Empl. Rights (BNA) 403 (D. Fla. 1987).

7. Fuselier, Ott & McKee v. Moeller, 3 Indiv. Empl. Rights (BNA) 197 (Miss. Sup. Ct. 1987).

8. Metcalf v. Intermountain Gas Co., 4 Indiv. Empl. Rights (BNA) 961 (Idaho Sup. Ct. 1989).

9. Morris v. Lutheran Medical Center, 115 L.R.R.M. (BNA) 4966 (Neb. Sup. Ct. 1983); Salimi v. Farmers Ins. Group, 116 L.R.R.M. (BNA) 3230, 3231 (Colo. Ct. App. 1984); Brudnicki v. General Electric, 115 L.R.R.M. (BNA) 4919, 4921 (D. Ill. 1982).

10. EEOC v. International Business Machine Corp., 34 Empl. Prac. Dec. (CCH) 34,391 at 33,549 (D. Md. 1984).

11. Salimi v. Farmers Insurance Group, 116 L.R.R.M. (BNA) 3230, 3231 (Colo. Ct. App. 1984).

12. Toussaint v. Blue Cross & Blue Shield, 115 L.R.R.M. (BNA) 4708, 4715 (Mich. Sup. Ct. 1980).

13. Goff v. Mass. Protective Assoc., 115 L.R.R.M. (BNA) 5016 (Wisc. Sup. Ct. 1970).

14. Bennett v. Eastern Rebuilders, 115 L.R.R.M. (BNA) 4444 (N.C. Ct. App. 1981).

15. O'Shea v. RCA Global Communications, 117 L.R.R.M. (BNA) 2880, 2882–83 (D. N.J. 1984).

16. Brannan v. Wyeth Laboratories Inc., 3 Indiv. Empl. Rights (BNA) 609 (La. Sup. Ct. 1988); Harris v. Mardan Business Systems Inc., 3 Indiv. Empl. Rights (BNA) 474 (Minn. Ct. App. 1988).

17. Panto v. Moore Business Forms Inc., 3 Indiv. Empl. Rights (BNA) 1025 (N.H. Sup. Ct. 1988); Livernois v. Medical Disposables Inc., 2 Indiv. Empl. Rights (BNA) 1832 (11th Cir. 1988).

18. Panto v. Moore Business Forms Inc., 3 Indiv. Empl. Rights (BNA) 1025 (N.H. Sup. Ct. 1988).

19. Bowen v. Wohl Shoe Co., 115 L.R.R.M. (BNA) 4758 (D. Tex. 1975).

20. Savodnik v. Korvettes, Inc., 115 L.R.R.M. (BNA) 4601, 4604 (D. N.Y. 1980); See also McGlendon v. Ingersoll-Rand Co., 779 S.W.2d 69 (Tex. Sup. Ct. 1989).

21. Ch. 4, fn. 110–129.

22. Langdon v. Saga Corp., 115 L.R.R.M. (BNA) 4975, 4978 (Okla. Ct. App. 1977).

23. Magnan v. Anaconda Industries, Inc., 101 Lab. Cas. (BNA) 55,485 at 76,182 (Conn. Sup. Ct. 1984).

24. Fortune v. National Cash Register Co., 115 L.R.R.M. (BNA) 4658, 4663 (Mass. Sup. Ct. 1977).

25. Mid-States Paint & Chemical v. Herr, 3 Indiv. Empl. Rights (BNA) 270 (Mo. Ct. App. 1988).

26. Payne v. K-D Mfg. Co., 2 Indiv. Empl. Rights (BNA) 459 (R.I. Sup. Ct. 1987); Courts Skeptical of 'Non-compete' Pacts, Wall Street J., B1, C3 (Jan. 11, 1989).

27. Paramount Termite Control Co. v. Rector, 4 Indiv. Empl. Rights (BNA) 791 (Va. Sup. Ct. 1989); Ingersoll-Rand Co. v. Ciavatta, 3 Indiv. Empl. Rights (BNA) 1285 (N.J. Sup. Ct. 1988); Owens v. The Penn Mutual Life Ins. Co., 3 Indiv. Empl. Rights (BNA) 1144 (8th Cir. 1988); B. Cantrell Oil Co. v. Hino Gas Sales, 3 Indiv. Empl. Rights (BNA) 869 (Tex. Ct. App. 1988); Modern Telecommunications v. Zimmerman, 3 Indiv. Empl. Rights (BNA) 741 (N.Y. Sup. Ct. App. Div. 1988); Marshall v. Gore, 2 Indiv. Empl. Rights (BNA) 318 (Fla. Ct. App. 1987).

28. Data Management Inc. v. Greene, 3 Indiv. Empl. Rights (BNA) 796 (Alaska Sup. Ct. 1988).

29. Hekimian Laboratories v. Domain Systems, 2 Indiv. Empl. Rights (BNA) 928 (D. Fla. 1987).

30. Brown v. General Electric Co., 3 Indiv. Empl. Rights (BNA) 1720 (N.Y. Sup. Ct. App. Div. 1988); Schuler v. Polaroid Corp., 3 Indiv. Empl. Rights (BNA) 532 (1st Cir. 1988); Funk v. Sperry Corp., 3 Indiv. Empl. Rights (BNA) 469 (9th Cir. 1988).

31. Schuler v. Polaroid Corp., 3 Indiv. Empl. Rights (BNA) 532 (1st Cir. 1988).

32. Brown v. General Electric Co., 3 Indiv. Empl. Rights (BNA) 1720 (N.Y. Sup. Ct. App. Div. 1988).

33. Funk v. Sperry Corp., 3 Indiv. Empl. Rights (BNA) 469 (9th Cir. 1988).

34. Malmstrom v. Kaiser Aluminum & Chemical, 2 Indiv. Empl. Rights (BNA) 180 (Cal. Ct. App. 1986).

35. D'Ulisse-Cupo v. Board of Directors, 2 Indiv. Empl. Rights (BNA) 948 (Conn. Sup. Ct. 1987).

36. Evans v. Einhorn, 855 F.2d 1245 (7th Cir. 1988).

37. C. Morris, 1 *The Developing Labor Law* 600–604 (1983).

38. Berda v. CBS Inc., 4 Indiv. Empl. Rights (BNA) 904 (3d Cir. 1989). See also Anderson v. Ford Motor Co., 803 F.2d 953 (8th Cir. 1986); Bale v. General Telephone Co. of Cal., 795 F.2d 775 (9th Cir. 1988); Central States, Southeast and Southwest Pension Fund v. Gerber Truck Service, Inc., 111 Lab. Cas. (CCH) 11,090 (7th Cir. 1988).

39. Caterpillar Inc. v. Williams, 482 U.S. 386 (1987); Malai v. RCA Corp., 794 F.2d 909 (3d Cir. 1986).

40. Caterpillar Inc. v. Williams, 482 U.S. 386, 396 (1987).

41. Wells v. General Motors, 881 F.2d 166 (5th Cir. 1989).

42. City of Miami, 131 L.R.R.M. (BNA) 3171 (Fla. Ct. App. 1989).

43. National Treasury Employees Union v. Von Raab, 109 S. Ct. 1384 (1989).

44. Heller v. Dover Warehouse Market, Inc., 515 A.2d 178 (Del. Super. Ct. 1986); Ambroz v. Cornhusker Square Lmt'd., 416 N.W.2d 510 (Neb. Sup. Ct. 1987).

45. Quinn v. Limited Express, Inc., 715 F. Supp. 127 (D. Pa. 1989).

46. Nat'l Treasury Employees Union v. Von Raab, 109 S. Ct. 1384 (1989).

47. Moore v. American Barnag Corp., 710 F. Supp. 1050 (D. N.C. 1989).

48. Doe v. Cheney, 885 F.2d 898 (D.C. Cir. 1989).

49. Fowler v. N.Y. City Dep't of Sanitation, 704 F. Supp. 1264 (D. N.Y. 1989).

50. Morris v. Penn Mutual Life Insur. Co., 51 Empl. Prac. Dec. (CCH) 39,345 (D. Pa. 1989).

51. F.L.R.A. v. U.S. Dep't of the Treasury, 884 F.2d 1446 (D.C. Cir. 1989).

52. Alexander Proudfoot Co. World Headquarter v. Thayer, 877 F.2d 912 (11th Cir. 1989).

53. Wall v. Dep't of Health and Human Services, 871 F.2d 1540 (10th Cir. 1989).

54. U.S. v. United Seafood Workers, Smoked Fish, and Cannery Union, 889 F.2d 1232 (2d Cir. 1989).

55. Hearing Centers of America, Inc., 106 Bankr. 719 (Bankr. Ct. Fla. 1989).

56. Adams v. Bainbridge-Decatur Co. Hospital Authority, 888 F.2d 1356 (11th Cir. 1989).

57. Dole v. Haulaway Inc., 29 Wage & Hour Cas. (BNA) 873 (D. N.J. 1989).

58. Luedtke v. Nabors Alaska Drilling, Inc., 768 P.2d 1123 (Alaska Sup. Ct. 1989).

59. Ellis v. Buckley, 1989 WL 138981 (Westlaw) (Colo. Ct. App. 1989).

60. Morton Thiokol, 89 Lab. Arb. (BNA) 572 (Nicholas, Arb. 1987).

61. Fowler v. N.Y.C. Dep't of Sanitation, 4 Indiv. Empl. Rights (BNA) 81, 87 (D. N.Y.).

62. Lockheed Missiles & Space Co., 89 Lab. Arb. (BNA) 506 (Wyman, Arb. 1987).

63. Fong v. U.S. Dep't of the Treasury, 705 F. Supp. 41 (D. D.C. 1989).

64. Zaccardi v. Zale Corp., 856 F.2d 1473 (10th Cir. 1988).

65. Berube v. Fashion Centre Ltd., 4 Indiv. Empl. Rights 353, 357 (Utah Sup. Ct. 1989).

66. Mechanics Lumber Co. v. Smith, 3 Indiv. Empl. Rights (BNA) 891 (Ark. Sup. Ct. 1988) (no tort of outrage where ill employee refused polygraph); Johnson v. Delchamps Inc., 3 Indiv. Empl. Rights (BNA) 560 (5th Cir. 1988) (Polygraph release lacked consideration); Gordon v. Tenneco Retail Service Co., 2 Indiv. Empl. Rights (BNA) 1027 (D. Miss. 1987) (Employee properly discharged when refused to sign statement admitting theft).

67. Myers v. Western-Southern Life Ins. Co., 3 Indiv. Empl. Rights (BNA) 723 (6th Cir. 1988) (contractual six month limitation on suits against employer not unreasonable); Thomson v. Weinberger, 3 Indiv. Empl. Rights (BNA) 7 (D. Md. 1988) (Federal Government requirement that employees sign drug testing consent form for random testing involves unreasonable search); Bateman v. Florida, 2 Indiv. Empl. Rights (BNA) 1075 (Fla. Ct. App. 1987) (Regulations required employee to consent to search of desk, search invalid).

68. Springer v. Weeks and Leo Co., 3 Indiv. Empl. Rights (BNA) 1345 (Iowa Sup. Ct. 1988). One court indicated that under the Fair Labor Standards Act, a person could waive factual elements, but not the right to full recovery. Runyan v. Nat'l Cash Register Corp., 787 F.2d 1039 (6th Cir. 1986).

69. Stewart v. The Pantry Inc., 4 Indiv. Empl. Rights (BNA) 526 (D. Ky. 1988).

70. McGonagle v. Union Fidelity Corp., 556 A.2d 878 (Pa. Super. Ct. 1989).

71. Delaney v. Taco Time Int'l., Inc., 670 P.2d 218 (Or. Ct. App. 1983).

72. Sides v. Duke Univ., 328 S.E. 2d 818 (N.C. Ct. App. 1985).

73. Shebar v. Sanyo Business Systems, 3 Indiv. Empl. Rights (BNA) 1380 (N.J. Super. Ct. 1987).

74. D. Martino v. City of Hartford, 636 F. Supp. 1241 (D. Conn. 1986).

75. Stroman v. West Coast Grocery Co., 884 F.2d 458 (9th Cir. 1989).

76. Firefighters, Local 1285 v. City of Las Vegas, 764 P.2d 478 (Nev. Sup. Ct. 1988).

77. EEOC v. U.S. Steel Corp., 671 F. Supp. 351 (D. Pa. 1987).

78. Towns v. Emery Air Freight Inc., 3 Indiv. Empl. Rights (BNA) 911, fn.3 at 914 (D. Ohio 1988).

79. Myers v. Western-Southern Life Ins. Co., 3 Indiv. Empl. Rights (BNA) 723 (6th Cir. 1988); Samples v. Hall of Mississippi Inc., 2 Indiv. Empl. Rights (BNA) 799 (D. Miss. 1987); Arnold v. Diet Center Inc., 2 Indiv. Empl. Rights (BNA) 1531 (Idaho Sup. Ct. 1987); Davis v. Bronson Methodist Hospital, 2 Indiv. Empl. Rights (BNA) 376 (Mich. Ct. App. 1986).

80. Fleming Foods West, 92 Lab. Arb. (BNA) 168 (LaRocco, Arb. 1989).

81. Casse v. Louisiana General Services, 531 So. 2d 554 (La. Ct. App. 1988).

82. Ballaron v. Equitable Shipyards, Inc., 521 So. 2d 481 (La. Ct. App. 1988).

83. Berube v. Fashion Centre, Ltd., 771 P.2d 1033 (Utah Sup. Ct. 1989).

84. Elliott v. Shore Stop, Inc., 384 S.E. 2d 752 (Va. Sup. Ct. 1989); Cruz v. Burlington Northern Railroad Co., 773 P.2d 1117 (Colo. Ct. App. 1989).

85. Shaheen v. B.F. Goodrich Co., 873 F.2d 105 (6th Cir. 1989); EEOC v. Cosmair Inc., L'Oreal Hair Care Div., 821 F.2d 1085 (5th Cir. 1987); Riley v. Am. Family Mutual Insur. Co., 51 Empl. Prac. Dec. (CCH) 39,230 (7th Cir. 1989).

86. Runyan v. National Cash Register Corp., 787 F.2d 1039 (6th Cir. 1986).

87. EEOC v. Cosmair, Inc., L'Oreal Hair Care Div., 821 F.2d 1085 (5th Cir. 1987).

88. Shaheen v. B.F. Goodrich, 873 F.2d 105 (6th Cir. 1989).

89. Berube v. Fashion Centre Ltd., 4 Indiv. Empl. Rights (BNA) 353 (Utah Sup. Ct. 1989).

90. Heck's Inc., and UFCW, 293 NLRB No. 132 (1989).

91. Bormann v. AT&T Comm. Inc., 875 F.2d 399 (2d Cir. 1989); Stroman v. West Coast Grocery Co., 884 F.2d 458 (9th Cir. 1989).

92. Stroman v. West Coast Grocery Co., 884 F.2d 458 (9th Cir. 1989).

93. Stroman v. West Coast Grocery Co., 884 F.2d 458 (9th Cir. 1989).

94. Pears v. Spang, 718 F. Supp. 441 (D. Pa. 1989).

95. Pears v. Spang, 718 F. Supp. 441 (D. Pa. 1989).

96. Coleson v. Inspector General of the Dep't of Defense, 721 F. Supp. 763 (D. Va. 1989).

97. Telxon Corp. v. Hoffman, 720 F. Supp. 657 (D. Ill. 1989).

98. Riley v. Am. Family Mutual Ins. Co., 881 F.2d 368 (7th Cir. 1989).

99. Skinner v. Railway Labor Executives' Assoc., 109 S. Ct. 1402 (1989).

100. Bormann v. At&T Communic., 875 F.2d 399 (2d Cir. 1989).

101. Toledo Molding & Die Corp., 88 Lab. Arb. (BNA) 937 (Ipavec, Arb. 1987); Fong v. U.S. Dept. of the Treasury, 705 F. Supp. 41 (D. D.C. 1989).

102. Ch. 6, fn. 69–81.

103. Judd v. Billington, 863 F.2d 103 (D.C. Cir. 1988); see also Lavery v. Dep't of Highway Safety and Motor Vehicles, 523 So.2d 696 (Fla. Ct. App. 1988).

104. Orange Co. Transit Dist., 89 Lab. Arb. 544 (Brisco, Arb. 1987).

105. Ashland Petroleum Co., 90 Lab. Arb. (BNA) 681 (Volz, Arb. 1988).

106. Boise Cascade Corp., 90 Lab. Arb. (BNA) 105 (Hart, Arb. 1987).

107. Northwest Airlines, 89 Lab. Arb. (BNA) 268 (Flagler, Arb. 1987).

108. Basf Corp., 90 Lab. Arb. (BNA) 460 (Daniel, Arb. 1987).

109. Torgerson v. Goodwill Industries, Inc., 391 N.W.2d 35 (Minn. App. Ct. 1986); Packer v. Dana Corp., 385 N.W.2d 727 (Mich. Ct. App. 1986).

110. Compare, Burchell v. Dep't of the Army, 679 F. Supp. 1393 (D.S.C. 1988) (must accommodate) and Salazar v. Ohio Civil Rights Comm., 528 N.E.2d 1303 (Ohio App. Ct. 1987) (no accommodation).

111. Bradshaw v. General Motors, 2 Indiv. Empl. Rights (BNA) 1346 (3d Cir. 1986); Lavery v. Dep't of Highway Safety, 523 So. 2d 696 (Fla. Ct. App. 1988). See, Firms Debate Hard Line On Alcoholics, Wall Street J., B1, C3 (Apr. 13, 1989).

112. Holmes v. Union Oil of Cal., 3 Indiv. Empl. Rights (BNA) 1219 (Idaho Ct. App. 1987).

113. Id.

114. Prezzy v. Food Lion Inc., 4 Indiv. Empl. Rights (BNA) 996 (D. S.C. 1989).

115. McCall v. U.S. Postal Service, 839 F.2d 664 (Fed. Cir. 1988).

116. Young v. Anthony's Fish Grottos, 2 Indiv. Empl. Rights (BNA) 1086 (9th Cir. 1987); Stallcop v. Kaiser Foundation Hospitals, 2 Indiv. Empl. Rights (BNA) 1010 (9th Cir. 1987); Kern v. Steelworkers, Local 1688, 2 Indiv. Empl. Rights (BNA) 526 (D. Pa. 1987).

117. Postal Workers v. Postal Service, 2 Indiv. Empl. Rights (BNA) 1197 (D. Ohio 1987).

118. Cummings v. Amtrak, 2 Indiv. Empl. Rights (BNA) 1022 (Pa. Sup. Ct. 1987).

119. James B. Beam Distilling Co., 90 Lab. Arb. (BNA) 740 (Ruben, Arb. 1988).

120. Magnan v. Anaconda Indus., Inc., 479 A.2d 781 (Conn. Sup. Ct. 1984).

121. Railway Clerks v. Atchison, Topeka, and Santa Fe Railway Co., 109 Lab. Cas. (CCH) 10,541 (7th Cir. 1988).

122. Long v. Elec., Radio & Mach. Workers, 544 F. Supp. 1375 (D. Pa. 1982).

123. Food Marketing Corp., 88 Lab. Arb. (BNA) 98 (Doering, Arb. 1986).

124. Faust v. RCA Corp., 657 F. Supp. 614, (D. Pa. 1986).

125. Food Marketing Corp., 88 Lab. Arb. (BNA) 98 (Doering, Arb. 1986).

126. Alcan Aluminum Co., 88 Lab. Arb. (BNA) 386 (Kindig, Arb. 1986); Univ. of Cincinnati, 89 Lab. Arb. (BNA) 388 (Wren, Arb. 1987).

127. Tootsie Roll Indus., Inc., v. Local 1, Bakery, Confectionery and Tobacco Workers' Union, 832 F.2d 81 (7th Cir. 1987); Basf Corp., 90 Lab. Arb. (BNA) 460 (Daniel, Arb. 1987); S.E. Rykoff & Co., 90 Lab. Arb. (BNA) 233 (Angelo, Arb. 1987); Kaydon Corp., 89 Lab. Arb. (BNA) 377 (Daniel, Arb. 1987).

128. Callicotte v. Carlucci, 698 F. Supp. 944 (D. D.C. 1988).

129. S.D. Warren Co., 89 Lab. Arb. 688 (Gwiazda, Arb. 1985), rev'd on other grounds, 125 L.R.R.M. (BNA) 2086 (1st Cir. 1987).

130. Navistar Int'l Corp., 88 Lab. Arb. 179 (Archer, Arb. 1986).

131. Kelly-Springfield Tire Co., 88 Lab. Arb. (BNA) 201, 204 (Dean, Arb. 1986).

132. Ark. Power & Light Co., 89 Lab. Arb. (BNA) 1028 (Woolf, Arb. 1987).

133. For a state-by-state chart on the status of the covenant, see Lab. Rel. Rep. Indiv. Empl. Rights Manual (BNA) 505:51 (1989).

134. Stark v. Circle K Corp., 3 Indiv. Empl. Rights (BNA) 53 (Mont. Sup. Ct. 1988); La Barber v. Gould Inc., 2 Indiv. Empl. Rights (BNA) 433 (D. Cal. 1987); DeMinico v. Monarch Wine Co., 2 Indiv. Empl. Rights (BNA) 171 (D. Cal. 1986).

135. Foley v. Interactive Data Corp., 3 Indiv. Empl. Rights (BNA) 1729, 1745 (Cal. Sup. Ct. 1988).

136. Gerlund v. Electronic Dispensers Int'l, 2 Indiv. Empl. Rights (BNA) 120 (Cal. Ct. App. 1987).

137. Hoffman-LaRoche v. Campbell, 2 Indiv. Empl. Rights (BNA) 739, 749 (Ala. Sup. Ct. 1987).

138. Foley v. Interactive Data Corp., 3 Indiv. Empl. Rights (BNA) 1729 (Cal. Sup. Ct. 1988).

139. Lumber Workers v. Missoula White Pine, 116 L.R.R.M. (BNA) 2799, 2802 (9th Cir. 1984).

140. Summers v. Sears, Roebuck & Co., 115 L.R.R.M. (BNA) 4812, 4815 (D. Mich. 1982).

141. Crain v. Burroughs Corp., 115 L.R.R.M. (BNA) 5008, 5009 (D. Cal. 1983); see also Stevenson v. ITT Harper, Inc., 115 L.R.R.M. (BNA) 5053, 5054 (Ill. App. Ct. 1977).

142. Ch. 4, fn. 74–90.

143. Dalton v. Herbruck Egg Sales Corp., 2 Indiv. Empl. Rights (BNA) 1729 (Mich. Ct. App. 1987).

144. St. Yves v. Mid State Bank, 2 Indiv. Empl. Rights (BNA) 1550 (Wash. Ct. App. 1987), reversed, 3 Indiv. Empl. Rights (BNA) 1187 (Wash. Sup. Ct. 1988).

145. St. Yves v. Mid State Bank, 3 Indiv. Empl. Rights (BNA) 1187 (Wash. Sup. Ct. 1988).

146. Payne v. AHFI/Netherlands, B.V., 115 L.R.R.M. (BNA) 5085, 5088 (D. Ill. 1980).

147. Scott v. Lane, 115 L.R.R.M. (BNA) 4233, 4235 (Ala. Sup. Ct. 1982).

148. Chastain v. Kelly-Springfield Tire Co., 116 L.R.R.M. (BNA) 2682, 2687 (11th Cir. 1984); Green v. Oliver Realty Inc., 2 Indiv. Empl. Rights (BNA) 1333, 1339 (Pa. Super. Ct. 1987).

149. Aberman v. Malden Mills, 2 Indiv. Empl. Rights (BNA) 1430 (Minn. Ct. App. 1987); Chastain v. Kelly-Springfield Tire Co., 116 L.R.R.M. (BNA) 2682, 2687 (11th Cir. 1984).

150. Chastain v. Kelly-Springfield Tire Co., 116 L.R.R.M. (BNA) 2682, 2686–87 (11th Cir. 1984).

151. Gonzales v. United Southwest Nat'l Bank, 115 L.R.R.M. (BNA) 4853 (N.M. Sup. Ct. 1979).

152. United Security Life Ins. Co. v. Gregory, 115 L.R.R.M. (BNA) 4595, 4596 (Ala. Sup. Ct. 1967).

153. Page v. Carolina Coach Co., 115 L.R.R.M. (BNA) 4128, 4130 (4th Cir. 1982).

154. Gonzales v. United Southwest Nat'l Bank, 115 L.R.R.M. (BNA) 4853, 4855 (N.M. Sup. Ct. 1979).

155. Page v. Carolina Coach Co., 115 L.R.R.M. (BNA) 4128, 4130 (4th Cir. 1982).

156. Fn. 146, supra.

157. Wadeson v. American Family Mutual Insur. Co., 34 Empl. Prac. Dec. (CCH) 34,459 at 33,964 (N.D. Sup. Ct. 1984).

158. Chastain v. Kelly-Springfield Tire Co., 116 L.R.R.M. (BNA) 2682 fn. 7 at 2686 (11th Cir. 1984).

159. Heheman v. The E.W. Scripps Co., 92 Lab. Cas. (BNA) 13,089 (6th Cir. 1981).

160. Fn. 188, infra.

161. Terrebonne v. La. Ass'n of Educators, 115 L.R.R.M. (BNA) 5191 (La. Ct. App. 1983).

162. Halsell v. Kimberly-Clark Corp., 115 L.R.R.M. (BNA) 4476, 4483 (8th Cir. 1982).

163. Georgia Power Co. v. Busbin, 115 L.R.R.M. (BNA) 4310 (Ga. Sup. Ct. 1978); Holmes v. Union Oil Co. of Cal., 3 Indiv. Empl. Rights (BNA) 1219 (Idaho Ct. App. 1988).

164. Rabago-Alvarez v. Dart Industries, 115 L.R.R.M. (BNA) 4704 (Cal. Ct. App. 1976).

165. Hodge v. Evans Financial Corp., 115 L.R.R.M. (BNA) 4081 (D.C. Cir. 1983).

166. Lowenstein v. Harvard College, 115 L.R.R.M. (BNA) 4753 (D. Mass. 1970).

167. Holmes v. Union Oil of Cal., 2 Indiv. Empl. Rights (BNA) 1560 (Idaho Ct. App. 1987).

168. Hong v. Commodore International, Ltd., 115 L.R.R.M. (BNA) 4022 (D. Cal. 1982); Shah v. Am. Synthetic Rubber Corp., 99 Lab. Cas. (BNA) 55,423 (Ky. Sup. Ct. 1983).

169. Rabago-Alvarez v. Dart Industries, 115 L.R.R.M. (BNA) 4704, 4706 (Cal. Ct. App. 1976).

170. United Security Life Ins. Co. v. Gregory, 115 L.R.R.M. (BNA) 4595, 4596 (Ala. Sup. Ct. 1967); Scott v. Lane, 115 L.R.R.M. (BNA) 4233, 4234 (Ala. Sup. Ct. 1982).

171. Gonzales v. United Southwest Nat'l Bank, 115 L.R.R.M. (BNA) 4853, 4855 (N.M. Sup. Ct. 1979); Martin v. Federal Life Insur. Co., 115 L.R.R.M. (BNA) 4524, 4527 (Ill. App. Ct. 1982).

172. Rogers v. IBM, 115 L.R.R.M. (BNA) 4608, 4609 (D. Pa. 1980).

173. Pine River State Bank v. Mettille, 115 L.R.R.M. (BNA) 4493, 4497 (Minn. Sup. Ct. 1983).

174. Hodge v. Evans Financial Corp., 115 L.R.R.M. (BNA) 4081 (D.C. Cir. 1983).

175. Kitsos v. Mobile Gas Service Corp., 117 L.R.R.M. (BNA) 2336, 2337 (Ala. Sup. Ct. 1981).

176. Fn. 166, supra.

177. Beidler v. W.R. Grace, Inc., 115 L.R.R.M. (BNA) 4619, 4620 (D. Pa. 1978).

178. Forman v. BRI Corp., 115 L.R.R.M. (BNA) 5002, 5003 (D.Pa. 1982).

179. Roberts v. Wake Forest Univ., 115 L.R.R.M. (BNA) 4999 (N.C. Ct. App. 1982).

180. O'Neill v. ARA Services, Inc., 115 L.R.R.M. (BNA) 4846 (D. Pa. 1978).

181. McNulty v. Borden, Inc., 115 L.R.R.M. (BNA) 4563 (D. Pa. 1979).

182. Morris v. Park Newspapers, 115 L.R.R.M. (BNA) 4194 (Ga. Ct. App. 1979).

183. Gordon v. Matthew Bender & Co., 115 L.R.R.M. (BNA) 4100, 4107 (D. Ill. 1983).

184. Veno v. Meredith, 2 Indiv. Empl. Rights (BNA) 1702, 1708 (Pa. Super. Ct. 1986).

185. Darlington v. General Electric, 2 Indiv. Empl. Rights (BNA) 1666 (Pa. Super. Ct. 1986).

186. Engstrom v. Nureen & Co., 2 Indiv. Empl. Rights (BNA) 1205, 1210 (D. Pa. 1987).

187. Foley v. Community Oil Co., 115 L.R.R.M. (BNA) 4582, 4583 (D. N.H. 1974).

188. Eales v. Tanana Valley Medical Group, 115 L.R.R.M. (BNA) 4505 (Alaska Sup. Ct. 1983); See also K Mart Corp. v. Ponsock, 2 Indiv. Empl. Rights (BNA) 56 (Nev. Sup. Ct. 1987).

189. McKinney v. National Dairy Council, 115 L.R.R.M. (BNA) 4861, 4872 (D. Mass. 1980).

190. Geib v. Alan Wood Steel Co., 115 L.R.R.M. (BNA) 4843 (D. Pa. 1976); Engstrom v. Nuveen & Co., 2 Indiv. Empl. Rights (BNA) 1205 (D. Pa. 1987); Hunnewell v. Mfr. Hanover Trust Co., 2 Indiv. Empl. Rights (BNA) 933 (D. N.Y. 1986).

191. Walker v. Modern Realty, 115 L.R.R.M. (BNA) 4926 (8th Cir. 1982); Sullivan v. Heritage Foundation, 115 L.R.R.M. (BNA) 4621 (D.C. Cir. 1979); Lowenstein v. Harvard College, 115 L.R.R.M. (BNA) 4753 (D. Mass. 1970); Beidler v. W.R. Grace, Inc., 115 L.R.R.M. (BNA) 4619 (D. Pa. 1978); Hodge v. Evans Financial Corp., 2 Indiv. Empl. Rights (BNA) 395 (D.C. Cir. 1987); Johnston v. Panhandle Co-op Ass'n, 2 Indiv. Empl. Rights (BNA) 1080 (Neb. Sup. Ct. 1987); Roy v. Woonsocket Inst. for Savings, 3 Indiv. Empl. Rights (BNA) 314 (R.I. Sup. Ct. 1987); Cassel v. Ancilla Development Group, 4 Indiv. Empl. Rights (BNA) 221 (D. Ill. 1989).

192. S.D. Cod. Laws L. 60-1-3 (Supp. 1989).

193. Tipton v. Canadian Imperial Bank, 4 Indiv. Empl. Rights (BNA) 721 (11th Cir. 1989).

194. Toussaint v. Blue Cross & Blue Shield, 115 L.R.R.M. (BNA) 4708, 4718 (Mich. Sup. Ct. 1980).

195. Schroeder v. Dayton-Hudson Corp., 115 L.R.R.M. (BNA) 4365, fn. 3 at 4369 (D. Mich. 1977).

196. Bruffett v. Warner Communications, 115 L.R.R.M. (BNA) 4117, 4119 (3d Cir. 1982).

197. Hong v. Commodore Int'l Ltd., 115 L.R.R.M. (BNA) 4022 (D. Cal. 1982); Gordon v. Matthew Bender & Co., 115 L.R.R.M. (BNA) 4100 (D. Ill. 1983).

198. Pugh v. See's Candies, 3 Indiv. Empl. Rights (BNA) 945, 956 (Cal. Ct. App. 1988).

199. Diggs v. Pepsi-Cola, 3 Indiv. Empl. Rights (BNA) 1601, 1604 (6th Cir. 1988).

200. Turner v. I.B.M., 115 L.R.R.M. (BNA) 4887, 4892 (D. Ind. 1981).

201. Id. at 4891.

202. Geib v. Alan Wood Steel Co., 115 L.R.R.M. (BNA) 4843 (D. Pa. 1976).

203. Walker v. Modern Realty, 115 L.R.R.M. (BNA) 4926 (8th Cir. 1982).

204. Roberts v. Wake Forest Univ., 115 L.R.R.M. (BNA) 4999, 5000 (N.C. Ct. App. 1982).

205. Paice v. Maryland Racing Comm. 115 L.R.R.M. (BNA) 5004, 5005 (D. Md. 1982).

206. Darlington v. General Electric, 2 Indiv. Empl. Rights (BNA) 1666, 1670 (Pa. Super. Ct. 1986).

207. Payne v. K-D Mfg. Co., 2 Indiv. Empl. Rights (BNA) 459 (R.I. Sup. Ct. 1987).

208. Spearman v. Delco Remy, 4 Indiv. Empl. Rights (BNA) 843, 846 (D. Ind. 1989).

6

Just Cause and Evaluation

INTRODUCTION

A major emphasis to this point has been on the characteristics of the at will individual employment contract. There are, however, numerous examples of definite term or other employment contracts requiring just cause to discharge. This chapter focuses on the concept of just cause and the evaluation processes by which just cause may be determined. The continuing importance of the concept of employer rights is evident here, as it is throughout the whole range of employment issues. Just cause requirements (definite term contracts) potentially give greater job security to employees than at will contracts. Accordingly, this chapter is concerned with such things as the role of the employee's past work record, the accuracy of the employer's evaluation of the employee, and the employee's long-term service.

An at will employee can be discharged under the individual employment contract for any reason or no reason. Just cause is not required. For purposes of exercising the power of discharge, the employer has little need to evaluate the at will employee. However even where an at will discharge system exists, the employer may have to evaluate for other purposes, such as promotion, demotion, pay, and workforce morale. The use of an evaluation system may also be useful in an at will environment for the purpose of discharge. Virtually any employee can be discharged for just cause. Where the employer can show the existence of cause for the discharge of an employee, the employer has the strongest defense in the event of a wrongful discharge suit by either an at will or definite term employee. Just cause can, therefore, be a useful concept in the at will employment context.

Just cause restrictions on discharge and evaluation procedures to measure performance are common clauses in collective bargaining agreements. Just cause is usually a prerequisite for the discharge of an employee during the term of a fixed term, individual employment contract. In either the collective bargaining or the individual fixed term contract situation, the evaluation process is frequently the way in which just cause will be established. The purpose of this chapter is to consider some of the issues that may arise concerning the use of just cause and evaluations.

EMPLOYER AND EMPLOYEE INTERESTS

It is a basic right of the employer to evaluate employees. The right to make decisions concerning the efficiency of the business includes a right to direct the labor force.[1] A part of this inherent or entrepreneurial right is the power to promulgate and enforce rules pertaining to evaluation, discipline, and efficiency.[2] Presumably, the evaluation should reflect to the ability of the employees to contribute to the goal of business efficiency. The employee who cannot meet the employer's rules is subject to discharge, discipline, or other adverse personnel decisions. The employee who can meet the employer's requirements can often expect to be rewarded.

An adverse evaluation may lead to employee discipline. It is commonly stated that punishment is not the purpose of discipline.[3] Rather, the purpose of discipline is to cause the employee to realize that the employee's actions were improper and to provide an opportunity for change and improvement in the employee's conduct.[4] Another purpose of discipline is to inform other workers that certain actions are improper.[5] The definition of just cause is critical to making discipline decisions.

The employee can reasonably expect that favorable evaluations should contribute to job security. Similarly, where the employee avoids actions that might constitute just cause, the employee can reasonably expect a more secure job future. The long-term employee has a special interest in evaluations. The long-term employee, who may also be an older employee, usually has a historical record of acceptable or better job evaluations. The long-term employee has a significant investment in the evaluations. The employee can reasonably expect that accumulated, favorable evaluations should contribute to future job security. A just cause requirement may take into account these elements of long-term service and favorable evaluations.

A major interest of many employees is to obtain an "accurate" evaluation. Employees feel that an accurate evaluation will demonstrate that they are not the type of employee that should be subject to discharge or that they are the type that should be rewarded when the opportunity arises. In litigation with the employer over a discharge, employees will frequently attempt to show that the employer's negative evaluation is not accurate, or that there was no just cause, or that the favorable evaluations outweigh any unfavorable comments. Arguments made in litigation indicate that employees believe that accuracy in evaluation is a critical element in the personnel system.

SUBSTANCE AND PROCEDURE

The just cause concept is composed of at least two components. One is procedural and it is concerned with the evaluation process by which it will be determined that cause exists.[6] The second component is substantive and is concerned with the identification of specific employee actions or omissions that give the employer cause to discharge.

As indicated above, the employee owes a number of duties to the employer that are implied from the nature of an employment relationship in our economic system. Some of these duties are discussed in Chapter 3. In addition, the employer may have issued an employee handbook that lists specific duties or examples of just cause violations. Courts generally hold that such a handbook list is not necessarily the exclusive basis upon which a finding of just cause can be made.[7] The list may only be illustrative, not complete or exclusive. Extensive lists of specific offenses have also been identified in treatises.[8]

Employers are entitled to respond to changing economic conditions and take personnel actions related to relocation, reorganization, or reduction in force. Economic conditions have been identified as being an adequate basis for a finding of just cause.[9] Thus a significant aspect of the substantive component of just cause is employer rights. Where the employer is primarily and in good faith motivated by business judgment concerns, the employer has gone a long way toward taking personnel actions based on just cause.

In summary, just cause consists of procedural and substantive elements. Substantive elements may be found in the employer rights doctrine, the implied duties of employees, and the express duties owed by the employee to the employer. Just cause takes account of changing business conditions.

EVALUATION CRITERIA

Evaluations may be based on objective or subjective criteria, or some combination of the two. The use of subjective criteria makes it difficult for the employee to effectively challenge the decision and for a court to identify a basis on which to overturn an adverse personnel action, especially in light of the deference given to the employer's business judgment. In a discharge situation, the employee may try to challenge the substance of the evaluation. The less fact specific (more subjective) the evaluation, the more difficult it is for the employee to refute the employer's judgment. It becomes the employee's opinion against the employer's opinion in a system that does not usually permit second guessing employers. Where the basis of a complaint is conflicting opinions, the courts are likely to defer to the employer.

Greater reliance on vague and subjective criteria will be permitted when the employer is dealing with higher level employees. The courts acknowledge that those jobs have elements that are more difficult to describe with precision, giving the employer greater latitude in evaluating the higher level employee.[10] Such general notions as trust, confidence, and getting along become important criteria.

The employer handbook may be treated as a contract and may spell out criteria or procedures used to select employees for promotion, filling vacancies, or discharge. The mere identification of descriptive criteria alone is not likely to be treated as being the only element of the contract. The employer has the right to apply the criteria through an exercise of managerial judgment.[11] Even where the statements speak in terms of largely objective qualifications for a position, it does not mean that merely possessing the qualifications automatically entitles that employee to the position.

The handbook may be found not to be a contract. The court may find the language too vague to create a binding promise. The court may also say merely listing of criteria does not mean they are all of equal weight.[12] Implicit in any listing of criteria is the notion that a judgmental choice is to be made by the employer.[13] The employer is entitled to the use of managerial judgment in balancing the weight to be given the criteria.[14] In applying the criteria, the employer is permitted to make an honest mistake in the application of the criteria to the selected person's abilities.[15] Courts will be very reluctant to second guess even these mistaken judgments.

In summary, evaluations may involve subjective or objective criteria. Whereas subjective criteria give the employer the most decisional latitude, objective criteria still assume that the employer has a range of choices in which to exercise the employer's judgment about the employee.

PERSONALITY DISPUTES AND BIAS

Personality disputes and employee attitudinal problems are major topics in the case law of the workplace. The employee may attempt to downplay an adverse evaluation by claiming that the evaluation reflects only a personality dispute and it is not a true measure of the employee's performance. Such an attack on the evaluation will rarely be effective.

Employers are entitled to discharge employees who cannot get along. The career of an employee with a long record of favorable evaluations may be put in jeopardy when the personal relationship with the employer breaks down. An employer may be permitted to discharge a higher level employee when the trust relationship is destroyed.[16] Where there is a personality clash affecting business efficiency, the employer is permitted to take adverse action.[17]

Attitude becomes increasingly important as the employee moves to higher level positions.[18] The employer is entitled to employees who maintain a proper attitude toward their supervisors and their job.[19] The employee will not successfully diminish the evidentiary value of the employer's evaluation by attempting to dismiss the findings as a mere "personality dispute."

A personality dispute may manifest itself in a claim that the decider-evaluator was biased against the employee. Where there is clear evidence of bias, a court may listen to the argument.[20] However, clear evidence is likely to be the exceptional case. Showing the existence of a mere dislike between the two individuals, standing alone, is insufficient.[21] Showing a personality clash and a failure by the evaluator to follow promulgated guidelines may be insufficient when there is no evidence of disparate treatment.[22] Even under the constitutional standard of due process, it is said that "the law does not presume that a supervisor who proposes to remove an employee is incapable of changing his or her mind."[23] If there is evidence of personal dislike and evidence of unsatisfactory job performance, the evidence of unsatisfactory job performance may outweigh the personal dislike factor and be sufficient for the court to support the employer's overall decision to terminate the employee.

In summary, employees frequently seek to avoid the consequences of unfavorable evaluations by claiming they are a product of a personality dispute. However, getting along and having a proper attitude are criteria that the employer is permitted to judge. Courts usually will not find that an evaluation is the product of improper bias merely because the evaluator disliked the employee. Specific evidence of bias must be shown.

"FAULTY" EVALUATIONS

Employees may seek to demonstrate that the employer's evaluation was faulty. "Faulty" is used here in the sense that the employer has made an evaluation that does not reflect his or her actual contribution to business efficiency or does not reflect the employee's view of the employee's contribution. For example, the employee may have been efficient in fact, but the employer gave the employee an unfavorable evaluation.

There is case law that permits employers to discharge on the basis of questionable evaluations. These cases illustrate the courts' reluctance to second guess the employer. Courts or arbitrators have permitted discharges that they have described in the following terms: arbitrary and malicious,[24] shortsighted and narrowminded,[25] negligent,[26] inhumane,[27] hardhearted,[28] unfair,[29] and reprehensible.[30] The employee may indeed be able to show that the evaluation and resultant discharge were faulty, but that alone may not be sufficient to provide a remedy to the employee. The employee has to show breach of a contract or of some other duty before a legal remedy may be available. Good faith mistakes by the employer are permitted.[31] The at will employee, of course, can be discharged for no reason or for a faulty reason.

Not all cases are as pessimistic as the foregoing. Where an evaluation can be shown to be the product of the supervisor's personal dislike of the employee, rather than on the employee's performance, an arbitrator applying just cause may redress the wrong.[32] Where cause is at issue and the evaluation is made by a person who was not employee's supervisor and who did not have first-hand information, the evaluation may carry little weight.[33] Antidiscrimination statutes may become involved. Reliance on faulty reasons or on arbitrary reasons may help the employee prove a prima facie case. Where the employer simply fired the oldest workers without checking the employees' evaluations, the action was disallowed.[34] Where an employer had no written standards, no rationale for the evaluation, and no records of employee performance, a court disallowed the employer's action.[35] These cases, however, must be read in the light of a court's reluctance to second guess an employer, especially in close cases.

Where the employer has a contractual or other duty to the employee to conduct an evaluation, the employer may have a duty to use reasonable care in performing the evaluation. Negligence in conducting the evaluation may be a breach of that duty.[36] However, this is merely a variation of the larger point that an employee has greater rights under a contract with specific terms than under an oral contract or under a noncontractual handbook.

Where state law permits a discharged employee to request a "service letter" from the employer, the employer is required to give the employee the reasons for the discharge. Punitive damages may be awarded under the statute if the employer is not truthful in the letter concerning the reasons for personnel action.[37]

The employer runs other risks by relying on a flawed evaluation. Courts often permit the use of subjective criteria,[38] and the employer may prefer the looser subjective system. However, if a claim of protected class discrimination is made, it may be easier for the employee to substantiate the prima facie case of the discrimination claim when the employer uses subjective or at will criteria. The employee may be able to show that the proffered reasons were a pretext for discrimination when the employer cannot come forward with a specific business or other legitimate, nondiscriminatory reason for the decision.[39] However, merely because subjective criteria were used does not necessarily prove that discrimination occurred.[40] A jury might be permitted to find discrimination based upon a discharge for recent "poor performance" where there is a prior history of favorable evaluations.[41] The faulty evaluation might be damaging to the employer if it was used in an attempt to conceal the real reason for the discharge, and the real reason was contrary to public policy.[42]

In summary, employees frequently complain that an unfavorable evaluation or personnel decision was faulty or incorrect. The courts are generally unwilling to second guess the employer even when they might disagree with the decision. The courts do not remedy bad judgment. They are concerned with only a narrow range of specific legal rights. Where the evaluation is totally baseless the court may permit redress. Where there are merely conflicting opinions between the employer and the employee, the courts will usually side with the employer. Other sources of rights, such as antidiscrimination statutes may pay greater attention to arbitrary evaluations.

NONWORK ACTIVITIES

Generally, an employee's conduct away from the workplace is not a matter that the employer can consider in the workplace evaluation, especially in arbitration.[43] However, where the outside conduct actually impacts on the workplace, the employer may properly consider it. In one such situation, an off duty employee made harassing telephone calls to the home of a supervisor. Discharge of the employee was upheld because of the carryover effect on the workplace.[44] Criteria to test the on duty impact of off duty activity include the following: whether the actions of the employee harmed the employer's reputation or product, whether the actions rendered the employee unable to perform his or her duties or to appear for work, or whether the activities led to the refusal, reluctance, or inability of other employees to work with the employee in question.[45] These are, of course, traditional matters of concern for conduct in the workplace, too.

TALENT AND COMPETENT PAST PERFORMANCE

A talented employee will usually expect to receive a favorable evaluation. However, the evaluation process is more than a measure of pure talent. For example, a gifted employee may be of little value to an employer if that employee cannot work effectively with others. Such an otherwise talented employee may be dismissed, not withstanding unrefuted proof of a high level of talent.[46] Evaluation of personality or attitudinal matters is always permitted as part of the overall evaluation and it is permitted to involve some degree of subjective determination.

In the same vein, past favorable evaluations may not guarantee success in the future. In many personnel systems, an employee is doubtlessly justified in relying on past good evaluations as some protection against adverse personnel decisions or as a favorable element for advancement. However, an employee who has favorable evaluations and who has received pay increases or promotions may still be subject to discharge on performance grounds.[47] An employee evaluated as competent may still be passed over for a promotion, where the employer feels that the selected employee will perform in a "better" manner.[48]

The past favorable evaluations may still serve protective functions. If the employer has charged the employee with a specific offense such as incompetence (just cause for discharge), past favorable evaluations can be viewed by the jury as a basis for saying that the discharge was not actually based on the specific charge of incompetence.[49] If the employer's basis for decision is found to be erroneous, then the employee was not discharged for cause, and the employer may be in violation of the employment contract. The past evaluations may be considered where a discharged employee seeks an injunction to remain working pending the outcome of the dispute,[50] or where an employer is seeking a judgment notwithstanding a jury verdict in favor of the employee.[51] A favorable evaluation followed by a discharge may be some evidence of the minimal prima facie case needed to be shown by the employee in age discrimination suits.[52]

In summary, a solid past work record is a valuable asset for the employee. However, there are numerous instances where the employer has been permitted to take adverse personnel action in the face of such a record. The employer is permitted to evaluate past performance in the light of present or changed workplace circumstances.

EMPLOYEE AND OUTSIDER EVALUATIONS

When employees are in competition for a position or promotion, the losing worker may feel that the decision was improperly or unfairly made. The losing employee may attempt to show that he or she was more qualified than the winner. In other words, the losing employee may offer the employee's own evaluation of the relative qualifications of the two contenders. Courts are reluctant to accept this argument involving comparative qualifications. This reluctance may be expressed by procedural rulings. When the issue of comparative qualifications is raised, courts may put the burden of proving the point on the complaining employee rather than on the employer who actually made the determination.[53] In close cases, the party with the burden of proof is likely to lose. Carrying the burden of proof usually means proving the point by a preponderance of the evidence. Because objective standards for the precise measure of qualifications in many jobs are frequently lacking, this becomes a very difficult burden. There is little to indicate that a long, favorable past record, standing alone, will meet this comparative qualifications burden when two employees were in competition.

By the same token, the view of most courts is that the employer's evaluation is the only measure of importance.[54] The employee's own evaluation of him- or herself is not given much weight.[55] The evaluation of coworkers is similarly not given much weight.[56] Courts also express little interest in how other outsiders view the employee's work record.[57] The courts are reluctant to second guess the employer, and are reluctant to accept measurements of the employee made by anyone other than the authorized employer.[58] In the absence of discrimination, emphasizing the positive side of a mixed work record will not convince the court that there has been an error.[59]

In an ironic twist, one court used the employee's self-evaluation as evidence of propriety of the discharge. The employer in the case had a system whereby employees prepared a written self-evaluation, which became part of their personnel record. One employee noted in the self-evaluation that the employee could improve some aspects of the employee's performance. The court used the employee's own evaluation statement on improvement as evidence to partially justify upholding the employer's discharge action.[60] The result can be read as a caution to all employees who write self-evaluations.

In summary, courts will not give weight to an evaluation presented by someone other than the employer. They weigh only the employer's evaluation in discharge disputes. Comparative evaluations are seldom convincing.

RELEVANT TIME

A major issue for the long-term employee concerns the relevant time period to consider in an evaluation. There are at least two choices. One is making each evaluation a review of the total performance of the employee up to that date. Another is making the evaluation a review of the most immediate period of performance since the last evaluation. In some workplaces the collective bargaining contract may provide that prior offenses can be "wiped clean" after the passage of a specified time period.[61]

The cases are inconsistent in their approach to the relevant time period. One series of cases permits consideration of only the current period of performance. This may benefit some long-term employees in special cases. A look at the entire record may show some prior blotches. If the employer cannot consider them because they are ancient history and the recent performance has been acceptable, the employer may not be permitted to take adverse action. For example, an employee who had falsified the original employment application and whose falsification was not discovered until years later was protected by an arbitrator who found that the recent performance was a better indication of employee performance.[62] In another situation, a court accepted the arbitrator's finding that actual recent performance was a better measure than looking to an employee's reasons for leaving prior jobs and an arrest record that occurred many years ago.[63]

In the second series of cases, the courts have emphasized the employee's total record. For example, an employer sought to deny a merit pay increase on the basis of a teacher's prior three years of performance. The court affirmed an arbitrator's decision that rejected this approach. The arbitrator said that the teacher's tenure would be illusory if the employer could disregard the long-term record of performance.[64] In contrast, another court stated that prior long-term performance does not entitle the employee to a special status.[65] A court found a 1982 evaluation not relevant to a 1984 discharge.[66]

One court discussed the use of a "recency" factor in the following terms: "While a recency factor may sometimes be justifiable . . . the

disparate impact on older persons is patent. Older persons, by definition, are more likely than younger persons to have older work experience, and such experience is discounted when a recency factor is
used."[67]

For other measurements, the most recent data may be needed.
Health records are an example.

> However, even where the contract does not contain the physical
> ability requirement, it has been said that the term "ability" in-
> cludes physical (and mental) ability. Health records showing an
> employee's physical condition have been considered as "tangible
> and objective" evidence of fitness and ability; but "old" records
> as to an employee's physical condition ordinarily may not be
> relied upon, arbitrators favoring more recent medical evidence
> concerning such matters.[68]

In summary, there are mixed results on the issue of the relevant time
frame for evaluations. The two choices are the full record and the more
recent record of the employee. The mixed results seem to be a reflection of the immediate issue being considered. Some long-term
employees benefit the most if the entire record is considered; others
may benefit if the more recent record is considered.

DUTY TO WARN, INVESTIGATE CHANGES, OR TRAIN

A long-term employee will usually have an overall favorable record
and will expect that current and past evaluations will be of a similar
character. It may come as a great surprise if the employer now finds
that performance to be lacking. The question arises as to whether the
employer is under a duty to warn the employee if the employee's
performance begins to slip. The general rule appears to be that the
employer is under no duty to warn the employee about complaints
about the employee's performance.[69]

A few cases, however, suggest that the employer may have some
duty to warn the long-term employee. One has stated that a failure to
inform a long-term employee of the possibility of discharge for the
employee's performance is negligence.

> The court does not hold that a particular length of service always
> and necessarily creates a duty to give prior notice of discharge.
> Each case is decided on its own facts. The court merely considers
> length of service to be a relevant factor in deciding whether the

failure to give notice was careless or negligent in a particular case.[70]

Some promulgated personnel policies may create a reasonable expectation of notice and opportunity to improve before a discharge will occur.[71] A court found strong evidence suggesting discrimination when the employee with favorable evaluations was demoted without notice of needed improvement.[72] The duty to warn may relate to the duty to evaluate. There may be a contractual or handbook obligation to evaluate.[73] In such a case, there may also be found to be a contractual duty to warn the employee.

Related to the issue of a duty to warn a long-term employee about sinking evaluations is the question of whether the employer has a duty to probe sudden changes in the employee's performance. In general, there is no such duty. One court, however, did find that an employer is under a duty to investigate the reasons underlying a sudden change in the performance of a long-term employee.[74] This is consistent with the occasionally expressed notion that a long-term employee is entitled to a greater degree of care than other employees in the evaluation process.[75] One arbitrator has indicated that basic fairness requires that the employer attempt to ascertain the reason for a sudden change in attitude or performance that is out of character for the employee. The employer should then attempt to remedy the problem.[76] For example, the sudden change may indicate emotional problems that may be subject to resolution.[77] The test for remedial action becomes whether the employee could be rehabilitated to become an effective employee once again.[78] However, the duty to probe and warn is generally an exception.

A sudden change in the evaluations of an employee may become a red flag for a court considering a charge of discrimination against the employer. A dramatic change in evaluations may provide evidence toward the minimal prima facie case that an employee must show in order to overcome an employer's motion to dismiss.[79] A sudden change may also indicate some evidence of unlawful discrimination itself.[80]

An employee may be subject to discharge for poor performance. The employee may challenge the discharge by claiming that he or she received inadequate training. A court responded to that defense by stating that, absent a special duty in contract, the employer had no duty to train.[81]

In summary, courts are generally reluctant to impose a duty on the employer to warn employees of a slipping work record, to investigate obvious changes in employee performance, or to adequately train an employee. Arbitrators may be less reluctant to impose some of these duties.

FAILURE OF EMPLOYER TO FOLLOW POLICIES OR STATEMENTS

When there is no contractual duty involved, an employee will not be able to effectively challenge an evaluation or discharge by reason of the employer's failure to follow the employer's own personnel procedures.[82] The mere promulgation of handbook procedures does not constitute the making of a contract with the employees, in the absence of additional evidence.[83] In one situation, an employee was told that he could be fired "should you not achieve." a certain rating by November 1. Later, but prior to November 1, the employee was discharged. The court held that it was not a wrongful discharge because the warning did not constitute a contract of employment until the November 1 date.[84] The employee continued to be an at will employee and could be discharged at any time for any reason. Some courts have held that even a discharge resulting from the employer's own negligence does not alter this rule.[85]

An at will employee is subject to discharge without reason. A court may find that the employer's failure to follow the employer's layoff procedures does not change this status.[86] However, an at will employee is not prohibited from contracting job security provisions.[87] Where there is no contract, such as the use of an employee handbook that has effective disclaimers, there is no contractual duty to follow the handbook procedures.[88]

The failure to follow procedures may be raised in the context of a past practice where the employer has never before disciplined an employee for the specific act at issue. An employer will not be prevented from acting in such a first time case where it is acting on the basis of new information that causes it to change its past policy.[89] Similarly, an employer who was lenient in the past may have had enough and will be permitted to tighten up the standards.[90] An employer is also permitted to make some mistakes.[91] A failure to enforce a policy in the past may not be found to be a waiver in all future cases.[92]

In arbitration, disparate treatment in like cases will be a basis on which an arbitrator might overturn or mitigate an employer action. However, to find disparate treatment, the facts of the cases must be similar.[93]

Discharge may result from the cumulative effect of a progression of employee actions or from a single act of gross misconduct. Some employee handbooks may provide for a series of disciplinary steps, commonly called progressive discipline, before issuing a final discharge. Where an employee is discharged without an opportunity to go through progressive discipline, the employee may be able to prove a violation of the handbook. However, if the action of the employee was particularly heinous or serious, courts will not require the employer to use progressive discipline.[94] Thus some failures to use progressive discipline are evidence of having followed the promulgated procedures, and not evidence of disparate treatment.

In summary, the failure of the employer to follow existing procedures in evaluating employees is not improper where there is no contractual duty to follow a handbook or past practice. The mere promulgation of handbook procedures does not necessarily create a contractual duty. Inaction in enforcing procedures in the past is not necessarily viewed as a waiver. Arbitrators might provide a remedy where there is disparate treatment of employees.

EXPLICIT AND IMPLICIT JUST CAUSE

One court defined a just cause discharge in terms of a cause finding based on facts supported by substantial evidence, facts reasonably believed by the employer to be true, and not done for any arbitrary, capricious, or illegal reason.[95] A determination of just cause for an employer is a very central finding in employment contract litigation. A just cause discharge is valid regardless of whether the employee is an at will employee or is under a definite term contract.[96] There are numerous acts that violate an employee's basic obligations and will constitute cause whether they are mentioned in a contract or not. Some are obvious, such as absenteeism, theft, and fighting.[97] Others are not always so clearly defined. The just cause requirement obviously applies where the contract demands it. However, just cause requirements may also be implied.

An employer might fall under a just cause requirement because of an explicit clause in a contract with the employee. Such a contract clause may be implied where the employer has not properly disclaimed the contractual character of the handbook.[98] The contract does not have to use the magic words "just cause."[99] In arbitration, an arbitrator dealing with a contract that has no just cause clause might imply such a clause.[100] The mere presence of an arbitration clause in the absence of a just cause clause may imply that just cause requirements are nonetheless applicable. One arbitrator stated that when a seniority clause and a grievance arbitration clause are found in a contract, a just cause provision can be implied.[101] If just cause were not implied, there would be little meaning in the seniority provision and little for the arbitrator to do.

To the contrary, a court has indicated that courts do not have the same power to imply just cause in the way an arbitrator might.[102] However, once a just cause requirement is found, the substantive definition of just cause is probably the same under collective bargaining contracts and individual contracts.[103] A progressive discipline clause cannot be the basis of judicially implying a just cause requirement.[104]

In summary, an arbitrator may be able to imply a just cause clause into a contract if other related clauses are present. Courts generally will not imply such a clause.

Where just cause applies, courts and arbitrators use similar definitions of the substance of just cause, but they may have different procedural requirements.

HIGHER LEVEL EMPLOYEES

Determining cause can be a complex process. Cause for discharge from a higher level job involves different factors than those used in lower level jobs. The number of higher level discharges may be small because of the limited number of higher level employees. This means that there will be fewer precedents and that instances of disparate treatment will be more difficult to prove. Where there are few examples, it may be that no clear good cause definitions or practices have been developed by a particular employer.[105] When an employer in such a circumstance claims to have cause to discharge the higher level employee, the courts may be even more reluctant to second guess the employer's judgment. Courts say that an employer must be given greater latitude in the discharge of higher level employees than with lower level employees.[106] Courts permit less specific job descriptions in evaluating the higher level positions. In lower level jobs, by comparison, arbitrators have identified a variety of topics that constitute cause.[107]

LONG-TERM EMPLOYEES

One court suggested that a different cause standard should be adopted for long-term employees than that used for other workers. However, there is no general requirement for this and no clear indication what the different standard would be. Nonetheless, the court stated that "good cause" in the context of being a manager after 32 years was different from the standard applicable in determining the propriety of an employee's termination under a contract for a specified term.[108] The court did not make it clear whether the difference would be in substance, procedure, or both.

In collective bargaining arbitration, long-term service is a factor of mitigation that is given significant attention.[109] Long-term service considerations have been found to be appropriate beginning at the six-year mark, at least.[110]

PROVING FACTS: EMPLOYER, COURTS, AND JURIES

The just cause requirement can involve at least two different levels of accuracy. One level would require that the employer have a factual basis for the just cause finding. The second level would require that the employer need only have a reasonable belief in the existence of facts leading to just cause. Many courts accept the reasonable belief approach.

A number of courts apply the rule that where just cause applies, the employer need only act on a reasonable belief that just cause exists. The employer does not have to show that the general reason that is being relied upon is provable by a preponderance of the evidence or is commonly accepted in the overall community as adequate grounds for discharge.[111] The discussion becomes further complicated by using language that includes the phrases of reasonableness, good faith, bad faith, and just cause as though the terms were interchangeable.

The complexity of the arguments is suggested by the following comment:

> The focus of the inquiry . . . was not a determination of whether [the employee] was in fact performing his job adequately, but rather, whether there was sufficient evidence of unsatisfactory performance to be a legitimate concern of his employer. This differs from a determination that just cause existed for the termination because of unsatisfactory job performance, which would necessitate a finding that his job performance was unsatisfactory.[112]

What the court seems to be saying is that if the employer discharged in the reasonable belief that there was inadequate performance, the discharge would be valid regardless of whether there were actual facts objectively demonstrating adequate or inadequate performance. This comports with the doctrine that the employer is entitled to make a good faith mistake.[113]

Another court described the question of whether just cause involves an objective or subjective standard in reference to the role of the jury. The presence of a jury complicates the expression of the matter. The court stated, in part:

> While the promise to terminate employment only for cause includes the right to have the employer's decision reviewed, it does not include a right to be discharged only with the concurrence of the communal judgment of the jury. Nevertheless, we have considered and rejected the alternative of instructing the jury that it may not find a breach if it finds that the employers decision to discharge the employee was not unreasonable under the circumstances. Such an instruction would transform a good cause contract into a satisfaction (at will) contract.[114]

The court seems to be saying that the contract can define good cause and the jury's role is applying that definition to the facts. The jury cannot make up its own definition and cannot second guess the employer.[115] If it can be demonstrated that the employer acted in bad faith, then the good cause standard has not been met.[116] Bad faith was described as meaning reasons that "are trivial, capricious, unrelated to business needs or goals, or pretextual."[117]

The suggestion has been made in some cases that where the just cause is based solely on an identified, specific reason such as dishonesty, the employee can attempt to show that the specific reason did not exist.[118] This may be another way of saying that a discharge based on a nonexistent reason is not a good faith discharge. It treats cause based on a single, specific reason different from where a more general basis of cause is alleged. It is not clear why this distinction exists, given the doctrines of reasonable belief and good faith mistakes.

The following description was offered by another court:

> When reviewing a discharge decision of a private employer in a contract case ... [the company handbook required cause] the court need only find that there was substantial evidence to support the employer decision and that the employer believed that evidence and acted in good faith in discharging the worker. It need not also determine that what the employer believed was true.[119]

This court would permit actions based on cause to turn essentially on the employer's reasonable belief, so long as there was some evidence to support the employer's decision. Substantial evidence is usually defined as a reasonable amount of evidence that may be less than a preponderance or 51 percent of all of the evidence.[120]

When the employee claims a discharge was based on prohibited discrimination, the employer may need to show some nondiscriminatory reason for the action. This may be a subjective reason. The nondiscriminatory reason need not be one that can be demonstrated to be factually true, because the issue is whether there was a mental intent to discriminate. Even if the employer acts on the basis of false facts, the employer may not have acted on the basis of an intent to discriminate. Where specific intent to discriminate is required, that state of mind can be overcome so long as the employer subjectively believes a certain set of facts existed. In one case an employer received complaints concerning an employee and the employee was discharged. The discharge was permitted to stand, on the rationale that the important element was that complaints were received and considered, thus showing that an intent to discriminate was not present.[121]

Where there is no factual basis whatsoever for the discharge decision and cause is required, the employer's action may be disapproved by the courts. There may be no basis for the decision where the employer has no immediate knowledge about the performance of the employee. For example, a discharge was not permitted to stand where the employer testified that the employer could not, in fact, recall the employee's performance.[122]

The arbitration authorities Elkouri and Elkouri state:

> Little if any weight has been accorded supervisory opinion where the company relied upon such opinion concerning one of the bidders while not consulting supervisors of another bidder at all, and where the supervisors consulted had little or no opportunity to observe the men they were rating and were not familiar with the requirements of the job being bid upon.[123]

In the same vein, that Elkouris' treatise also states: "While the opinion of supervisors regarding the ability of the employee is considered important and is entitled at least to some consideration, such opinion without factual support will not be deemed conclusive."[124] The role of the arbitrator is to find the facts. The arbitrator may require a higher level of proof than the courts require.

In summary, employers are permitted to use objective or subjective standards of just cause. The courts will not require factual proof of job inadequacy, only enough proof to cause the employer to be reasonably concerned. Neither courts nor juries will substitute their judgment for that of the employer. However, bad faith decisions may not constitute just cause. A total lack of factual basis for a decision is not just cause. The arbitration hearing is designed to find facts and reasonable employer belief may be insufficient. In addition, an arbitrator can apply the mitigation doctrine where the facts and the penalty do not match.

GOOD FAITH AND JUST CAUSE

The covenant of good faith and the doctrine of just cause are frequently seen by the employee as being related. That is not the reality seen by the courts. The covenant implies the exercise of good faith, but the application of that good faith does not require that the employer show just cause for a discharge.[125] One court has stated that "termination in the absence of good cause does not establish bad faith."[126] The absence of good faith does not necessarily imply bad faith, but rather it apparently relates to some ill defined middle ground. Presumably, proof of actual bad faith would show a breach of the covenant. The good faith requirement relates only to terms in an existing employment agreement and is not a vehicle used to bring in additional terms or general morality terms not contained in the contract.[127]

As discussed above, the courts prefer to play a limited role in reviewing the employer's decisions. The courts reject the notion that the employer must always act in good faith, even under the covenant of good faith. The employee who can only show a lack of good faith on the part of the employer usually has not helped advance the case. The courts will usually require the employee to show actual bad faith before they will consider overturning the employer's decision under the covenant. Bad faith may be shown by a violation of public policy or actions intended to deny contractual rights to the employee.

Bad faith is difficult to prove. Employees frequently feel or allege that there has been bad faith, but they are usually unable to prove it. Bad faith has been shown in a few situations, such as those involving pensions and sales commissions. In one, an employer discharged the employee shortly before the vesting of the employee's pension. The court determined this to be abusive and in violation of the state's public policy.[128] In another, an employer fired a salesman shortly after the salesman obtained a large order. The court determined that part of the reason for the discharge was to minimize the bonus the employee would receive.[129]

The absence of good faith alone is usually insufficient proof that bad faith was present. The expression of an efficiency or business related basis for the decision would seem to be enough to overcome bad faith in many disputes. The following statement was made on this topic by one court:

> But to imply into each employment contract a duty to terminate in good faith would seem to subject each discharge to judicial incursions into the amorphous concept of bad faith. We are not persuaded that the protection of employees requires such an intrusion on the employment relationship or such an imposition on the courts.[130]

This statement should be compared with the following, which is doubtlessly a minority notion: "We hold that a termination by the employer of a contract of employment at will which is motivated by bad faith or malice or based on retaliation is not in the best interest of the *economic system* or the public good and constitutes a breach of the employment contract."[131] (Emphasis added.) This is also a rare example of a court using a balance that includes a public interest, namely the economic system.

In summary, employees frequently claim that a discharge not solidly based on factual reasons lacks good faith and therefore is not based on just cause. Courts defer to the employer's judgment and are unwilling to equate the absence of good faith with the presence of bad faith. Courts say that the covenant of good faith and fair dealing is separate and distinct from a just cause requirement. Bad faith will not constitute just cause. Bad faith must be shown to affirmatively exist. Bad faith is not proved, courts say, merely by showing that good faith was lacking. The application of doctrines of good faith, bad faith, and just cause is a complex subject. The differences between them is often measured in terms of shades of gray, and it is not capable of being expressed in terms of black and white.

MITIGATION

To the extent that the court will review the employer's decision, it will usually only review to determine if there was just cause for the discharge. It will not review whether discharge is too severe a discipline, given the nature of the cause. An arbitrator under a collective bargaining contract, however, will usually review the work record to determine if the discharge is appropriate or whether it is too harsh.[132] This reflects, in part, the different role of the arbitrator, as compared to the court. The collective bargaining arbitrator has usually been invited into the dispute under the terms of the contract as agreed to by the parties.[133]

SPECIFIC OFFENSES AND SPECIFIC KNOWLEDGE

An employment agreement may contain both a just cause provision and a list of specific employee offenses. No general just cause question arises where the employee is discharged for one of the specified reasons in the list of offenses. The employee may also be discharged for reasons not included in the list of offenses, but included in generally accepted definitions of just cause.[134] The use of the list of offenses may give rise to issues that are separate and distinct from those found in just cause. The specific (list) does not control the general (just cause).

Where a specific offense is given as the basis of the discharge, one court described the role of the jury in the following terms. "Where the employer claims that the employee was discharged for specific misconduct—intoxication, dishonesty, insubordination—and the employee claims that he did not commit the misconduct alleged, the question is one of fact for the jury: Did the employee do what the employer said he did?"[135] Courts have indicated, as stated above, that where general just cause is involved, the jury may not be permitted to decide whether the employee actually did what the employer said the employee did. The jury may only decide if the employer's action based on that belief was reasonable. Where a specific, objectively ascertainable offense is charged, the role of jury seems to be more of that of a factfinder. The decisions are not entirely clear on this point.

Just cause also contains an important procedural element in addition to the substantive element. Employee knowledge of specific personnel rules is an important element for some courts in just cause situations. A court has stated: "'Just cause' includes only conduct that employee knows is subject to discipline."[136] The court would impose a duty on the employer to make work rules and to properly promulgate them to the employees. However, as indicated above, a number of courts permit vague personnel standards or subjective personnel evaluations which the employer might not be able to fully define and cannot fully promulgate.

In the public sector, statutes may require a showing of just cause. One court defined this statutory just cause in the following terms:

In cases involving statutory protection for public employees, "cause" has been defined as a substantial shortcoming which renders the employee's continuance in his position in some way detrimental to the discipline and efficiency of the employer and which the law and sound public policy recognize as good cause for no longer holding the position.[137]

In summary, an employer who discharges for a specifically identified offense may have to prove the employee committed that action. Where more general reasons are given, the employer may need only a reasonable belief to support the discharge. Just cause procedural elements may require that the employer promulgate rules so that the employee has more specific knowledge of what is prohibited. Statutes requiring just cause in the public sector may require a greater factual showing of proof of the employee's shortcomings and require more than reasonable employer belief.

DISPARATE TREATMENT

Just cause requirements may be violated if there are certain types of disparate enforcement of the work rules.

> An employee discharged for violating a selectively enforced rule or policy would be permitted to have the jury assess whether his violation of rule or policy amounted to good cause. Rules and policies uniformly applied are, however, as much a part of the "common law of the job" and a part of the employment contract as a promise to discharge only for cause.[138]

Where several employees may have been involved in an incident, punishing only those few who were actually identified is not evidence of disparate treatment.[139]

A common claim of perceived (or actual) disparate treatment is found in a number of cases. It involves the employee who feels that the employer has singled out the employee for discharge. Rather than immediately discharging the person, the employer makes work life uncomfortable or unbearable until there is a quit or an alleged basis for discharge. An external whistleblower is a typical example.[140] An internal whistleblower who only relates the bad news within the company is also a common example.[141] Despite some egregious fact patterns, courts seem very reluctant to allow recovery in these cases, absent statutory protection.[142] Occasionally a court will allow an employee to get past a motion for summary judgment on a claim for intentional infliction of emotional distress.[143] Whistleblower statutes may make a difference in some of these outcomes. The employee may also rely on the constructive discharge doctrine in some situations where the employee quits. However, in many cases the employee who feels singled out will have no effective remedy because the employee will not have enough proof to convince a court.

NEW REASONS

An employer may assign a given reason for a discharge. Subsequently, new information may be found that gives additional reasons for the discharge. Courts and arbitrators will permit the employer to also rely on the new rationale.[144]

"NO FAULT"

Just cause may be seen as a process of determining whether the employee was at fault for not doing better. One of the elements of the determination seems to be that the employee who can do better is at fault for not doing so. This person is seen as more accountable than an employee who has less control of his or her circumstances. However, the "no fault" employee may also be subject to discharge.[145] "(W)hen neither party is at fault . . . at some time the employee must bear the burden. That is, in some cases, the employer's interest will outweigh the need for a showing of personal fault."[146] Adverse employee action can be based upon the "no fault" actions of the employee.[147] For example, an employee who is injured and unable to work, or an employee who is ill and unable to work may nevertheless be discharged.[148] The employer is entitled to an employee who can perform, regardless of the reason for the nonperformance.[149] If the employee cannot perform, for whatever reason, the employer is entitled to continue the business. Legitimate absences that become excessive can still be a ground for discharge.[150] The employer is ultimately entitled to have employees who get the job done.

An incompetent employee may still be doing the absolute best that employee can. If the job is not properly done, the employer is entitled to take adverse action.[151] Such an employee may not be morally at fault, because the employee can do no better. This inability may not become evident for some period. It may not occur until the employee has merited promotions that take the employee beyond the employee's skill level.

When an employer's business turns down, the employer may have less need for the same number of employees. Good evaluations will not necessarily prevent a discharge based on economically induced, "no fault" reduction in force.[152] Adverse economic circumstances constitute just cause for layoffs.[153] A business decision to reorganize provides just cause.[154] An employee challenge of the actual existence of economic decline is not likely to succeed. Courts do not second guess the employer's judgment and discretion.[155] However, an employer cannot use the economic circumstances rationale where it is only a pretext to discharge.[156]

ARBITRATION, COURTS, AND JUST CAUSE

There is a pronounced difference between the judicial application and some arbitral applications of just cause. One arbitrator has used the following list of questions to apply the just cause principle from the arbitrator's point of view:

> A negative response to any one or more usually indicates that just cause does not exist. (1) Did the Company give the employee forewarning or foreknowledge of the possible or probable disciplinary consequences of the employee's conduct? (2) Was the Company rule or managerial order reasonably related to the orderly, efficient, and safe operation of the Company's business? (3) Did the Company, before administering discipline to an employee, make an effort to discover whether the employee did in fact violate or disobey a rule or order of management? (4) Was the Company investigation conducted fairly and objectively? (5) At the investigation did the judge obtain substantial evidence of proof that the employee was guilty as charged? (6) Has the Company applied its rules, orders, and penalties evenhandedly and without discrimination to all employees? (7) Was the degree of discipline administered by the Company in a particular case reasonably related to (a) The seriousness of the employee's proven offense and (b) The record of the employee in his service with the Company?[157]

The arbitrator using these guidelines would require employee knowledge and factual proof that the employee acted in the charged manner. Courts do not use this intensive analysis in applying just cause. The arbitrator's analysis puts the burden of proof in a discharge case on the employer, not the employee. In a judicial action for action, the employee has the burden of proof. The arbitrator will measure the discharge punishment against the employee action. If the discharge seems too severe, the arbitrator may apply mitigation and reduce it to a suspension or some lesser discipline. Courts do not exercise a mitigation role. Although the substantive definitions of acts that constitute just cause may not greatly vary between courts and arbitration, the procedural aspects vary greatly between the two forums.

DISCHARGE AND DEMOTION

The just cause dispute typically involves a discharge. However, the employee may attempt to use a just cause argument when the employer makes a personnel decision that is less than discharge, such as a demotion or transfer. The first point of reference is always the contact, if there is one. In one case the argument that just cause applied to demotions was rejected on the basis of the language of the contract in question. The language was clear that the employee was at will and that there were no implied agreements or understandings beyond the written contract.[158]

Some courts permit virtually any personnel action, including discharge, to be at will, absent contract restrictions.[159] Other courts are more restrictive. In one case an employee based the claim regarding demotion on the employer's personnel manual. The court held that the claim would survive the employer's motion to dismiss. The lower court, which was reversed, had ruled that the entire job status, including demotion, was determinable at will.[160] The reversal of the lower court's rationale would appear to be correct because at will status should not be viewed as a substantive limitation on the ability of the parties to make a contract concerning other terms. The same rationale should apply to other personnel actions not involving discharge, but involving other adverse actions toward the employee, even when the employee is at will.

Part of the answer to the question of whether the employer can demote at will depends in part on the definition of what is a demotion. In one instance, a long-term employee was transferred. The employee considered it to be a demotion, "put out to pasture," and refused to report for duty. The employee was eventually discharged.[161] The court found that the ultimate problem here was not whether the employer could demote at will, but whether the employee's reaction ultimately gave the employer cause to discharge. The refusal to work was a violation of the duty owed to the employer, unless it was the result of a constructive discharge. Once cause for discharge had been established, the at will question became moot.

A job may consist of the fact of employment, a certain salary, and certain authority and responsibility. Some courts and arbitrators question whether a demotion occurs when an employee is transferred and loses some authority and responsibility but retains the same salary.[162] Another court relied on the opening the floodgates argument. It stated that to require a trial in every public or private sector transfer would create "chaos both in the workplace and in the courts."[163] Related issues arise under claims of retaliation, such as an alleged demotion because of the employee's exercise of first amendment speech rights. Various tests for demotion have been enunciated, such as "substantial equivalent of dismissal,"[164] where the employer deliberately brings about a "substantial and permanent lessening of both the internal satisfactions . . . and the external prestige,"[165] or "formal personnel actions that have an effect on either compensation or job rank."[166]

In summary, at will status or just cause status is usually a discharge issue. Personnel actions that are less than discharge may, however, raise the same problems. Some courts treat all elements of the employment relationship as at will where the discharge can be at will, although this result fails to distinguish between an at will durational term and other clauses in the contract. Where an alleged demotion is at issue, part of the answer lies in defining demotion. A number of courts use salary level as a prime determinant of whether a demotion has occurred.

EXECUTION OF PERSONNEL DECISIONS

An employer may be fully justified in the personnel decision that was reached, but the execution of that decision in an outrageous manner may subject the employer to liability. For example, an employer may be able to discharge for violations of the sick leave policy. However, monitoring the sick leave policy by peering through the windows of the home of the employee to determine if the employee is really ill may be an invasion of the privacy of the employee.[167] Discharging an employee may be permissible, but pursuing the employee to subsequent employers and seeking to have those employers also discharge the employee may also lead to liability.[168]

Setting an employee up for discharge may lead to liability for intentional infliction of emotional distress.[169] Altering an employment record to justify termination in court proceedings may also lead to liability.[170]

CONCLUSION

Just cause may be required for a valid discharge where there is a fixed term contract or other specific requirement. Whereas just cause requirements are substantial limitations on the power to discharge at will, protection of basic employer rights is broadly recognized as part of the just cause concept. The just cause concept includes both fault and no fault elements on the part of the employee and changing business conditions.

Employees commonly raise a number of arguments that are not generally accepted when the employer acts on the basis of cause. These include alleged personality (not performance) conflicts, "faulty" evaluations, emphasis on past record, long-term status, comparative evaluations, a duty to warn or train the employee, and others.

These are generally rejected by courts. However, under an employ-ment related statute such as employment discrimination, some of these arguments may be helpful to the plaintiff employee. Figure 6.1 summarizes some of these arguments.

Just cause concepts highlight differences between dispute resolu-tion forums. The arbitration forum will commonly use a penalty mitigation approach, will require that there be no disparate treatment of like cases, and will imply the requirement of just cause where the actual clause may be missing but where other terms imply its exist-ence. Courts will rarely do any of these things.

Just cause and the arbitral forum become increasingly significant in the light of actual and proposed statutory modification of the common law at will doctrine. Whether arbitration and just cause under those proposals will be more judicial or more like traditional collective bargaining arbitration remains to be determined.

As an overall generalization, many courts seem inclined to view the entire contractual relationship as being at will. There are, however, a number of courts that will distinguish the discharge term of the contract from the other terms and conditions of employment, where that is warranted. In the latter situation, an at will discharge status does not necessarily mean that demotions, transfers, and other actions should be treated as at will.

Figure 6.1   Challenging Cause

WEAKER	STRONGER
Beyond Employee Control	Contract Not Followed
Cause Required For Nondischarge	Disparate Treatment
Duty to Train	Mitigation, If Arbitration
Duty to Warn	No Factual Basis
Employer Error	Nonwork Activities
Employer Policy Not Followed	Objective, Not Subjective,
Factual Error	Standard
General Bias	Specific Bias
Generally Good Evaluations	Standards Not Promulgated
Generally Talented Employee	Statutory Rights
Long Service, Special Status	
Not Acting In Good Faith	
Not Employee's Fault	
Personality Dispute	
Self Evaluation	
Third Party Evaluation	

NOTES

1. F. Elkouri and E. Elkouri, *How Arbitration Works* 553 (4th ed. 1985).

2. Trojan Luggage Co., Inc., 81 Lab. Arb. (BNA) 409, 412 (Lane, Arb. 1983).

3. Youngstown Hospital Assoc., 82 Lab. Arb. (BNA) 31, 35 (Miller, Arb. 1983).

4. Stauffer Chemical Co., 83 Lab. Arb. (BNA) 332, 336 (Blum, Arb. 1984); Post-Newsweek Stations, 82 Lab. Arb. (BNA) 386, 389 (Daniel, Arb. 1984).

5. Stauffer Chemical Co., 83 Lab. Arb. (BNA) 332, 336 (Blum, Arb. 1984).

6. Montana Dep't of Highways, 90 Lab. Arb. (BNA) 1257, 1260–61 (Tilbury, Arb. 1988).

7. Ch. 5, fn. 72.

8. E.g., F. Elkouri and E. Elkouri, *How Arbitration Works* 691–707 (4th ed. 1985).

9. Boynton v. TRW, Inc., 858 F.2d 1178 (6th Cir. 1988).

10. Ch. 3, fn. 42–58.

11. Dabrowski v. Warner-Lambert Co., 2 Indiv. Empl. Rights (BNA) 99 (6th Cir. 1987); MacGill v. Blue Cross of Maryland Inc., 3 Indiv. Empl. Rights (BNA) 1850 (Md. Ct. App. 1989).

12. Stewart v. Chevron Chemical Co., 3 Indiv. Empl. Rights (BNA) 1552 (Wash. Sup. Ct. 1988).

13. MacGill v. Blue Cross of Maryland Inc., 3 Indiv. Empl. Rights (BNA) 1850 (Md. Ct. App. 1989).

14. Dabrowski v. Warner-Lambert Co., 2 Indiv. Empl. Rights (BNA) 99 (6th Cir. 1987).

15. Id.

16. Pugh v. See's Candies, Inc., 3 Indiv. Empl. Rights (BNA) 945 (Cal. Ct. App. 1988).

17. Burrows v. Chemed Corp. dba Vestal Laboratories, 35 Empl. Prac. Dec. (CCH) 34,631 at 34,841 (8th Cir. 1984).

18. Ch. 3, fn. 42–58.

19. Ch. 3, fn. 122–125.

20. Baldwin v. Sisters of Providence, 4 Indiv. Empl. Rights (BNA) 208 (Wash. Sup. Ct. 1989).

21. Northrup Corp., 90 Lab. Arb. (BNA) 724, 728 (Weiss, Arb. 1987).

22. Id.

23. Hanley v. GSA, 2 Indiv. Empl. Rights (BNA) 892, 893 (Fed. Cir. 1987).

24. Snyder v. Washington Hosp. Center, 35 Empl. Prac. Dec. (CCH) 34,786 at 35,428 (D. D.C. 1984).

25. EEOC v. Trans World Airlines Inc., 30 Empl. Prac. Dec. (CCH) 33,011 at 26,838 (D. N.Y. 1984).

26. Palazon v. KFC Management Co., 29 Empl. Prac. Dec. (CCH) 32,744 at 25,509 (D. Ill. 1981).

27. Pacific Tel. & Tel. Co., 81 Lab. Arb. (BNA) 259, 264 (Connors, Arb. 1983).

28. Hanlon & Wilson Co. v. NLRB, 101 Lab. Cas. (CCH) 11,093 at 22,431 (3d Cir. 1984).

29. Mellitt v. Schrafft Candy Co., 115 L.R.R.M. (BNA) 4195, 4198 (D. N.H. 1981).

30. Mallard v. Boring, 115 L.R.R.M. (BNA) 4750, 4751 (Cal. Ct. App. 1960).

31. Dabrowski v. Warner-Lambert Co., 2 Indiv. Empl. Rights (BNA) 99 (6th Cir. 1987).

32. Oklahoma City Air Logistics Center, 82 Lab. Arb. (BNA) 240, 244 (Williams, Arb. 1984).

33. Dep't of Health & Human Services, 82 Lab. Arb. (BNA) 771, 778 (Aronin, Arb. 1984).

34. Duffy v. Wheeling Pittsburg Steel Corp., 34 Empl. Prac. Dec. (CCH) 34,527 at 34,318-319 (3d Cir. 1984).

35. Crawford v. Western Electric Co., Inc., 35 Empl. Prac. Dec. (CCH) 34,908 at 36,020 (11th Cir. 1984).

36. Haslam v. Pepsi Cola Co., 117 L.R.R.M. (BNA) 2950, 2952 (D. Mich. 1984).

37. Labrier v. Anheuser Ford, Inc., 95 Lab. Cas. (CCH) 55,368 (Mo. Sup. Ct. 1981); Harch v. K.F.C. Nat. Manag. Corp., 94 Lab. Cas. (CCH) 55,352 (Mo. Sup. Ct. 1981).

38. Mozee v. Jeffboat, Inc., 35 Empl. Prac. Dec. (CCH) 34,719 at 35,202 (7th Cir. 1984); Yartzoff v. State of Oregon, 35 Empl. Prac. Dec. (CCH) 34,737 (9th Cir. 1984); Casillas v. U.S. Navy, 34 Empl. Prac. Dec. (CCH) 34,394 (9th Cir. 1984).

39. Meschino v. International Tel. & Tel. Co., 35 Empl. Prac. Dec. (CCH) 34,926, fn. 9 at 36,093 (D. N.Y. 1983).

40. Haskell v. Kaman Corp., 35 Empl. Prac. Dec. (CCH) 34,613 at 34,716 (2d Cir. 1984).

41. O'Donnell v. Georgia Osteopathic Hosp., 35 Empl. Prac. Dec. (CCH) 34,863 at 35,784 (11th Cir. 1984). See also detailed discussion in LaMontagne v. American Convenience Products, Inc., 35 Empl. Prac. Dec. (CCH) 34,914 (7th Cir. 1984).

42. Cort v. Bristol-Meyers Co., 115 L.R.R.M. (BNA) 5127, 5128 (Mass. Sup. Ct. 1982).

43. F. Elkouri & E. Elkouri, *How Arbitration Works* 656–658 (4th ed. 1985); Trailways, Inc., 88 Lab. Arb. (BNA) 1073, 1080 (Goodman, Arb. 1987). But see, Iowa State Penitentiary, 89 Lab. Arb. (BNA) 956, 960 (Hill, Arb. 1987) (law enforcement employee).

44. Hayes Int'l Corp., 81 Lab. Arb. (BNA) 99, 103 (Van Wart, Arb. 1983).

45. Mich. Dep't of Mental Health, 82 Lab. Arb. (BNA) 1306, 1309 (Borland, Arb. 1984); Whirlpool Corp., 90 Lab. Arb. (BNA) 41, 44 (Holley, Arb. 1987); Genesee County, 90 Lab. Arb. (BNA) 48, 54 (House, Arb. 1987). But see, Pagdilao v. Maui Intercontinental Hotel, 3 Indiv. Empl. Rights (BNA) 1628 (D. Haw. 1988).

46. Ch. 3, fn. 129.

47. Everett v. Comm. Satellite Corp., 33 Empl. Prac. Dec. (CCH) 34,120 at 32,252-253 (D. D.C. 1983); Linn v. Beneficial Commercial Corp., 3 Indiv. Empl. Rights (BNA) 1557 (N.J. Super. Ct. 1988); LaBarber v. Gould Inc., 2 Indiv. Empl. Rights (BNA) 433 (D. Cal. 1987).

48. Burrows v. Chemed Corp. dba Vestal Lab., 35 Empl. Prac. Dec. (CCH) 34,631 (8th Cir. 1984).

49. Washington Welfare Assoc. v. Poindexter, 116 L.R.R.M. (BNA) 3438, 3441 (D.C. Cir. 1984).

50. EEOC v. Target Stores, Inc., 35 Empl. Prac. Dec. (CCH) 34,654 (D. Minn. 1984).

51. Cazzola v. Codman & Shurtleff, Inc., 35 Empl. Prac. Dec. (CCH) 34,857 (1st Cir. 1984); Koyen v. Consol. Edison Co. of New York, Inc., 33 Empl. Prac. Dec. (CCH) 34,189 (D. N.Y. 1983).

52. LaMontagne v. American Convenience Products, Inc., 35 Empl. Prac. Dec. (CCH) 34,914 at 36,050 (7th Cir. 1984).

53. Young v. Lehman, 35 Empl. Prac. Dec. (CCH) 34,809 (4th Cir. 1984).

54. E.g., City of North LarVegal, 90 Lab. Arb. (BNA) 563, 567 (Richman, Arb. 1988).

55. Moon v. Transport Drivers, Inc., 2 Indiv. Empl. Rights (BNA) 1502 (6th Cir. 1987); DeMinico v. Monarch Wine Co., 2 Indiv. Empl. Rights (BNA) 171 (D. Cal. 1986); U.S. Tobacco Co., 89 Lab. Arb. (BNA) 611, 615 (Clarke, Arb. 1987).

56. Okla. City Air Logistics Center, 82 Lab. Arb. (BNA) 240, 242 (Williams, Arb. 1984).

57. Criddle v. Hickory Hill Furniture Co., 34 Empl. Prac. Dec. (CCH) 34,547, at 34,443 (D. Miss. 1984).

58. Moylan v. Nat'l Westminister Bank, 3 Indiv. Empl. Rights (BNA) 1015 (D. N.Y. 1988).

59. Schoen v. Consumers United Group, Inc., 2 Indiv. Empl. Rights (BNA) 1905 (D. D.C. 1986).

60. Snyder v. Washington Hosp. Center, 35 Empl. Prac. Dec. (CCH) 34,786, fn. 2 at 35,428 (D. D.C. 1984).

61. Babcock & Wilcox Co., 90 Lab. Arb. (BNA) 606, 611 (Ruben, Arb. 1987).

62. Wine Cellar, 81 Lab. Arb. (BNA) 158, 164 (Ray, Arb. 1983); See also Lockheed Corp. 83 Lab. Arb. (BNA) 1018, 1023 (Taylor, Arb. 1984).

63. Devine v. Sutermeister, 116 L.R.R.M. (BNA) 2495, 2497 (Fed. Cir. 1983).

64. Iowa City School Dist. v. Educ. Ass'n, 116 L.R.R.M. (BNA) 2832, 2837 (Iowa Sup. Ct. 1983).

65. Walton v. Avant Dev. Corp., 115 L.R.R.M. (BNA) 4084, 4087 (D. Ga. 1983).

66. Menard v. First Security Corp., 3 Indiv. Empl. Rights (BNA) 591 (1st Cir. 1988).

67. Haskins v. Sec'y Health and Human Services, 35 Empl. Prac. Dec. (CCH) 34,902 at 35,983 (D. Mo. 1984).

68. F. Elkouri and E. Elkouri, *How Arbitration Works*, 639–640 (4th ed. 1985).

69. Pierce v. New Process Co., 35 Empl. Prac. Dec. (CCH) 34,864 at 35,788 (D. Pa. 1984); Butler v. Westinghouse Electric Corp., 3 Indiv. Empl. Rights (BNA) 1430 (D. Md. 1987); Kohler v. Ericsson Inc., 3 Indiv. Empl. Rights (BNA) 721 (9th Cir. 1988).

70. Chamberlain v. Bissell Inc., 115 L.R.R.M. (BNA) 4137, fn. 2 at 4150 (D. Mich. 1982).

71. Id. at 4150.

72. Sebastian v. Texas Dep't of Corrections, 29 Empl. Prac. Dec. (CCH) 32,716 at 25,340 (D. Tex. 1982).

73. Haslam v. Pepsi-Cola Co., 117 L.R.R.M. (BNA) 2950, 2952 (D. Mich. 1984); Murray v. Bridgeport Hosp., 117 L.R.R.M. (BNA) 3111, 3112 (Conn. Super. Ct.

1984); Loftis v. G.T. Products Inc., 3 Indiv. Empl. Rights (BNA) 641 (Mich. Ct. App. 1988).

74. Cazzola v. Codman & Shurtleff, Inc., 35 Empl. Prac. Dec. (CCH) 34,857 at 35,709 (lst Cir. 1984).

75. Chamberlain v. Bissell Inc., 115 L.R.R.M. (BNA) 4137, 4150 (D. Mich. 1982).

76. Cazzola v. Codman & Shurtleff, Inc., 35 Empl. Prac. Dec. (CCH) 34,857 at 35,709, 710 (1st Cir. 1984); Steiger Tractor, Inc., 83 Lab. Arb. (BNA) 966, 971 (Jacobowski, Arb. 1984).

77. Porvene Roll-A-Door, Inc., 81 Lab. Arb. (BNA) 1016, 1019 (Maxwell, Arb. 1983).

78. Fn. 3–5, supra.

79. Avakian v. Trinity Memorial Hospital of Cudahy, Inc., 31 Empl. Prac. Dec. (CCH) 33,396 at 28,784 (D. Wis. 1981).

80. Cazzola v. Codman & Shurtleff, Inc., 35 Empl. Prac. Dec. (CCH) 34,857 (1st Cir. 1984); Koyen v. Consol. Edison Co. of New York, Inc., 33 Empl. Prac. Dec. (CCH) 34,189 (D. N.Y. 1983).

81. Budd v. American Savings & Loan Ass'n, 3 Indiv. Empl. Rights (BNA) 740 (Or. Ct. App. 1988).

82. Boresen v. Rohm & Haas, 115 L.R.R.M. (BNA) 4336, 4340 (D. Pa. 1981); see also Johnson v. Lehman (Hidalgo) 29 Empl. Prac. Dec. (CCH) 32,700 at 25,288 (D.C. Cir. 1982) (failure to follow employer's own regulations may not be sufficient evidence of age discrimination when standing alone, but is a factor to consider).

83. Kohler v. Ericsson Inc., 3 Indiv. Empl. Rights (BNA) 721 (9th Cir. 1988).

84. Aldahir v. Mobil Oil, Inc., 115 L.R.R.M. (BNA) 4472 (La. Ct. App. 1982).

85. Palazon v. KFC Management Co., 29 Empl. Prac. Dec. (CCH) 32,744 at 25,509 (D. Ill. 1981).

86. Bethea v. Levi Strauss & Co., 2 Indiv. Empl. Rights (BNA) 734 (8th Cir. 1987).

87. Ch. 5, fn. 5–13.

88. Morgan v. Harris Trust & Savings Bank, 2 Indiv. Empl. Rights (BNA) 577 (D. Ill. 1987); Eldridge v. Evangelical Lutheran, 2 Indiv. Empl. Rights (BNA) 1506 (N.D. Sup. Ct. 1987).

89. Hillsboro Glass Co., 88 Lab. Arb. (BNA) 107 (Traynor, Arb. 1986).

90. Gen. Tel. Co. of Cal., 89 Lab. Arb. (BNA) 867, 872 (Collins, Arb. 1987); Muskin, Inc., 89 Lab. Arb. (BNA) 297, 299 (DiLauro, Arb. 1987); Miss. Forestry Comm'n v. Piazza, 3 Indiv. Empl. Rights (BNA) 236 (Miss. Sup. Ct. 1987).

91. Santa Monica Hosp. v. Superior Court, 2 Indiv. Empl. Rights (BNA) 1899, 1904 (Cal. Ct. App. 1985).

92. Postal Workers v. Postal Service, 2 Indiv. Empl. Rights (BNA) 1197, 1202 (D. Ohio 1987).

93. Kable Printing Co., 89 Lab. Arb. (BNA) 314, 319 (Mikrut, Arb. 1987); TRW, Inc., 90 Lab. Arb. (BNA) 31, 35 (Graham, Arb. 1987).

94. Loftis v. G.T. Products Inc., 3 Indiv. Empl. Rights (BNA) 641 (Mich. Ct. App. 1988); Silkworth v. Ryder Truck Rental Inc., 2 Indiv. Empl. Rights (BNA) 1015 (Md. Ct. App. 1987); Brumbaugh v. Ralston Purina Co., 2 Indiv. Empl. Rights (BNA) 877 (D. Iowa 1987).

95. Baldwin v. Sisters of Providence, 4 Indiv. Empl. Rights (BNA) 208 (Wash. Sup. Ct. 1989).

96. Luft v. Sears, Roebuck and Co., 117 L.R.R.M. (BNA) 2704, 2707 (Iowa D. Ct. 1984).

97. F. Elkouri and E. Elkouri, *How Arbitration Works*, 691–707 (4th ed. 1985).

98. McCarthy v. Cycare Systems, Inc., 2 Indiv. Empl. Rights (BNA) 680 (D. Ill. 1986) (distinguishing between a contract and a "code of conduct"); Golden v. Worldvision Enterprises, Inc., 2 Indiv. Empl. Rights (BNA) 1468 (N.Y. Sup. Ct. App. Div. 1987) (distinguishing between a satisfaction contract and a cause contract).

99. Diggs v. Pepsi-Cola, 3 Indiv. Empl. Rights (BNA) 1601 (6th Cir. 1988).

100. Shell Oil Co., 90 Lab. Arb. (BNA) 112, 114 (Massey, Arb. 1988).

101. North American Fencing Corp., 81 Lab. Arb. (BNA) 92, 94 (Hart, Arb. 1983).

102. Brevik v. Kite Painting Inc., 2 Indiv. Empl. Rights (BNA) 211, 213 (Minn. Ct. App. 1987).

103. Burlington Northern, 90 Lab. Arb. (BNA) 585, 591 (Goldstein, Arb. 1987).

104. Alexander v. Phillips Oil Co., 2 Indiv. Empl. Rights (BNA) 824 (Wyo. Sup. Ct. 1987).

105. Chamberlain v. Bissell Inc., 115 L.R.R.M. (BNA) 4137, 4148 (D. Mich. 1982).

106. Pugh v. See's Candies, Inc., 115 L.R.R.M. (BNA) 4002, 4010–4011 (Cal. Ct. App. 1981); Williams v. Maremont Corp., 4 Indiv. Empl. Rights (BNA) 799, 806 (10th Cir. 1989).

107. F. Elkouri and E. Elkouri, *How Arbitration Works*, 691–707 (4th ed. 1985).

108. Pugh v. See's Candies, Inc., 115 L.R.R.M. (BNA) 4002, 4010 (Cal. Ct. App. 1981).

109. Shell Oil Co., 90 Lab. Arb. (BNA) 112 (Massey, Arb. 1988); S.E. Rykoff & Co., 90 Lab. Arb. (BNA) 233 (Angelo, Arb. 1987); Pennwalt Corp., 89 Lab. Arb. (BNA) 585 (Kanner, Arb. 1987).

110. Pennwalt Corp., 89 Lab. Arb. (BNA) 585 (Kanner, Arb. 1987); Foley v. Interactive Data Corp., 3 Indiv. Empl. Rights (BNA) 1729, 1740 (Cal. Sup. Ct. 1988). But see, DeMinico v. Monarch Wine Co., 2 Indiv. Empl. Rights (BNA) 171, 179 (D. Cal. 1986) (7 years insufficient time).

111. Simpson v. Western Graphics, 115 L.R.R.M. (BNA) 4605, 4608 (Or. Ct. App. 1981).

112. Douglas v. Anderson, 115 L.R.R.M. (BNA) 4906, fn. 5 at 4909 (9th Cir. 1981). See also Gordon v. Matthew Bender & Co., 115 L.R.R.M. (BNA) 4100, 4104 (D. Ill. 1983); Rabago-Alvarez v. Dart Industries, 115 L.R.R.M. (BNA) 4704, 4706 (Cal. Ct. App. 1976).

113. Dabrowski v. Warner-Lambert Co., 2 Indiv. Empl. Rights (BNA) 99 (6th Cir. 1987).

114. Toussaint v. Blue Cross & Blue Shield, 115 L.R.R.M. (BNA) 4708, 4719 (Mich. Sup. Ct. 1980). See also the discussion of Toussaint in Pugh v. See's Candies Inc., 3 Indiv. Empl. Rights (BNA) 945, 957 (Cal. Ct. App. 1988); Hodge v. Evans Financial Corp., 2 Indiv. Empl. Rights (BNA) 395, 403 (D.C. Cir. 1987); Kestenbaum v. Pennzoil, 4 Indiv. Empl. Rights (BNA) 67, 73 (N.M. Sup. Ct. 1988).

115. Cox v. Resilient Flooring, 2 Indiv. Empl. Rights (BNA) 1757, 1762 (D. Cal. 1986).

116. Pugh v. See's Candies Inc., 3 Indiv. Empl. Rights (BNA) 945, 959 (Cal. Ct. App. 1988).

117. Id. at 958.

118. Diggs v. Pepsi-Cola, 3 Indiv. Empl. Rights (BNA) 1601, 1606 (6th Cir. 1988); Prout v. Sears, Roebuck and Co., 4 Indiv. Empl. Rights (BNA) 193, 196 (Mont. Sup. Ct.)

119. Simpson v. Western Graphics, 115 L.R.R.M. (BNA) 4605, 4608 (Or. Ct. App. 1981).

120. B. Schwartz, *Administrative Law* 599–600 (1984).

121. Snyder v. Washington Hosp. Center, 35 Empl. Prac. Dec. (CCH) 34,786 at 35,428 (D. D.C. 1984).

122. Krodel v. Young, 35 Empl. Prac. Dec. (CCH) 34,861 at 35,773 (D.C. Cir. 1984). See also Dep't of Health & Human Services, 82 Lab. Arb. (BNA) 771, 778 (Aronin, Arb. 1984).

123. F. Elkouri and E. Elkouri, *How Arbitration Works* 631 (4th ed. 1985).

124. Id. at 630.

125. Magnan v. Anaconda Indus., 117 L.R.R.M. (BNA) 2163, 2169 (Conn. Sup. Ct. 1984).

126. Gram v. Liberty Mutual Ins. Co., 115 L.R.R.M. (BNA) 4152, 4156 (Mass. Sup. Ct. 1981). See also Siles v. Travenol Laboratories, 115 L.R.R.M. (BNA) 4178, 4181 (Mass. App. Ct. 1982).

127. Ch. 5, fn. 135.

128. Savodnik v. Korvettes, Inc., 115 L.R.R.M. (BNA) 4601 (D. N.Y. 1980).

129. Fortune v. National Cash Register Co., 115 L.R.R.M. (BNA) 4658 (Mass. Sup. Ct. 1977).

130. Parnar v. Americana Hotels, Inc., 115 L.R.R.M. (BNA) 4817, 4821–22 (Haw. Sup. Ct. 1982).

131. Monge v. Beebe Rubber Co., 115 L.R.R.M. (BNA) 4755, 4757 (N.H. Sup. Ct. 1974).

132. Fisher Foods, Inc., 82 Lab. Arb. (BNA) 505, 512 (Abrams, Arb. 1984).

133. Ch. 2, fn. 26.

134. Hinson v. Cameron, 4 Indiv. Empl. Rights (BNA) 266 (Okla. Sup. Ct. 1987); Fink v. Revco Discount Drug Centers, 3 Indiv. Empl. Rights (BNA) 115 (D. Mo. 1987).

135. Toussaint v. Blue Shield & Blue Cross, 115 L.R.R.M. (BNA) 4708, 4719 (Mich. Sup. Ct. 1980).

136. Staton v. Amax Coal Co., 116 L.R.R.M. (BNA) 2517, 2519 (Ill. App. Ct. 1984).

137. Id.

138. Toussaint v. Blue Shield & Blue Cross, 115 L.R.R.M. (BNA) 4708, 4720 (Mich. Sup. Ct. 1980).

139. Peninsular Steel Co., 88 Lab. Arb. (BNA) 391, 395 (Ipavec, Arb. 1986).

140. E.g., Smalley v. Fast Fare Inc., 4 Indiv. Empl. Rights (BNA) 105 (D. S.C. 1988).

141. Foley v. Interactive Data, 3 Indiv. Empl. Rights (BNA) 1729 (Cal. Sup. Ct. 1988).

142. Potter v. Village Bank of N.J., 3 Indiv. Empl. Rights (BNA) 1076 (N.J. Super. Ct. 1988); Sterling Drug Inc. v. Oxford, 3 Indiv. Empl. Rights (BNA) 1060 (Ark. Sup. Ct. 1988).

143. Minniti v. TRW, 2 Indiv. Empl. Rights (BNA) 765 (D. Cal. 1987).

144. Leahy v. Federal Express, 3 Indiv. Empl. Rights (BNA) 927 (D. Va. 1988); Homestake Mining Co., 90 Lab. Arb. (BNA) 720, 722 (Fogelberg, Arb. 1987). See also Mt. Healthy City School Dist. Board of Educ., 429 U.S. 274 (1977).

145. Copperweld Bimetallies Group, 83 Lab. Arb. (BNA) 1024, 1028 (Denison, Arb. 1984) (incompetent employee who could do no better).

146. Linn Co., Iowa, 81 Lab. Arb. (BNA) 929, 933 (Sinicropi, Arb. 1983).

147. Coca-Cola Bottling Co., 81 Lab. Arb. (BNA) 56, 58 (Berger, Arb. 1983).

148. Stokely Van Camp, Inc., 81 Lab. Arb. (BNA) 677, 680 (Schaffer, Arb. 1983); see also Hansome v. Northwestern Cooperage Co., 101 Lab. Cas. (CCH) 55,464 (Mo. Ct. App. 1984).

149. Peabody Coal Co., 83 Lab. Arb. (BNA) 1138, 1143 (Roberts, Arb. 1984).

150. Coca-Cola Bottling Co., 81 Lab. Arb. (BNA) 56, 58 (Berger, Arb. 1983); Stokely Van Camp, Inc., 81 Lab. Arb. (BNA) 677, 680 (Schaffer, Arb. 1983).

151. Municipality of Anchorage, 82 Lab. Arb. (BNA) 256, 263 (Hauch, Arb. 1983).

152. Rompf v. Hammons Hotels, 117 L.R.R.M. (BNA) 2185, 2189 (Wyo. Sup. Ct. 1984).

153. Delminico v. Monarch Wine Co., 2 Indiv. Empl. Rights (BNA) 171, 179 (D. Cal. 1986); Malmstrom v. Kaiser Aluminum & Chemical, 2 Indiv. Empl. Rights (BNA) 180, 189 (Cal. Ct. App. 1986); Burdette v. Mepco/Electra, Inc., 2 Indiv. Empl. Rights (BNA) 214, 218 (D. Cal. 1987).

154. Clutterham v. Coachmen Indus., Inc., 2 Indiv. Empl. Rights (BNA) 164 (D. Cal. 1985); Dabrowski v. Warner-Lambert Co., 2 Indiv. Empl. Rights (BNA) 99 (6th Cir. 1987).

155. Nixon v. Celotext Corp., 3 Indiv. Empl. Rights (BNA) 1391, 1397 (D. Mich. 1988).

156. Coelho v. Posi-Seal Int'l, 3 Indiv. Empl. Rights (BNA) 821, 827 (Conn. Sup. Ct. 1988); Stark v. Circle K Corp., 3 Indiv. Empl. Rights (BNA) 53, 57 (Mont. Sup. Ct. 1988).

157. Air Treads of Atlanta, Inc., 83 Lab. Arb. (BNA) 1323, 1326 (Yancy, Arb. 1984).

158. Summers v. Sears, Roebuck & Co., 115 L.R.R.M. (BNA) 4812, 4815 (D. Mich. 1982); Salimi v. Farmers Insurance Group, 116 L.R.R.M. (BNA) 3230, 3231 (Colo. Ct. App. 1984).

159. Summers v. Sears, Roebuck & Co., 115 L.R.R.M. (BNA) 4812 (D. Mich. 1982).

160. Salimi v. Farmers Insurance Group, 116 L.R.R.M. (BNA) 3230, 3231 (Colo. Ct. App. 1984).

161. Doscherholmen v. Walters, 35 Empl. Prac. Dec. (CCH) 34,685 (D. Minn. 1984).

162. Shamley v. City of Chicago, 2 Indiv. Empl. Rights (BNA) 1236 (Ill. App. Ct. 1987); Los Angeles Police Dep't, 89 Lab. Arb. (BNA) 1091 (Koven, Arb. 1987); Rutan v. Republican Party of Ill., 3 Indiv. Empl. Rights (BNA) 569, 577 (7th Cir. 1988); Lowe v. Kansas City, 3 Indiv. Empl. Rights (BNA) 1339 (8th Cir. 1988); Greenberg v. Kmetko, 840 F.2d 467 (7th Cir. 1988); Lombardo v. Oppenheimer, 701 F. Supp. 29 (D. Conn. 1987). On failure to promote, see Wygant v. Jackson, 476 U.S. 267 (1986); Rutan v. Republican Party of Illinois, 4 Indiv. Empl. Rights (BNA) 445 (7th Cir. 1989).

163. Sager v. Reynolds, 3 Indiv. Empl. Rights (BNA) 1023, 1023–24 (Mo. Ct. App. 1988).

164. Rutan v. Republican Party of Ill., 3 Indiv. Empl. Rights (BNA) 569, 575 (7th Cir. 1988).

165. Agosto De Feliciano v. Aponte, 2 Indiv. Empl. Rights (BNA) 1350 (1st Cir. 1987).

166. Zamboni v. Stamier, 3 Indiv. Empl. Rights (BNA) 417, 424 (3d Cir. 1988).

167. Cokely v. Pacific Gas & Electric Co., 35 Empl. Prac. Dec. (CCH) 34,746 at 35,298 (D. Cal. 1984).

168. Yaindl v. Ingersoll-Rand Co., 115 L.R.R.M. (BNA) 4738, 4748 (Pa. Super. Ct. 1981).

169. McCool v. Hillhaven Corp., 97 Or. App. 536 (1988).

170. Skirpan v. United Air Lines, 4 Indiv. Empl. Rights (BNA) 929, 933 (D. Ill. 1989).

7

Statutes and At Will

INTRODUCTION

The law of individual contracts of employment can be divided into two distinct areas. One area is governed by the common law, the general law applicable to all contracts. This includes the contract at will approach and the interpretation given to definite term contracts. Courts are the primary dispute resolution forum that interprets the contract. This area of the law of individual contracts has been the primary subject of these materials up to this point. The second area of individual employment contract law is governed by the relationship between the individual employment relationship and employment related statutes. Many new employment related statutes have been enacted at the state and federal levels in recent years and many more are coming. One overall impact of this legislation generally has been to limit the application of the at will doctrine in specific narrow areas. The judicial common law at will doctrine has been effectively modified so that it now means that the employer can discharge at any time for any reason unless otherwise limited by statute. The purpose of this chapter is to look at some aspects of the relationship between statutes and statutory proposals and individual contracts of employment.

The existence of these statutes is reflected in the multiple causes of action in employment contract litigation. Plaintiff employees frequently bring cases alleging multiple causes of action, based on both contract and statutory violations. Allegations may include six, eight, or more causes of action against the employer.[1]

TYPES OF STATUTES

There are at least two general types of statutes that relate to the individual contract. One consists of those statutes whose major focus is directly related to employment. For example, Title VII[2] prohibits certain types of employment discrimination in the workplace. Such statutes both create specific employee rights and often include nonretaliation provisions to give protection to employees who use the statutes, whether the statute was otherwise violated or not.[3] Thus the statutes provide both for protection against actual discrimination and they provide protection for persons seeking to exercise rights under the statute, such as those who file charges involving allegations of discrimination that have yet to be proved. The employer who discharges with mixed motives, such as arbitrary at will without a reason, but also with possible retaliation may be put in a difficult position to defend the discharge under the statutes. The employer who relies heavily upon rights given the employer by the at will doctrine may be put into jeopardy under these statutes. The at will doctrine permits arbitrary discharges or unexplained discharges. If the employer discharges on that arbitrary basis, these statutes might subsequently require the employer to give a nondiscriminatory explanation for the discharge. Where the discharge was originally arbitrary or without reason, it may be difficult at a later date to give a credible reason for the discharge that will meet statutory standards.

The second type of statute is not necessarily employment related as its primary focus. Rather the statute seeks to promote some non-employment public policy such as safety in transportation, or in nuclear energy, or promote efficient government.[4] As part of this protection, employees who act in a manner to promote the public policy may have a remedy against arbitrary retaliatory action by the employer. The employee, for example, who refuses to drive an allegedly unsafe truck,[5] or the whistleblower who reports unsafe nuclear industry conditions, may be given some protection against discharge when the employee seeks to advance the protected public policy. Whistleblower legislation need not be solely aimed at blowing the whistle on violations of employment related legislation.[6]

Protective legislation may also take the form of statutes that permit public sector collective bargaining.[7] These statutes permit public sector employees to move from civil service or at will status to the possibility of having an arbitration grievance mechanism with cause based discharge. In addition, these statutes may provide for special agency forums instead of judicial forums for statutory violations.

Other protections might also be added, such as a right to engage in organizational or union activities.[8]

In addition to legislation, the expansion of constitutional due process concepts in the public sector gave many public employees hearing rights when they were terminated. A due process hearing right might be invoked by the employee who has less than a formal, written contract but whose employment is such that a property interest is found.[9] The property right might be based on an express or implied a contract right or on a statutory right. Where a liberty (or reputational) interest is involved, the employee might be entitled to at least a name clearing type of hearing.[10] Public policy employment considerations may also be found in the public sector in other parts of the constitution, such as the right of free speech under the First Amendment.[11]

These statutes might be seen by some as unwarranted limitations on employer rights or as undesirable limits on the employer's exercise of entrepreneurial control. Others may see them as a limitation on some employer abuses under the at will doctrine. The statutes might also be seen as a legislative effort to balance employer and employee rights in a way that courts have been reluctant to do on their own. Statutes may impose a requirement of balancing not only the employment interests, but also require giving significant weight to various public policy interests, including the public policy interest in preserving entrepreneurial controls.

In summary, employment related legislation might be seen as involving two types of statutes. Either type of statute may have the effect of benefiting certain at will employees who have been discharged without cause. However, the purposes of the statutes may be entirely different. One type of statute is aimed at protecting employees, and the employee beneficiary is the object of the statute. Another type of statute seeks to primarily protect a public policy not related to employment, but protecting employees who are policing that public policy may be one of the ways the statute is enforced. The distinction is important. Where employee protection is the primary goal, courts may wish to give significant balance to employer rights, as is traditionally done. Where a larger public interest is involved, the court may have to make a clear balance between three elements, the employer, the employee, and the public interest. Courts are historically reluctant to make either a two- or threefold balance in employment disputes. In addition, courts are historically reluctant to act in other than a constrained manner in employment disputes, but statutes may compel them to relax the rule of restraint.

READING STATUTES

The diversity of content, style, and organization of legislation often makes it difficult to read. However, some content issues are common to many pieces of employment retaliation and whistleblower legislation. Identifying some of these more common elements can be an aid in more quickly getting a general understanding of the statute. Among the most important content elements are the definitions of employer and employee used in the statute, the procedure and forum provided by the statute, and the remedies that might be available. Another important element is whether the statute pre-empts other rights or whether it is an additional procedure on top of pre-existing rights. The pre-emption issue may be addressed directly in the statute, but frequently the statute is silent and the answer can only be found in case law, if at all. The following sections briefly discuss these content issues.

Definitions

The definitions of employer and employee are critical elements in understanding a statute. These definitions tell who is covered by the statute and who is not. Employer definitions commonly are expressed in terms of the number of employees the employer has and in terms of their public or private sector status. The difference between a large (covered by the statute) and a small (not covered by the statute) employer may be in the range of 15 to 20 employees.[12]

The definition of employee is also an important element in understanding the statute. The definition may distinguish between probationary and nonprobationary employees.[13] The definition may also distinguish between supervisory and nonsupervisory employees.[14]

Procedure

The procedural elements of the statute are important to identify. The statute may create rights and identify an agency forum in which those rights must be investigated or adjudicated. The power given to the agency may be only the power to investigate or it may be to investigate and adjudicate the complaints of the protected party. Other statutes may create a private right of action to be enforced in court. Another procedural element is identification of the period of limitations, or the

time in which an action must be started under the statute. In employment legislation, a common period of limitations is six months.[15]

Remedies

Another important element in the statute is the remedies that may
be provided for a violation of the protected rights. In employment
legislation, back pay is among the most common remedies.[16]
Reinstatement might also be provided. An especially important question for both employees and employers is whether the statute provides
for the recovery of punitive damages, beyond the recovery of back pay
and compensatory damages. Punitive damages, which can produce
six or seven figure recoveries in unusual cases, are a major source of
concern for employers.[17]

Pre-emption

A final item of importance for these purposes is to determine
whether the statute defines the relationship between the statutory
remedy that may be available and other remedies provided by other
statutes or judicial doctrines (common law). Part of this consideration
is sometimes expressed by the shorthand notion of "one bite" or "two
bite" remedies. A "one bite" remedy is where the employee is given
only one avenue of recourse; the first choice is the final choice. In a
"two bite" situation, the employee can bring an action under one
statute or contractual right, and, if the employee loses, the employee
can bring a second and separate action under another statute or
contractual system.[18] Also related to this pre-emption issue is the
situation where there are overlapping forums, such as comparable
federal and state statutes, or a possible right under a National Labor
Relations Act collective bargaining contract and state law. The question is often phrased in terms of whether one source of rights will
pre-empt the other. Employers may face potential liability from two
statutes, that is, the federal statute may not pre-empt the effect of the
state statute.[19] There may be a situation where there is a statutory right
and a contractual right. This combination raises the question of
whether the employee can proceed under either or both, or whether
the contractual right must be exercised first and will be essentially the
only available right. This latter situation is commonly found where
the employee has a right to arbitration under a private sector collective
bargaining agreement and a possible common law state action for
wrongful discharge.[20] Usually the employee must proceed under the

collective bargaining contract. Statutes may be silent on pre-emption and the employer and employee will have to wait until the courts announce the answer.

Pre-emption is a powerful doctrine whose form and force seems to change to meet different situations. Public policy may play a major role in it. It is one of the employer's stronger defenses to defeat an employee's effort to bring certain kinds of suits. Where there is a private sector collective bargaining contract, if the employee's state court claims for wrongful discharge would require an interpretation of a collective bargaining contract, the state claim will be pre-empted.[21] One court described the following test for collective bargaining pre-emption.

> In deciding whether a state law is pre-empted under section 301, therefore, a court must consider: (1) whether the collective bargaining agreement contains provisions that govern the actions giving rise to the state claim, and if so, (2) whether the state has articulated a standard sufficiently clear that the state claim can be evaluated without considering the overlapping provisions of the CBA, and (3) whether the state has shown an intent not to allow its prohibition to be altered by private contract. A state law will be pre-empted only if the answer to the first question is "yes," and the answer to either the second or third is "no."[22]

If the state claim is independent of the contract, it will not be pre-empted.[23] However, there is a great deal of variety in the judicial decisions.[24]

In summary, this chapter initially focuses on four elements of statutes relating to individual contracts of employment. They are the definitions, especially definitions of employer and employee; procedure, especially the forum for dispute resolution and the period of limitations; remedies, especially the absence or presence of punitive damages; and the relationship between the statute and other rights, especially the matter of pre-emption of other rights by the statute. These four aspects are among the most important elements that the legislation might have.

STATUTES AND EMPLOYER RIGHTS

One major effect of statutes on the employment relationship is that the statute may limit, to some extent, the court created doctrine of judicial restraint.[25] However, even under a statute, courts remain reluctant to second guess the business judgment of the employer. The

ADEA (Age Discrimination) is not intended as a vehicle for general, judicial review of business decisions.[26] A Title VII lawsuit is not about the defendant's business judgment or about the wisdom of that judgment.[27]

Judicial recognition of the central role of efficiency and profit must, under some statutes, be put into a balance with other elements. For example, efficiency may have to be balanced against a statutory need for accommodation of a handicap. "While the Court recognizes the difficulties caused by a less than 100% productive worker, the situation is generally short-term in nature and is a necessary consequence of any effort to accommodate."[28]

In contrast, employees seeking to claim statutory rights may be faced with difficult procedural hurdles created to protect entrepreneurial control. The requirement of showing a prima facie case of discrimination, for example, may be not only difficult to define,[29] but may also be difficult to demonstrate. Changing judicial attitudes on the meaning of statutes may also impact heavily on the efforts of the employee to prove violation of a right.[30]

Some statutes will give statutory recognition to special employment relationships. For example, the ADEA recognizes the higher level job (highly paid) category.[31] The Montana wrongful termination legislation has an exception for the probationary employee, preserving the employer's right to test the acceptability of the employee.[32]

Employee duties traditionally owed to the employer are largely unchanged by most statutes. The major exception is found in whistleblower legislation.[33] The protections given to employees under those statutes may override some aspects of the duty of loyalty commonly owed to the employer. Some of the whistleblower legislation is aimed at least as much at public protection or other public policy considerations as it is aimed at employee protection.[34] The employer-employee balance of rights has long been subject to some adjustment to accommodate larger public policy interests.[35] Whistleblower legislation expands the scope of the need to balance various interests.

Statutes may also be seen as giving some recognition to public policy values that may benefit an employer. Some of these values have been previously recognized by the courts.[36] Legislation may give protection to the employer interests in getting reasonably quick decisions and greater predictability about the level of damages or other recovery in employer-employee disputes. Employers have an interest in being able to make plans that are not contingent on too many unknowns. Final and binding arbitration may be encouraged under the statute[37] that has these characteristics. Of course, the employer may have preferred the option of choosing this procedure rather than having it imposed by statute, but the values incorporated in the statutes may nevertheless include some of these employer protections. The statutes may give recognition to inhouse methods of dispute resolution (employee manuals) to the benefit of employers who may wish to use such systems.[38] In addition, the statutes may require uniform, nondiscriminatory treatment of employees. This may be in the interests of some employers to the extent that it promotes the greater availability of more potential employees.[39]

The public sector is the product of constitutional and legislative mandates. Without statutes, it would not exist. It is commonly suggested that the public employer does not have the same interests in entrepreneurial rights as the private sector employer. Courts do not always recognize that there is a large difference in the two. "There is a tension inherent in the government's role as employer. In its capacity as government, its actions are constrained by the constitution in ways that the actions of private entities are not. In its proprietary capacity, however, it must be free to make efficient personnel decisions."[40] When courts discuss the government as employer, they look to many of the same factors that are used in the private sector. For example, when the U.S. Supreme Court considered the rights of public employees to speak out on matters of public concern, they used the following common concepts in balancing the rights of the employees and the government employers: harmony among co-workers, impact on close working relationships, and interference with operations of office.[41] These are well-known elements in the private sector. Private and public employees face many of the same employment problems. Concepts of employer rights recognized in the private sector are often used in the public sector to help resolve disputes over the employment relationship. A workplace is a workplace.

In summary, employer rights are the single most important element in the judicial resolution of individual contract disputes. When the contract dispute also involves a statutory right, employer rights concepts may also be incorporated into the statute and continue to play a dominating role in the interpretation of the statue. Of the three elements of employer rights—judicial restraint, entrepreneurial control and business judgment, and employee duties—statutes appear to have the greatest impact in lessening the element of judicial restraint. Specific statutes may have additional impacts, such as the impact of whistleblower statutes on the common notions of the employee's duty of loyalty. Public and private employers may be covered by some of the same legislation. This gives some additional credibility to the notion that public and private employers share the same interests in many employer rights. Figure 7.1 summarizes some of the statutory impacts.

Figure 7.1   Examples: Statutory Impacts on Employer Rights

```
Cause Replaces At Will
Constitutional Limits On Employer
Duty of Loyalty, Whistleblowers
Efficiency, Accommodation of Handicap
Judicial Restraint Limitations
Limitations On Punitive, Other Damages
Nondiscrimination Limits At Will
Nonretaliation Limits At Will
Required Balance of Public, Employee, and Employer Interests
Suspension, Demotion, Require Cause
```

STATUTES AND AT WILL CONTRACTS

Statutes may impact on individual employment contracts in both the private and the public sector. In the private sector, the scope of the statutes may vary. Some statutes apply generally to a large number of individual contracts of employment, some statutes apply to only a particular type of employment, and some are only indirectly concerned with the individual contract.

Some states have adopted the language of the common law at will employment doctrine in statutory form. California is one of these states,[42] but it has also been a leader in judicial reform of that doctrine. Another type of statute sets a definite term period for contracts that do not themselves specify the duration of employment. An example of this type is a state statute that adopts the salary period or pay period as being the duration of the fixed employment term.[43] If there is a monthly pay period the contract is month to month. A statute may provide for a week of notice for discharge or quitting, unless reasonable cause exists. Failure to give the week of notice will cause the obligated person to pay a week of wages.[44]

Montana

The most comprehensive private sector statute to date affecting individual contracts is the Montana legislation that substantially limits the common law at will doctrine and encourages use of the arbitration forum for employment dispute legislation. The statute was challenged in litigation after the legislature passed it, but the Montana Supreme Court upheld it against the challenge.[45]

The definitional section of the statute includes constructive and actual discharges.[46] Employer and employee are broadly defined. Wrongful discharges include retaliation for the employee's refusal to violate public policy, lack of good cause if the employee is beyond probation, and violation of the employer's own written policies. Discharges prohibited by other statutes, which provide a procedure for relief, employees covered by a collective bargaining agreement, and employees covered by an individual definite term contract, are not under the legislation.[47]

From the procedural perspective, the statute provides for a judicial forum, or for an arbitration forum where the parties agree.[48] There is a one year period of limitations after which the action cannot be brought.[49] If arbitration is used, the arbitrator's award is final and binding, with limited judicial review available.[50]

Remedies under the Montana statute include up to four years of back pay. Punitive damages are permitted only if there is clear and convincing evidence of actual fraud or malice.[51] The requirement of clear and convincing evidence is a much higher evidentiary burden than the preponderance of the evidence test that is commonly required in civil actions. The purpose of this higher requirement is to limit access to punitive damages.

The statute pre-empts all other tort or contract remedies for the discharge.[52] As indicated, where other remedial forums are provided by statute those forums must be used, not this special legislation.

The overall characteristics of the statute are to encourage the use of nonjudicial forums, to require that discharges must generally be based on cause, and to limit the remedies available to employees for wrongful discharge.

Virgin Islands

Less comprehensive but significant legislation is found in the Virgin Islands and Puerto Rico. The Virgin Islands legislation sets forth a detailed definition of just cause for discharge. Discharge for any other reason is deemed to be a wrongful discharge. An employee claiming a wrongful discharge has 30 days to request a hearing.[53] If the employee is found to have been wrongfully discharged, the hearing officer can award reinstatement with back pay.[54] Limited judicial review is available.[55] The wrongfully discharged employee may also bring an action in court for compensatory and punitive damages.[56]

Puerto Rico

The Puerto Rico legislation covers at will employees.[57] The statute defines good cause, with a list of examples.[58] If the at will employee has been discharged without good cause, the employee is entitled to one month's salary plus one week's salary for each year of service.[59] Constructive discharge is also covered.[60]

Miscellaneous Statutes

In the category of more limited impact legislation affecting the individual employment contract are statutes that speak to specific types of employment. One type of statute may provide for a cause based discharge after the employee has served a substantial probationary period.[61] Cause may be required in particular trades, such as a ship pilot.[62] Another statute provides limited protection for a very narrow type of employment, the lawyer inhouse corporate counsel position.[63] Under state and federal laws, certain bank officers may be prohibited from being employed on any basis other than common law at will.[64] State statutes must be carefully read to identify the narrow focus of the legislation.

Indirect Legislation

Other types of statutes may be only indirectly concerned with the individual employment contract, but may still play an important role in some situations. Mention will be made of whistleblower statutes that can intrude into an attempted at will discharge.[65] A statute may go only to the issue of remedies. Much of the individual contract at will litigation is fueled to some extent by the potential of large punitive damage awards. Legislation in one state seeks to put a cap on punitive damages. That limit on damages is likely to limit the volume of litigation that may arise in the future.[66]

Nonretaliation Legislation

Nonretaliation provisions found in a great variety of legislation will impact on the common law right of the employer to arbitrarily discharge the at will employee.[67] Under these provisions an employee may have a cause of action against an employer who disciplines an employee for seeking to exercise rights under the statute. These provisions may be closely related to whistleblower legislation.

Public Sector Legislation

In the public sector, legislation has long intruded into the individual contract relationship. Some of the legislation that affects the private sector may also apply to some aspects of the public sector, such as civil rights legislation.[68] State legislation may provide for job protection through tenure or merit systems that require just cause to discharge.[69] In addition, these statutes may set up forums for employment contract dispute resolution outside of the courts.[70] These statutes may go beyond the basic employer actions of discharge or dismissal and also provide that the employee cannot be "suspended, demoted, or dismissed" unless there is just cause.[71] Another broad scope statute provides that just cause is required if the employee is to be "reprimanded, discharged, suspended without pay, or demoted."[72] Another provides that the employee shall not be suspended, removed, fined or reduced in rank or in office, employment or position therein except for just cause.[73] It may be recalled that these topics going beyond discharge are those that are still in a state of flux in the courts in the private sector.[74]

The constitution itself plays a significant role. Due process may require hearings prior to discharge where property or liberty issues are raised.[75] In the public sector, the constitution has greatly limited the summary action that can be taken under the common law at will doctrine because pretermination or posttermination hearings may be required.

In summary, there are a variety of statutes that are aimed at altering some aspects of the individual contract of employment. In the private sector, the Montana legislation has the greatest scope of coverage concerning the individual contract. In the public sector, statutes and constitutional demands rule many aspects of the relationship, but there is strong recognition of the government's interests as an employer.

If one were identifying only three trends in statutes on individual contracts of employment, perhaps two of the most important would be the creation of new forums as alternatives to the courts and the limitation of damages, especially punitive damages, that might be available to the employee. The third is the growing use of provisions for nonretaliation when the employee seeks to exercise statutory rights, or whistleblower protection involving a public interest.

234 Individual Employment Disputes

PUBLIC POLICY AND AT WILL CONTRACTS

An increasing number of states recognize the doctrine that arbitrary discharges that violate public policy are improper.[76] The purpose here is not to plumb the depths of public policy exception to the at will contract doctrine, but only to consider a few examples. This is a rapidly changing area that must be watched in each state for new developments.

Although the recognition of the public policy doctrine is expanding, it is still a narrow doctrine. Not any reference to public policy argument will give rise to this at will contract exception. Where the doctrine is recognized, there is generally only a very narrow definition of public policy for these purposes. In general, the public policy must be clear and definite.[77] The public policy exception argument may be stronger where the employee faces personal liability if the employee follows the employer's orders to violate the public policy.[78] General notions of morality however valid and well recognized, such as reporting theft within a company, may not protect the employee under the employment doctrine of public policy.[79]

A statutorily defined public policy rather than a generalized statement of public policy may more easily fit the definition, but not all statutory policies will fit the public policy category. Statutory policies that seek to promote full employment concepts will not be recognized as a public policy basis for challenging a discharge.[80] A statute may contain a clear and definite public policy and may also include a dispute resolution mechanism within the statute. If a statutory forum is created, frequently the employee will have to use the statutory forum rather than rely on a common law public policy law suit in court to challenge the alleged breach of public policy aspect of the contractual relationship.[81]

The public policy evidenced in statutes may be seen as a legislative mandate to balance the interests of the employer and employee. This mandated balance may be, in part, a recognition of the general reluctance of courts to recognize a balancing of rights in the absence of statute.[82] The public policy of the statute may be a recognition of a public interest that is distinct from any direct interest in the employment relationship,[83] or it may be an interest in rearranging the employment contract relationship itself.[84] Where it is a public interest distinct from any direct interest in the employment relationship, it may require the courts to balance the interests of the public against the interests of both the employee and employer. Courts are generally reluctant to perform this type of balance in the absence of a statute.

In addition to public policy considerations that impact more heavily on the employee rights side, significant public policy considerations in statutes may also give recognition to employer rights. Those doctrines of public policy impacting on the employer rights side of an employment contract are frequently identified by the courts when interpreting the statute, rather than by explicit legislative language. As indicated above, the judicial policy of protecting employer business judgments and the public policies favoring doctrines that enhance the opportunity for the employer to operate a profitable and efficient business are strongly recognized, frequently enunciated policies repeated by most courts when interpreting statutes.[85]

In summary, statutes are increasingly used to create public policies that impact on the individual contract relationship. The public policy might be one aimed at the workplace, or it might be one that identifies an interest of the public beyond the workplace. Either of these types of statutes may have the effect of expanding the rights of the employee in a contract dispute. However, the at will doctrine and many other judicial doctrines involved in traditional individual contract analysis are recognition of a strong public policy interest in giving the employer an opportunity to run efficiently and make a profit. These employer related public policies must be given great weight even when a statute is put into the picture.

RETALIATION AND WHISTLEBLOWING STATUTES

Many statutory protections extend to both indefinite term and fixed term employees. Two types of provisions are especially broad in their potential impact. One type involves protection for employees from retaliation when they seek to exercise statutory rights, such as the antiretaliation provisions in equal employment legislation. The second type of statute protects employees who report illegal or improper actions of their employers to appropriate officials, such as the whistleblower statutes. There is some overlap between the antiretaliation and whistleblower statutes. There is also some overlap between these statutes and cases that recognize a judicially created public policy exception to the at will doctrine. The public policy exception recognized by a few courts protects employees who are discharged for reasons that violate public policy, similar to whistleblower statutes. There are many efforts to expand the scope of the judicially created public policy exception preventing retaliation, but relatively few succeed.[86] The primary focus here is on retaliation for exercising statutory rights rather than claims based on some broad general public policy.

A frequent claim of unlawful retaliation arises when an employee files a race or sex discrimination complaint and the employer retaliates by discharging the employee.[87] Another statute that is frequently involved is the worker compensation statute.[88] The retaliation claim is separate and distinct from the other claims. Thus where an employee claims discrimination action but cannot prove it, the employee may still be able to prove the separate claim of retaliation if the employer punished the employee for raising the claim.[89] In the discrimination area, persons who are not the victim of discrimination may attempt to promote the rights of others who are perceived to be victims. The advocates may be able to recover for retaliation if they are punished because of their advocacy.[90] Advocacy and protest must take place within limited bounds. Where the employee is making false and malicious statements, the reckless employee will not be able to claim protection under the retaliation clause of a statute.[91] Protection may also be lost where there is no factual or legal basis for the claims being made.[92] A variety of statutes may contain protection against retaliation.[93]

Whistleblowing legislation is aimed at protecting an employee who exposes certain defined types of illegal or improper activities. This legislation is frequently drafted to have narrow application and the courts may read it strictly. Employees who go beyond this narrow license will not be protected. Nuclear power workers have some protection under the Federal Energy Reorganization Act. However, this protection is available only from an administrative agency, not from the courts.[94] This protection was denied to an employee who left a work station without permission in order to do research on possible violation of industry codes.[95] The legislation may also pre-empt the nuclear employee's state claims.[96] The Federal Railroad Safety Act may have the same pre-emptive effect on state claims.[97]

Whistleblower legislation must be read carefully. Courts are inclined to read employment statutes in a narrow manner. For example, where the statute protects reporting unlawful activity that represents a "substantial and specific danger to the public health or safety," the employee must allege exactly that—substantial, specific, health, or safety. Possible illegality is not enough.[98] Only those public employees who report illegal activity to actual law enforcement authorities may be protected in some statutes.[99] Reporting the same improper activities to the employer may not be protected by statute or exceptions to the at will doctrine.[100] Efforts to have an employer comply with professional codes of ethics may not be protected.[101]

When the protected reporting of employer activity is limited to reporting illegal activity, the employee may be faced with a difficult problem of knowing whether the activity really is illegal. One recent court decision protected an employee from retaliation when the employee sought advice about the legality of the employer action.[102] If the employee reports the alleged illegal activity, as of yet there is no clear rule on whether protection is extended to the employee if it turns out that the action is not illegal. One court would require the report to involve an actual statutory violation and the employee's reasonable belief that there was a violation would be insufficient.[103] Another court would only require the employee to have a reasonable and good faith belief in illegality. If the reported action turned out to be legal, the reasonable and good faith belief would be sufficient for protection.[104] The making of such narrow distinctions illustrates the difficulties employees may face.

Some disclosures of information to public authorities are prohibited by law. Where an employee allowed county officials to look at patient records concerning patient care, the employee was not protected by the whistleblower statute because under another statute there was a prohibition on disclosure of the patient records.[105]

Whistleblower legislation seeks to protect both the employee and the public. Where a whistleblowing problem arises, an employer may seek to settle the matter quietly with the complaining employee. The settlement may include terms whereby the employee cannot reveal the subject of the whistleblowing to anyone. The Nuclear Regulatory Commission has identified the existence of several of these settlements relating to nuclear safety. The Commission has declared the settlements void under the Energy Reorganization Act.[106] Whistleblower legislation must also protect the legitimate rights of both public and private employers. Internal decision making processes may need to be confidential. Trade secrets require protection.

In summary, antiretaliation provisions and whistleblower statutes are major statutory exceptions to the at will employment contract doctrine. In addition, these statutory provisions require a balancing of employee, employer, and public interests that courts are not often willing to recognize in the absence of statutes. These provisions may be narrowly drafted and may be narrowly construed. This narrowness is a reflection of employer interests that need substantial protection. Protecting employer interests is also a public policy goal. However, as the Supreme Court has recognized, employment statutes may represent an explicit decision that courts should show less judicial restraint when interpreting statutes than they traditionally use in applying common law or judge made doctrine.

PROPOSALS FOR AT WILL MODIFICATION LEGISLATION

There are only a few examples of enacted statutes directly aimed at the individual at will contract, as indicated in a preceding section. There are, however, a great many proposals being considered in various states. This section looks at some aspects of these proposals. The purpose here is not to examine any one proposal in depth, but rather, to identify the range of issues that the proposals cover. By looking at the range of general issues, an employer or employee may be better able to judge the merits of proposals that may be under consideration in their jurisdiction. The same breakdown is used here that was used earlier in this section—definitions, procedure, remedies, and pre-emption.

Definitions

The definition of employer and employee is paramount. The major element in defining employer is the term relating to the size of the employer that will be covered by the statute. In a Massachusetts proposal, six or more employees define the covered employer.[107] Public employers are commonly excluded.[108] Covered employees may be described by reference to high or low income[109] or by reference to high level status.[110] Higher level or higher income employees may be excluded from protected coverage. Probationary employees are likely to be excluded.[111] Part-time employees will usually be excluded.[112] The proposals usually exclude employees under collective bargaining contracts, because they usually have a contractual grievance mechanism. Independent contractors are also excluded.[113]

Just cause may be defined in the proposal, using traditional concepts.[114] Notice and reasons for the discharge may be required to be provided and sent to the employee.[115]

Procedure

A major procedural issue is burden of proof. The legislative proposals variously put the burden of proof of wrongful discharge on the employee[116] or on the employer.[117] The period of limitations may range from a year[118] to 14 days.[119] Various dispute resolution forums may be involved. One proposal uses a government agency hearing process.[120] More commonly, mediation and arbitration forums would be used.[121] Costs of arbitration may be apportioned in various ways, depending on who wins and other elements.[122] Inhouse grievance mechanisms may be encouraged.[123] Limited judicial review and enforcement might be available.[124] Waivers of the protective legislation may or may not be prohibited.[125]

Remedies

Reinstatement and back pay are traditional remedies for improper discharge that are recognized in the proposals.[126] However, reinstatement need not be awarded where there is likely to be friction or other difficulties in the employment relationship.[127] Front pay of a limited duration or limited liquidated damages may be awarded in some proposals.[128] Nonretaliation provisions may also be included.[129]

Pre-emption

There is great variation in the pre-emption provisions of the legislative proposals. Some specifically provide for no pre-emption, that is, the full range of common law remedies would remain available.[130] This would not, however, permit the employee to recover more than once on the same cause of action. Others provide for complete pre-emption.[131] State legislation is not likely to eliminate federal remedies, so many issues of pre-emption are likely to remain to be resolved by the courts no matter how the legislation is phrased. Some proposals specifically preclude pre-emption of claims of employment discrimination.[132] Many proposals are silent on the subject.

In summary, the legislative proposals vary widely in many of the areas of definitions, procedure, remedies, and pre-emption. However, there are common themes. All proposals seek to reduce the employer's potential liability and the employee's potential recovery. They put a major emphasis on nonjudicial forums of dispute resolution, and often favor arbitration. Presumably these nonjudicial forums would concentrate more on actual employment issues than on the niceties of common law contract doctrine. Employer rights to exercise business judgments are generally given explicit protection and doubtlessly will be given implicit recognition by the dispute resolution forum.

National Conference of Commissioners on Uniform State Laws

Among the more important proposals is the one being drafted by the National Conference of Commissioners on Uniform State Laws. In the definitional section, employee is defined as an individual who works 20 hours or more per week, with an exception for high level employees. Employer is a person who employs 15 or more, thus exempting small employers. Termination includes the usual discharge, plus a constructive discharge, or a layoff for more than six months.[133] Employees under collective bargaining agreements or

under individual definite or specified term contracts are excluded.[134]
A one-year probationary period is not covered by the statute.[135]

By way of procedure, the aggrieved employee has a 180 day period
of limitations in which to bring the action.[136] The dispute resolution
process includes reference to inhouse procedures, filing with the appropriate agency, mediation,[137] and arbitration.[138] The employer has
the burden of proving the violation.[139] Limited judicial review is
permitted.[140]

For remedies, the proposal includes reinstatement, back pay, and a
possible liquidated damage not to exceed the amount of back pay. In
lieu of reinstatement, severance pay of up to two years total can be
allowed.[141] The usual nonretaliation provision is included.[142]

The proposal would pre-empt tort or contract claims based on the
same facts as the termination, but would not necessarily apply to or
pre-empt claims of discrimination.[143] The arbitrator's award is
deemed to be final and binding.[144]

The initial reaction to the commissioners' draft was mixed. However, the drafting effort continues. Many changes are expected in some
of the items described above.[145]

In summary, these various proposals to alter the at will contract will
not touch all workplaces, which will make careful reading of the
definition section extremely important. Among the major exceptions
are persons under collective bargaining contracts. It is useful to note,
however, that these proposals incorporate many of the elements found
in the collective bargaining contract relationship, most notably the
preference shown to arbitration and other nonjudicial forms of contract dispute resolution, and the requirement of cause. Figure 7.2
summarizes some of the issues arising in the debate over at will
modification.

The proposals also make it clear that there is great diversity in
approaches. Under existing judicial doctrine at the state level, each
state takes a somewhat different approach than other states. This
disparity of approaches is likely to find itself repeated among those
states that adopt a legislative method to resolving disputes about
individual contracts of employment.

ISSUES REMAINING UNDER STATUTORY TERMINATION
PROPOSALS

One purpose of the statutory proposals is to rebalance the rights of
employers and employees under indefinite term individual contracts.
Many other questions that have uncertain answers under current
judicial doctrine might be clarified by the statutory proposals. Like

Figure 7.2 Issues: At Will Modification Proposals

```
Definition:     Employer Size
                Public or Private Coverage
                Employee Definition, e.g., High Level
                Probationary Status
                Part time
                Discharge, Constructive Discharge
                Applicability to Fixed Term Contract
                Just Cause

Procedure:      Burden of Proof
                Period of Limitations
                Forum:   Arbitration, Court, Inhouse,
                            Agency
                Judicial Review, Availability, Scope
                Waivers Prohibited, Permitted

Remedies:       Reinstatement
                Punitive Damages
                Back Pay, Limitation on Length
                Front Pay
                Time Limits on Recovery
                Nonretaliation

Preemption:     Mentioned, Not Mentioned
                Total or Limited
```

any proposal or enacted statute, however, not all of the potential issues are addressed and the language used in many of the proposals may itself create some new issues. The purpose of this section is to identify some of these major issues that arise when looking at the proposals in general.

Many of the proposals include the use of arbitration as the forum for dispute resolution for individual contracts of employment. Arbitration can take many forms. A major question that the proposals do not address is how closely the proposed arbitration forum will follow the type of arbitration currently used under collective bargaining contracts in the private sector. Two of the major points here are whether the employer will have the burden of proof in discharge cases under the proposals and whether the arbitrator will have the power to mitigate the discharge decision into a lesser penalty, such as a suspension without pay for a period. Both of these concepts are commonly used in the private sector collective bargaining arbitration today. Other major issues include whether the arbitration under the proposals is essentially final and binding and whether it precludes the bringing of other actions, such as an action for discrimination against a protected class member.

Another large issue to consider is the role of any inhouse grievance mechanisms. Is the statutory forum the preferred forum, or does the statutory proposal seek to give greater recognition of and promote the use of any inhouse grievance mechanism? If the proposals give preference to inhouse grievance mechanisms, the proposals will reflect existing public policy efforts to encourage the creation of in-house grievance mechanisms in the nonunion employment sector. Where such preference is given, care will have to be given to such matters as whether the employer is permitted to unilaterally change the grievance mechanism (issue a new handbook), and if so, will the statutory proposal spell out minimal standards of protection to be included in the inhouse grievance mechanism. The scope of judicial review will also be important.

Another major area of questions concerns the scope of the statutory proposal. Will it cover only traditional discharges or terminations, or will it also cover constructive discharges, or will it will also cover demotions or transfers that have a punitive aroma? The treatment of releases or waivers of rights is another significant issue that should be resolved in the legislation.

In summary, a rash of proposals is being put forward to legislatively correct some of the perceived problems of the judicially created at will discharge doctrine. Although these proposals address many issues, they also raise a number of issues. The approach requiring just cause and arbitration appears to be the most popular, but it is still unclear whether the proposals also adopt the major elements of the arbitration system developed in the private sector. The role of inhouse grievance mechanisms is left uncertain in some proposals at a time when the courts have been putting more and more emphasis on such proce-dures.

CONCLUSION

It seems clear that the workplace experiences a high level of conflict and distrust between employees and employers in many circumstan-ces. This is reflected in a growing amount of litigation. Arguably, the rash of recent litigation arising under individual contracts of employ-ment does not reflect new problems in the workplace, but it is simply the mechanism through which long-standing conflicts and elements of distrust have been permitted to find voice. The statutory proposals are an effort to channel these problems into new forums and answer some of the many problems inevitably left open by the ad hoc nature of the courtroom trial and appellate processes. The choice at this point for states seems to be one between the continuation of ad hoc judicial policies based on turn of the century contract notions or more structured legislative attempts at providing a better balance between employee, employer, and public interests under individual contracts of employment.

The major characteristic exhibited by the judicial forum in this context is the great deference given to employer rights, based on judicially defined public policy factors. A major goal of most proposals is not only to continue to give great deference to employer rights, but also to create more of a balancing process when resolving disputes between the two parties to the employment contract. Employer rights are made up of three major elements: judicial restraint, entrepreneurial control or business judgments, and the duties owed by the employee to the employer. In general, the passage of legislation appears to have the most impact on lessening judicial restraint, and less impact on the protection given business judgments or the employees' duties.

There is a significant amount of legislation that already impacts directly or indirectly on limited elements of the individual employment contract. Some of it touches directly on the contract relationship and may mandate a certain relationship, such as nondiscrimination. Some of it also creates special forums for employment dispute resolution. A larger area of existing legislation creates public policies that courts may apply to the individual contract relationship. Some of this policy is directly aimed at the employment relationship, such as antidiscrimination statutes, and some of it is aimed at larger public policy issues, such as the various whistleblower statutes.

Many new legislative proposals are being considered that focus directly on individual at will contracts of employment. The future of these at will contract proposals is uncertain, but the fact of increasing legislative impact on the individual contract is certain. The thrust of the statutory proposals is to require far more use of cause as the basis of discharge, to provide a new forum, often arbitration, for dispute resolution, and to limit the amount of potential employee recovery.

Discharge is the main focus of these contract proposals. The judicial case law shows that many courts apply the at will discharge approach to many nondischarge facets of the employment relationship. This broader use of the at will approach can leave many questions unanswered if the legislative proposals neglect to cover such issues as constructive discharges, punitive demotions, punitive transfers, and related personnel decisions.

At present, a major concern of employers who are sued on the basis of employment contract is the question of whether they will be subject to the potential of enormous punitive damages that go far beyond compensatory damages. Under the legislative proposals, a common theme is to reduce this potential. The proposals attempt to strike a balance by recognizing an employer's right to be free of excessive damage awards while providing the employees with a dispute resolution forum that gives a more balanced, faster, and cheaper look at the employment dispute.

Up to this point in time, the courts have been the primary interpreters of individual contracts of employment. The courts created the at will doctrine and some of them have modified it. Legislation, not courts, is likely to have the greatest impact on individual contracts of employment in the future. Legislation may be of two types. One type deals with a specific problem and rearranges the employment relationship on that issue, such as whistleblower or nonretaliation provisions in statutes. The second type deals broadly with the at will doctrine by changing the rules as to forum, procedure, and remedy. The question in each jurisdiction is whether they will adopt an increasing number of limited application statutes or whether they will deal comprehensively with the at will relationship.

The adoption of a general application statute changing the judicial at will employment relationship may have a significant impact beyond the obvious creation of new forums and limitations on recovery. The general requirement of good cause for discharge is one example. Good cause is a concept that includes recognition of significant public policy elements of employer interests. It also has a large general public policy overtone. Whereas many collective bargaining arbitrators seemed historically reluctant to recognize it, it cannot be doubted today that a discharge based on discrimination cannot be based on just cause. The continued development of public policy through the just cause requirement will be interesting. Historically, arbitration has been defined by what the limited number of private sector collective bargaining arbitrators have done. The noncollective bargaining workforce that might be reached by arbitrators under some of the statutory proposals is immensely larger than the collective bargaining population. The revitalization and challenge to the arbitration process that we know today will be another enormously interesting evolution.

Adoption of a statutory limitation on the at will doctrine may create a new interest in the use of fixed term contracts that can be arbitrarily nonrenewed at the end of the term. It will be an ironic outcome if the legislative fix for the current furor over the at will contract is replaced by a similar furor over arbitrary action coming at the renewal point of fixed term contracts.

NOTES

1. DiTomaso v. Electronic Data Systems, 3 Indiv. Empl. Rights (BNA) 1700 (D. Mich. 1988); U.S. v. Garde, 3 Indiv. Empl. Rights (BNA) 1109 (D.C. Cir. 1988); Chrisman v. Philips Indus. Inc. 181 (Kan. Sup. Ct. 1988).

2. Equal Employment Opportunity Act, 42 U.S.C.A. 2000e-2(a) (1989).

3. Id. at 42 U.S.C.A. 2000e-3(a) (1989).

4. Norris v. Lumbermen's Mutual Casualty, 4 Indiv. Empl. Rights (BNA) 1030 (1st Cir. 1989); Cox v. Radiology Consulting Assoc., Inc., 2 Indiv. Empl. Rights (BNA) 233 (D. Pa. 1987); Nietert v. Overby, 2 Indiv. Empl. Rights (BNA) 89 (10th Cir. 1987).

5. NLRB v. City Disposal Systems, 465 U.S. 822 (1984); Brock v. Roadway Express, Inc., 481 U.S. 252 (1987).

6. Smith v. Travelers Mortgage Services, 3 Indiv. Empl. Rights (BNA) 1706 (D. N.J. 1988); Tyrna v. Adamos Inc., 2 Indiv. Empl. Rights (BNA) 407 (Mich. Ct. App. 1987).

7. E.g., O.R.S. 243.650 243.782 (1989).

8. E.g., O.R.S. 243.662 (1989).

9. Board of Regents of State Colleges v. Roth, 408 U.S. 564 (1972); Perry v. Sinderman, 408 U.S. 593 (1982).

10. Lyons v. Barrett, 3 Indiv. Empl. Rights (BNA) 780 (D.C. Cir. 1988).

11. Berg v. Hunter, 3 Indiv. Empl. Rights (BNA) 1317 (7th Cir. 1988).

12. Equal Employment Opportunities Act, 42 U.S.C.A. 2000e(b) (1989).

13. Mont. Code Ann. 39–2-904(2), Lab. Rel. Rep. Indiv. Empl. Rights Manual (BNA) 567:5 (1989).

14. Labor Management Relations Act, 29 U.S.C.A. 152(11) (1989).

15. "There is nothing inherently unreasonable about a six-month limitations period. For example, six months is the time limit within which claims must be brought for breach of the duty of fair representation under the Labor Management Relations Act." Myers v. Western-Southern Life Insur. Co., 3 Indiv. Empl. Rights (BNA) 723, 725 (6th Cir. 1988).

16. Mont. Code Ann. 39–2-905, Lab. Rel. Rep. Indiv. Empl. Rights Manual (BNA) 567:5 (1989).

17. Id. at 39–2-905(2).

18. Alexander v. Gardner-Denver Co., 415 U.S. 36 (1974).

19. Occupational Safety and Health Act, 29 U.S.C.A,. 667 (1989).

20. Miller v. AT&T Network Systems, 3 Indiv. Empl. Rights (BNA) 966 (9th Cir. 1988); Young v. Anthony's Fish Grottos, 2 Indiv. Empl. Rights (BNA) 1086 (9th Cir. 1987).

21. Paradis v. United Technologies, 2 Indiv. Empl. Rights (BNA) 1221 (D. Conn. 1987); Paige v. Henry J. Kaiser Co., 2 Indiv. Empl. Rights (BNA) 705 (9th Cir. 1987).

22. Miller v. AT&T Network Systems, 3 Indiv. Empl. Rights (BNA) 967, 969–970 (9th Cir. 1988).

23. Krasinski v. United Parcel Service Inc., 3 Indiv. Empl. Rights (BNA) 1674 (Ill. Sup. Ct. 1988).

24. Baldracchi v. Pratt & Whitney Aircraft, 2 Indiv. Empl. Rights (BNA) 572 (2d Cir. 1987).

25. "Courts are generally less competent than employers to restructure business practices, and unless mandated to do so by Congress they should not attempt it." Furnco Const. Corp. v. Waters, 438 U.S. 567, 578 (1978).

26. Douglas v. Anderson, 115 L.R.R.M. (BNA) 4906, 4911 (9th Cir. 1981).

27. Criddle v. Hickory Hill Furniture Co., 34 Empl. Prac. Dec. (CCH) 34,547 at 34,443 (D. Miss. 1984).

28. Callicotte v. Carlucci, 698 F. Supp. 944, 951 (D. D.C. 1988).

29. Furnco Constr. Corp. v. Waters, 438 U.S. 567 (1978).

30. Patterson v. McLean Credit Union, 109 S. Ct. 2363 (1989).

31. Age Discrimination in Employment Act, 29 U.S.C.A. 623(i)(5).

32. Mont. Code Ann. 39–2-904(2), Lab. Rel. Rep. Indiv. Empl. Rights Manual (BNA) 567:5 (1989).

33. E.g., Michigan Whistleblower Discrimination, Lab. Rel. Rep. Indiv. Empl. Rights Manual (BNA) 563:7 (1989).

34. Norris v. Lumbermen's Mutual Casualty, 4 Indiv. Empl. Rights (BNA) 1030 (1st Cir. 1989).

35. Nees v. Hocks, 272 Or. 209 (1975).

36. First Nat'l Maintenance Corp. v. NLRB, 452 U.S. 666 (1981).

37. Mont. Code Ann. 39–2-914, Lab. Rel. Rep. Indiv. Empl. Rights Manual (BNA) 567:6 (1989).

38. Id. at 39–2-911, Lab. Rel. Rep. Indiv. Empl. Rights Manual (BNA) 567:6 (1989).

39. "[The] . . . available manpower should be used to the fullest extent possible." ORS 659.015 (1989).

40. Arvinger v. City of Baltimore, 3 Indiv. Empl. Rights (BNA) 1801, 1801–802 (4th Cir. 1988).

41. Rankin v. McPherson, 483 U.S. 378 (1987).

42. Calif. Employment at Will, Lab. Rel. Rep. Indiv. Empl. Rights Manual (BNA) 545:23 (1989).

43. South Dakota, Employment at will, Lab. Rel. Rep. Indiv. Empl. Rights Manual (BNA) 583:2 (1989).

44. Me. Rev. Stat. Ann. Tit. 26, 625-B (Supp. 1989).

45. Meech v. Hillhaven West Inc., 4 Indiv. Empl. Rights (BNA) 737 (Mont. Sup. Ct. 1989).

46. Mont. Code Ann. 39–2-903, Lab. Rel. Rep. Indiv. Empl. Rights Manual (BNA) 567:5 (1989).

47. Id. at 39–2-912, at 567:6.

48. Id. at 39–2-914, at 567:6.

49. Id. at 39–2-911, at 567:6.

50. Id. at 39–2-914, at 567:6.

51. Id. at 34–2-905, at 567:5.

52. Id. at 39–2-913, at 567:6.

53. V.I. Code Ann. Tit. 24, 77 (Supp. 1987).

54. Id. at 77.

55. Id. at 78.

56. Id. at 79.

57. P.R. Laws Ann. Tit. 29, 185a.

58. Id. at 185b.

59. Id. at 185a.

60. Id. at 185e.

61. Shell v. Metropolitan Life. Insur. Co., 4 Indiv. Empl. Rights (BNA) 579 (W. Va. Sup. Ct. 1989).

62. Ala. Code 33–4-33 (1975).

63. Ill. Senate Bill 13 Enrolled (1989).

64. Citizens State Bank of N.J. v. Libertelli, 2 Indiv. Empl. Rights (BNA) 116 (N.J. Super. Ct. 1987); Zatkin v. Bank of the Commonwealth, 2 Indiv. Empl. Rights (BNA) 1466 (Mich. Ct. App. 1987); Trujillo v. FDIC, 3 Indiv. Empl. Rights (BNA) 38 (D. Cal. 1988); but see Potter v. Village Bank of N.J., 3 Indiv. Empl. Rights (BNA) 1076 (N.J. Super. Ct. 1988).

65. Fn. 86–106, infra.

66. Punitive Damages, 7 BNA Employee Rel. Weekly 711 (1981).

67. Equal Employment Opportunities Act, 42 U.S.C.A. 2000e-3(a) (1989).

68. Garcia v. San Antonio Metro Transit Auth., 469 U.S. 528 (1985).

69. E.g., O.R.S. 342.845 (1989).

70. E.g., O.R.S. 342.905 (1989).

71. Mass. Ann. Law ch. 31A, 7 (Law. Co-op. 1983).

72. Minn. Stat. Ann. 43A.33 (West 1988).

73. N.J. Stat. Ann. 40A: 14–19 (West 1980).

74. Ch. 6, fn. 158–166.

75. Board of Regents of State Colleges v. Roth, 408 U.S. 564 (1972); Perry v. Sinderman, 408 U.S. 593 (1972).

76. 9A Indiv. Empl. Rights Manual (BNA) 505:51 (1989).

77. Johnson v. Kreiser's Inc., 3 Indiv. Empl. Rights (BNA) 1767 (S.D. Sup. Ct. 1988).

78. McClanahan v. Remington Freight Lines Inc., 2 Indiv. Empl. Rights (BNA) 1888 (Ind. Sup. Ct. 1988).

79. Smalley v. Fast Fare Inc., 4 Indiv. Empl. Rights (BNA) 105 (D. S.C. 1988).

80. Maxwell v. Ross Hyden Motors Inc., 2 Indiv. Empl. Rights (BNA) 1342 (N.M. Ct. App. 1986).

81. Walt v. Alaska, 3 Indiv. Empl. Rights (BNA) 649 (Alaska Sup. Ct. 1988); Hunnewell v. Mfr. Hanover Trust Co., 2 Indiv. Empl. Rights (BNA) 933 (D. N.Y. 1986).

82. Ch. 3, fn. 193–208.

83. Norris v. Lumbermen's Mutual Casualty, 4 Indiv. Empl. Rights (BNA) 1030 (1st Cir. 1989).

84. E.g., Michigan Whistleblower Discrimination, Lab. Rel. Rep. Indiv. Empl. Rights Manual (BNA) 563:7–8 (1989).

85. See ch. 3.

86. Maus v. National Living Centers, Inc., 663 S.W. 2d 674 (Tex. Ct. App. 1982); Morton v. Hartigan, 495 N.E. 2d 1159 (Ill. App. Ct. 1986).

87. Bailey v. USX Corp., 850 F.2d 1506 (11th Cir. 1988).

88. Burrow v. Westinghouse Electric Corp., 363 S.E.2d 215 (N.C. Ct. App. 1988).

89. Sparrow v. Piedmont Health Systems Agency, Inc., 593 F. Supp. 1107 (D. N.C. 1984).

90. Spence v. UAW, Local 1250, 595 F. Supp. 6 (D. Ohio 1984).

91. Barnes v. Small, 840 F.2d 972 (D.C. Cir. 1988).

92. Kern v. DePaul Mental Health Services, 529 N.Y.S.2d 265 (N.Y. Sup. Ct. 1988).

93. Shores v. Senior Manor Nursing Center, Inc., 518 N.E.2d 471 (Ill. App. Ct. 1988) (Nursing Home Care Reform Act); Sheets v. Teddy's Frosted Foods, 427 A.2d 385 (Conn. Sup. Ct. 1979) (Food, Drug, and Cosmetics Act).

94. Norman v. Niagara Mohawk Power Corp., 873 F.2d 634 (2d Cir. 1989).

95. Lockert v. U.S. Dep't of Labor, 867 F.2d 513 (9th Cir. 1989).

96. English v. General Electric Co., 871 F.2d 22 (4th Cir. 1989).

97. Rayner v. Smirl, 873 F.2d 60 (4th Cir. 1989).

98. Leibowitz v. Bank Leumi Trust Co., 548 N.Y.S.2d 513 (N.Y. Sup. Ct. App. Div. 1989).

99. Winters v. Houston Chronicle Pub. Co., 781 S.W.2d 408 (Tex. Ct. App. 1989).

100. Wiltsie v. Baby Grand Corp., dba Maxim Hotel and Casino, 774 P.2d 432 (Nev. Sup. Ct. 1989).

101. Wieder v. Feder, Kaszovitz, Isaacson, Weber & Skala, 544 N.Y.S.2d 971 (N.Y. Sup. Ct. 1989).

102. Johnston v. Del Mar Distrib. Co., 776 S.W.2d 768 (Tex. Ct. App. 1989).

103. Remba v. Federation Employment and Guidance Service, 545 N.Y.S.2d 140 (N.Y. Sup. Ct. App. Div. 1989).

104. Johnston v. Del Mar Distrib. Co., 776 S.W.2d 768 (Tex. Ct. App. 1989).

105. Hill v. Iowa Dep't of Employment Services, 442 N.W.2d 128 (Iowa Sup. Ct. 1989).

106. BNA-Daily Labor Report, 228 DLR A-1 1989, (Nov. 29, 1989) (Text in Westlaw).

107. Mass. Senate Bill No. 72, 2 (c) (1989).

108. Cal. Senate Bill No. 222, 2881 (d) (Jan. 19, 1989).

109. (Cal. Senate Bill No. 282, 2880 (a) (Jan. 26, 1989).

110. Mass. Senate Bill No. 72, 2 (b) (1989).

111. Mass. Senate Bill No. 72, 4(b) (1989).

112. Cal. Senate Bill No. 282, 2880(a) (Jan. 26, 1989).

113. Model Unif. Employment Termination Act. 1(b), 2(b) (Draft 1989), Lab. Rel. Rep. Indiv. Empl. Rights Manual (BNA) 540:51 (1989).

114. Cal. Senate Bill No. 282, 2881 (b) (Jan. 26, 1989).

115. Cal. Senate Bill No. 282, 2882 (Jan. 26, 1989).

116. Cal. Senate Bill No. 222, 2883 (Jan. 19, 1989).

117. Cal. Senate Bill No. 282, 2889 (Jan. 26, 1989).

118. Mass. Senate Bill No. 72, 5 (a) (Jan. 1989).

119. Cal. Senate Bill No. 282, 2884 (a) (Jan. 26, 1989).

120. Iowa House File 7, 3 (Jan. 10, 1989).

121. Mass. Senate Bill No. 72, 5–6 (1989).

122. Cal. Senate Bill No. 282, 2890 (c) (Jan. 26, 1989).

123. Model Unif. Employment Termination Act 3 (Draft 1989), Lab. Rel. Rep. Indiv. Empl. Rights Manual (BNA) 540:51 (1989).

124. Cal. Senate Bill No. 282, 2891 (Jan. 26, 1989).

125. Mass. Senate Bill No. 72, 11 (1989).

126. Cal. Senate Bill No. 222, 2884 (Jan. 19, 1989).

127. Cal. Senate Bill No. 222, 2884 (Jan. 19, 1989).

128. Mass. Senate Bill No. 72, 7 (a) (1989).

129. Mass. Senate Bill No. 72, 10 (1989).

130. Mass. Senate Bill No. 72, 13 (1989).

131. Cal. Senate Bill No. 222, 2884 (d) (Jan. 19, 1989).

132. Model Unif. Employment Termination Act 2 (Draft 1989), Lab. Rel. Rep. Indiv. Empl. Rights Manual (BNA) at 540:52 (1989).

133. Model Unif. Employment Termination Act 1 (Draft 1989), Lab. Rel. Rep. Indiv. Empl. Rights Manual (BNA) 540:51 (1989).

134. Id. at 2 at 540:52–540:53.

135. Id. at 3 at 540:53.

136. Id. at 4 at 540:54.

137. Id. at 4 at 540:54.

138. Id. at 5 at 540:54–540:55.

139. Id. at 5 at 540:55.

140. Id. at 7 at 540:56.

141. Id. at 6 at 540:55–540:56.

142. Id. at 9 at 540:56.

143. Id. at 2 at 540:52.

144. Id. at 6(c) at 540:56.

145. 7 BNA Employee Rel. Weekly 973 (July 31, 1989).

8

Conclusion

THE EMPLOYER

The predominant judicial and arbitral theme is the emphasis on employer rights. The theme is most pronounced in discharge cases but it is never far from the from the surface in other employment disputes. Juries that award employees large punitive damages may be somewhat less enthusiastic about the doctrine than courts, but the appellate courts remain strong in their emphasis. Employer rights is at its judicial zenith in at will discharge cases. The result is that courts have made the finding of a fixed term contract extremely difficult in the absence of a clear writing. It is not entirely clear whether all courts will apply the employer rights with the same rigor in nondischarge cases. Employers in some jurisdictions may find that a less strict view is taken on clauses in the contract that are less concerned with such a fundamental employer right as discharge.

One aspect of employer rights focuses primarily on the right of the employer to make the decisions necessary to operate an efficient and profitable business. This element of the employer rights doctrine is described in such a way as to make it an innate characteristic of our form of economic organization. Because of this fundamental quality, courts are unlikely to alter their basic approach to these employer rights. Similarly, legislatures are unlikely to attempt to alter this aspect of employer rights in any effort to reform the at will discharge situation. If a legislature attempts to modify the basic doctrine of employer rights, it will have to be done with very explicit language, which is unlikely. Whereas new theories may be recognized by some courts to limit some of the harshness of the at will doctrine, courts are unlikely to fundamentally modify their well-established and long-established judicial restraint approach. Legislation may modify the judicial restraint doctrine if it is sufficiently specific in that regard. When there are well-established judicial patterns, legislative history must be clear to effect any major changes. Statutes that modify the at will doctrine may be aimed as much at protecting employer rights as they are at providing for less harshness for employees. Public policy arguments can be used to support both employer interests employee interests.

Judicial recognition of the employer rights doctrine manifests itself, in part, in the judicial restraint expressed by courts when they deal with individual contract disputes. As the at will reform movement slowly gathers steam, a major question for employers is whether the alternative, nonjudicial forums for contract dispute resolution will show the deference to employer rights that the courts have. Arbitration is the most commonly considered alternative forum and the question becomes one of whether the individual contract arbitrator will treat the dispute more like a collective bargaining arbitrator (somewhat less employer deference) or more like the courts (greater employer deference). Statutory restrictions or submission agreement restrictions on the arbitrator or limited remedial arbitration authority may play a major role here.

Cause is the broadest defense that employers can use in an individual contract dispute. If cause can be established, it is a complete defense in the contract dispute, as well as in most other employment disputes. Cause has been relatively well defined in hundreds of collective bargaining arbitration cases. These definitions are unlikely to greatly change. They will continue to recognize the employer's right to make fundamental business judgments despite the impact on the individual employee. Where statutory methods of altering the at will doctrine are used, the definition of cause in the statute will be of critical importance to the parties. Statutes could restrict the common meaning of the term and give rise to another round of judicial interpretations aimed at interpreting what the statutory definitions mean. If the arbitrator's determination is not given the finality that is recognized in the collective bargaining area, this could also lead to another round of litigation after the arbitrator has rendered his or her award.

Courts frequently point out that if the employee wants more job security than an at will contract, then the employee should attempt to negotiate a suitable contract with the employer. By the same token, if employers seek relief from some of the frustrations caused by at will litigation, they are also free to attempt to negotiate with the employees. These negotiations can take at least two directions from the employer perspective. One is to negotiate written contracts with explicit at will terms. If a dispute arises, such a contract would increase the employer's chances of winning at the motion to dismiss stage. The other direction would be for the employer to negotiate relatively short duration fixed term contracts. During the life of the contract, the employer would be bound by the requirement of cause for discharge. When the contract has expired, however, the employer could renew or not renew on whatever basis the employer desires. If the contracts are of relatively short duration, the employer would not have to keep an undesirable employee very long, even if cause could not be proved. The nonrenewal of the expired contract would mean that the employment was over. The result might well be that the situation would look much like the current at will doctrine. In jurisdictions recognizing the covenant of good faith, however, the employer may have to be more cautious.

Cause is the strongest defense in support of an employer's decision to discharge. An employer has cause when the employee, for example, fails to meet the standards of the position, that is, the duties owed to the employer. There are many employees whose jobs give them a special status because of the characteristics of their work. Employers can scrutinize the various positions to determine whether special characteristics exist that can be used as a possible basis for finding cause if the employee does not work out. The changing nature of our economy may put greater emphasis on this factor. In a service based economy, more of the jobs may involve contact with the public. Courts frequently find employees in these public contact positions more vulnerable than whose only contact is with other employees. Higher level employees are also subject to greater employer controls. Criteria are difficult to enunciate and the employer will be given fairly wide latitude. Employers who are concerned about a cause basis for discharge should be careful to fully identify all of the characteristics of the job that may be relevant. If the employee violates one of these duties, the employer may discharge. In the case law, there is little in the opinions to suggest that the courts will permit the employee to require the employer to give detailed proof of the validity of the job description.

The use of the extended probationary period is a concept that has not been widely tested. Employers who want greater control over discharge decisions might gain from this by extending their probationary periods. In addition, employers may be able to put longer term employees into a probationary status when they change positions or as a result of discipline. If the employer were to use the probationary status as a bad faith gesture, courts may be less lenient in their recognition of the status. At present, however, there is little in the case law that limits the employer's use of probationary status.

One growing trend is for employers to seek waivers of rights or consents or releases of claims from employees. This may be attempted at the point of hire, during the term of hire, or at the point of discharge or other termination. Courts have had mixed reactions to some of these attempts, but on the whole the courts have not been hostile toward the employer's attempts. This trend is likely to continue. It is an approach that employers should consider if they risk high liabilities in the event of a successful employee suit. This is another example of where the courts seek to encourage the parties to negotiate, but ignore the issue of whether any real negotiations are possible, that is, whether the employee has any individual bargaining strength.

Where mutuality concepts are given great weight, it follows that if the employee can sue on the contract of employment, then the employer also ought to have some contract grounds that might use to sue the employee. However, there have been surprisingly few examples of employer suing employee types of suits. There may be greater movement in this direction in the future. So long as the suit is not frivolous, it may not matter whether the employer wins or loses. Even an unsuccessful suit may convey the message to other employees to think twice before bringing a suit. The covenant of good faith has not been tested in this context.

Employee litigation may be viewed by some employers as merely another cost of doing business. However, if a big, punitive damage verdict is levied against the employer, it may make the cost of business too high. Part of the legislative efforts to reform the at will doctrine is aimed at reducing or eliminating large punitive damages recoveries. The punitive damages battle is also being waged in other areas of the law. If punitive damages are reduced or eliminated, it is likely to have a major impact on who can afford to challenge the employer. There is evidence in many areas of law beyond employment law that punitive damages are being challenged. This trend is likely to accelerate. Employers may eventually feel some relief from punitive damages from these nonemployment activities in unrelated areas of law may spill over to employment law.

Employers should give serious consideration to the establishment of inhouse grievance mechanisms. More employers are probably interested in nonbinding forms than in final and binding mechanisms. However, the final and binding versions may substantially reduce or eliminate the concern over punitive damages. Where such mechanisms exist, the employee may be required to exhaust them before moving into court, although this is still an open question in most jurisdictions. The court may give weight to the decisions rendered in fairly reached decisions. The law is far from certain in most states on the exhaustion and two bite remedy issues. The availability of some form of inhouse review, however, may reduce the number of employees who otherwise might go directly to court. The U.S. Supreme Court has indicated that the results of fair inhouse procedures may be viewed with favor by courts where there are claims of discrimination, especially harassment claims. The increasing movement toward alternative dispute resolution devices in areas outside of employment law will doubtlessly affect how courts view inhouse employment dispute procedures.

A major decision for an employer is whether or not to issue an employee handbook. Courts have recognized the utility of handbooks but have also found that they may constitute a binding contract of employment. At this juncture, it appears that most courts will find that a properly disclaimed handbook usually is not binding as a contract. Where the handbook is not a binding contract it leaves the door open for the employee to claim that a post handbook contract was made. A nonbinding handbook also raises the general question of why publish an unenforceable document. Once employees find out about its true legal character, they may largely ignore it. Where the manual contains an inhouse grievance procedure, it is especially important that the employer identify the intent of the publication. If it is not binding, the employer will not be able to take advantage of those court decisions that look with favor on inhouse grievance mechanisms.

THE EMPLOYEE

The judicial case law makes it clear that all clauses of the individual contract of employment are not read in the same manner. The durational term (fixed or indefinite term) is read in the strictest possible manner, whereas other terms may be read with a balancing of employer and employee interests in mind. One obvious conclusion is that the employee should carefully consider all the clauses of the contract. If claims can be based on clauses other than the durational clause, the employee should emphasize them where possible. The chances of getting more detailed consideration by the courts seem much higher.

One way for the employer to attempt to minimize litigation is to have a written contract that clearly spells out the status of the employee. This same approach can be used by that small number of employees who have some negotiating power. Because of the broad range of potential clauses, employees should look beyond simply trying to negotiate a fixed term contract where that is difficult and seek to get other contractual elements of job security, such as a notice period, a grievance mechanism, or severance pay. For long-term employees, it is especially important that they identify whatever vested rights they may have when they are discharged or when the employer seeks to impose a disclaimed handbook. New employees should seek to obtain early vesting of important rights.

The list of employee duties owed to the employer is long and the list of employer duties owed to the employee is short. Where negotiations are possible, employees should attempt to create employer contractual duties. Employees may seek to negotiate clauses that impose a duty on the employer to give warnings if the employee's performance is slipping or seek to impose a duty to conduct regular evaluations so that the employee will have an up to date indicator of where he or she stands.

Where grievance mechanisms involving arbitration are being negotiated, it is important that the agreement spell out that the arbitrator should act in the manner of a collective bargaining arbitrator. The power of the arbitrator to mitigate the employer's personnel action should be specifically considered. Arbitrators are as aware of employer rights as courts are. There is little for employees to gain in arbitration if the arbitration system or other grievance mechanism that is established shows the same level of restraint that the courts usually show.

Discharge is the major subject matter of the cases considered in these materials because it is the major topic of the case law. However, there are many actions that affect employees that are less than discharge. If the employee is at will for purposes of duration, attention should be given to whether that at will approach will be used for all adverse personnel decisions in that jurisdiction. The arguments about implied, unwritten contracts might be more helpful here, although that is an uncertain conclusion. Where negotiations about a contract are underway, even if the employee has to concede an at will durational term, it does not inevitably follow that the employee must also give the employer arbitrary decision making authority on all other terms and decisions. Some courts might hold to the contrary, but it is clear that different contract clauses are given different treatment by courts. A noncompetition clause, for example, is viewed by most courts as requiring a balancing of the interests of the employee, the employer, and the public. One of the strongest cases that the employee can have is where the employee can show that the employer intentionally acted in a certain manner. The intentional infliction of emotional distress is one of these situations. In addition, protected class discrimination often must be shown to be intentional. The cases reflect a very mixed picture here. If the employee can show intent, the court has less trouble offering remedies. Intent is very difficult to prove in the law, whether here or in other areas of law. What makes the topic confusing is that the case law is full of employee statements suggesting that the employer was out to get the employee, or that the employer was setting the employee up. Despite the frequency of the claim, the employee is rarely able to prove it. It is not clear what this frequent reference to distrust of the employer means in the overall employment relationship picture. For these purposes, however, where facts showing the employer intent are available, they are a strong case where the court is less likely to show restraint.

Employees must be increasingly concerned about the efforts of employers to make the employee sign releases, waivers of rights, and consents. Where the employee does sign such a document, many courts are willing to take it on face value. Many courts refuse to seriously consider whether it was voluntary or involuntary. Employer drafted documents seem to be given far less scrutiny than employee claims for a fixed term contract. The increasing use of these clauses may result in courts starting to give them greater scrutiny in some jurisdictions. It is a matter of major concern in this era of drug and alcohol testing and last chance agreements. Employees should be cautious about such documents when they have a real choice. Where new statutory rights are being created, consideration should be given to a statutory prohibition on waivers other than those that are truly voluntary and in the best interests of all parties, including the public.

Where employee rights are measured more by statutory rights than common law rights, the employee is likely to receive greater protection than the common law gives. Whistleblower and antiretaliation provisions in statutes become very important. Statutes and case law should be scrutinized to determine whether such rights exist or can be implied. Whereas many employers are increasingly cautious in their relations with employees on many topics, some employers seem unfamiliar with the nonretaliation provisions included in many statutes. Where new legislation is being drafted, nonretaliation provisions should be sought. For at will employees, nonretaliation may be their best case if the facts fit. Whistleblower statutes may have a similar impact. However, the language of whistleblower statutes varies greatly and employees should be fully familiar with the specific language of their statute before acting. For example, many statutes do not protect employees whose whistleblowing is solely internal or where the disclosure does not directly affect a matter of major public health or safety.

Remedies are a major issue for employees as well as employers. Most employees cannot afford to get a lawyer to go into court unless there is the prospect of a large recovery from which the lawyer can be paid on a contingent fee contract. If punitive damages, the usual source of large recoveries, are eliminated the employee will need to have another forum substituted for courts that is cheaper and faster. Reinstatement is a traditional remedy for many employees. However, in a number of situations reinstatement will not work because of the animosity that has been generated. Under these circumstances, employees should be greatly concerned about the availability of frontpay to permit transition to another job. The balancing of reduced remedies and more accessible forums is one of the most critical issues to be watched in the legislative efforts to alter the common law at will doctrine.

The temper of a significant portion of the case law suggests that employees are sometimes seeking a forum that will give a factually correct answer to the question of whether the employee was properly evaluated or discharged. In many of these cases, the employee seems to have greater expectations than the legal system will ever be able to deliver. Courts in this area, as in other areas, are willing to tolerate a high degree of employer error, so long as the decision is essentially reasonable. In addition, courts are always going to give the benefit of the doubt to the employer. Employees should be careful to match their expectations with the reality of what the dispute resolution forum can really offer. Fully accurate decision making is rarely on the menu of most forums. Another error that many employees make is to attempt to show that the employer acted in bad faith when the employee does not have evidence of particular facts to show bad faith. Employees seem to rely on more subtle things that seek to show there was an atmosphere of ill will. Courts in this area and in many other areas of law are disinclined to find bad faith in specific situations when only general allegations are being made. The remarkable level of mistrust shown in many cases may well exist in the workplace, but it will take specific and not general allegations to prove that it exists to the satisfaction of the courts. Part of the reason that employees should be interested in nonjudicial forums is to seek a forum that will permit these allegations to be more easily shown, if they can really be demonstrated.

Cases are replete with situations where employees have quit because they feel that they were forced out in a constructive discharge. It is another example of the remarkable level of distrust that appears in the case law of the workplace. This is the problem of the constructive discharge. Courts respond to these claims in diverse ways, but almost always put a heavy burden on the employee to prove specific facts showing that there was a constructive discharge. General allegations will be insufficient. Frequently the employee cannot make the showing to the satisfaction of the courts. In the legislative efforts to alter the common law at will rule, careful attention needs to be given to the inclusion of and definition of constructive discharge. It may not be sufficient from the employee perspective to simply use the reasonable person approach because courts tolerate many strained working relationships as being reasonable, given the general difficult situations most employees find in the usual workplace.

Many employees seem to be put to the difficult choice of following an employer's order or being discharged for insubordination. The employee, for example, may have to sign a consent to a drug test or acknowledge a handbook that releases an employer from various liabilities. Courts have not been receptive to arguments of economic duress, that is, the employee needs the job and could not afford to quit over the issue. This issue frequently goes beyond at will status, because the employee's refusal may be deemed to be insubordination, which gives the employer cause to discharge. To the extent that the matter goes beyond at will status, the employee must give careful consideration to whistleblower and nonretaliation statutes. The creation of rights means little if the exercise of the rights leads to discipline. As the law develops in this area, it may turn out that whistleblower concepts and nonretaliation doctrines are more important than contract status or the forum in which contract status may be determined.

The difficulties over the at will doctrine are more likely to be lessened or resolved through legislation, rather than through the courts. Judicial efforts will always be hampered by the restrained approach that the courts have historically followed. Statutes can either limit the exercise of judicial restraint or remove the matter from the courts and put the dispute in another forum. The current trend in legislative proposals is toward resolving the individual contract disputes in forums other than the courts. The tradeoff is usually that the employee will be limited in the amount of damages that he or she might be able to recover. If statutes are passed that still make the court a major player and do not limit judicial restraint, then little will be gained by these efforts. If a forum other than the courts is created but the forum exercises the same restraint that the courts often exercise, then little will be gained in the new forum. If the statutes do not protect the employees from involuntary waivers, the statute will have added nothing to the employee side of the ledger. If the statutes make exceptions for fixed term contracts, then the statute will have added little unless some way is given for most employees to have some bargaining power. This will be very difficult.

Statutes can be passed for at least two reasons. One is to limit the impact of the common law at will doctrine. The other reason is to give the employer greater protection from the increasing number of law suits and the risk of heavy punitive damages. The employee does not gain where the statute seeks primarily to protect the employer's historical status quo.

THE PUBLIC

At various times in individual employment disputes, either the employer or the employee may feel that their interests are being overlooked. That may indeed be true in a given case. However, the public also has some interests involved in these disputes, but few courts have recognized this. One public interest is in productivity and efficiency. Many factors must come together to make a workplace productive and efficient. It must be asked, however, whether a system of job security based on common law contract considerations or a system based on greater use of cause contributes most to production and efficiency. Common law contract notions are far removed from the workplace and do not consider whether the employee was a contributing member of the work force. The common law is more concerned about what was said and how it was said at a time that is months or years earlier when the parties first talked about employment. Cause more nearly focuses on the whether the employee was an efficient contributor and more nearly focuses on the employer's vital interests, such as the state of the economy or the business changes the employer may be trying. A greater judicial response to these issues would seem to be the better vehicle to reach the public's goal of a competitive economy.

Reform in this area of law, as in most areas of law, involves a balance of procedural, substantive, and remedial rights. There are no obvious answers. Current reform proposals affecting the at will doctrine ease procedural hurdles, lessen potential substantive rights of employees, and limit the remedial rights of employees. For employers, the effects are approximately the opposite, if one assumes the usual adversarial relationship exists between the two. In practice, it is relatively clear that procedural access to the courts is governed in large measure by remedies that permit the recovery of enough funds to make the case profitable for lawyers. Thus remedies might be seen by some to be the public policy key. Employers seem to have the greatest concern about the potential of facing a six figure payout if they lose the case. From a public policy perspective, it needs to be asked which of these elements is the most important. Limiting remedies may eliminate the forum. A balancing approach suggests that if remedies are limited, the forum should be changed to permit the employee to have access to a dispute resolution forum.

It can be argued, of course, that the only important issue in dispute resolution is the outcome, how much was won or lost. However, a great deal of public policy suggests that fair procedures or the opportunity for a fair review may be the most important element in a great many dispute resolution systems. Nothing in the law generally requires totally accurate fact finding and the existence of possible error is readily conceded by courts and arbitrators. However, a fair procedure or a fair review system is seen as essential, as a general matter. It will be important to watch how courts and legislatures respond to the many changes being experienced in the employment relationship. Perhaps a fair procedure is most that can be reasonably expected. In the workplace context, a fair procedure should reflect values and considerations found in the workplace and should provide an accessible forum that does not feel unduly restrained. There is a common interest in production, efficiency, and profitability for all of the participants.

Most members of the public are going to be involved in the workforce at one time or another. There is doubtlessly a common interest in seeing that the employment relationship is not something that only the most sophisticated can navigate. Part of this common interest would be to make the rules of the game as consistent across workplaces as possible. Courts have certainly stated that employers have a strong interest in this type of consistency and predictability. One element of this goal would be to lessen the gulf between the individual contract of employment and the collective bargaining agreement. In some areas, this has been done. The collective bargaining definitions of cause are commonly recognized in statutes and by many courts. The use of releases and similar individual agreements are common in collective bargaining. The collective bargaining contract is read as being more than merely a contract. The individual contract could benefit from an approach more nearly like that of its collective counterpart, and less like a 19th-century contract. Emphasizing the shared points instead of differences between collective and individual employment relationships could usefully alter some approaches in both categories. The differential treatment that courts give to different clauses in the individual contract is largely unexplained. Whereas the courts suggest that if the parties want greater job security or some other working condition they can contract about it, the courts have created such a complex system of contract interpretation that every employee and employer would need a lawyer if they were to seriously negotiate in the way that most courts suggest.

Very few courts are willing to balance a public interest as part of the process of resolving an individual contract of employment dispute. A greater recognition of the public interest is desirable, just as it is in the collective bargaining arena. Of course, it is necessary to consider what the court might mean by the public interests. Certainly a number of courts believe that maximizing the employer's rights through the application of the presumption of at will status is a reflection of the public interest. However, if that really is the only element, the workplace would not be experiencing the litigation that is being seen. Identifying the public's real interests is never an easy task, but a near total failure to look to the broader view cannot be the best approach, especially given the public's growing concern with the productivity and efficiency of the economy.

A number of states are or will be considering a major policy issue. That issue is whether employment disputes should continue to be resolved in the courts or whether there is a better forum, such as arbitration. The choice is not always an easy one, particularly given the nonpublic, confidential approach commonly used in arbitration. However, arbitration has worked well in the collective bargaining arena, and the problems of individual, nonunion employees are often the same as the workers under a collective contract. If one follows the advice of the courts who state the at will problem is a legislative problem, then another forum must be the answer. Judicial restraint is based, in part, on the complex nature of the employment relationship that the courts seem to feel ill equipped to handle, or so they say. Many courts have said that they cannot change their self created at will doctrine, it is a legislative matter. If the courts cannot change, perhaps the message to the legislature is that the courts really are the wrong forum. That was the result in collective bargaining where, in most situations, arbitration has replaced courts. The die is likely cast in favor of nonjudicial forums in many areas in the future. The public will have to keep a wary eye on that new forum to determine whether it will be considering the public's very real interests in these issues.

The visibility of the dispute resolution forum can be a factor of considerable concern to the public. Inhouse and arbitration dispute resolution forums are among the more common suggestions as better places to resolve employment disputes than the courts. The courts have one advantage in that they are open to public view. Inhouse and arbitration systems are not necessarily as visible, especially if judicial review of the results is limited. It seems likely that there is some correlation between the resolution of disputes in the workplace and productivity and efficiency. The public has an interest in maintaining a strong economy. Whatever dispute resolution forums are adopted, attention should be given to the visibility of the forum so that the overall performance of the forum can be monitored.

Employment disputes often involve consideration of the nature of our economic system. The Supreme Court has frequently described those elements that are essential to management in our system. State courts have gone so far as to suggest that the justification for the continuance of the common law at will doctrine is that it promotes economic development. Employees may not always share these views. At best, the judicial views are based upon casual observation and not on empirical evidence presented and tested in the litigation or in the marketplace. Much of what courts say may be justified on the basis of common sense experience that may be valid. However, where fundamental economic policy is being used to resolve important individual employment disputes, it is reasonable to ask whether the judicial forum is really the place to define the nature of our economics. When there is consideration being given to removing the employment disputes to less public forums, the question becomes more important. Perhaps what is needed is greater attention to be given to the employment factor in making basic economic judgments. What is not needed is to determine the rights of employers and employees on the basis of unprovable theories of economics.

Statutes provide greater protection for employees than the common law does. For example, nonretaliation provisions in legislation will provide increasingly meaningful protection to workers. However, merely tacking a nonretaliation provision into a broader statute may be insufficient. The courts have announced many of their predilections in employment cases. If the legislative body fully accepts those views, the stand alone nonretaliation clause is not needed. If, however, those views are being challenged, as they are in the at will area, the addition of a nonretaliation provision to be administered in a judicial forum that has a basic stance of restraint may change little. The problem of employee rights often masks larger social and economic issues. The statutory provisions need to be drafted with a view to some of these larger issues. It is particularly important that some of these larger issues be debated in those jurisdictions that are considering the wholesale change of the at will doctrine. In the absence of the identification of some of these larger economic and social issues, the result might be a lot of work for a minimum amount of actual change because of the premises traditionally used by the judicial dispute resolution forum. Greater attention needs to be directed toward the way that various forums approach economic issues if real changes are being sought.

The case law evidences high levels of distrust and animosity between employers and employees. Because the case law is only a relatively thin slice of the real world, it is difficult to know how representative of the larger picture it really is. However, the persistence of the issue should raise some questions about the basic approaches to employer and employee relationships in the nonunion area. A popular buzzword in collective bargaining is the notion of collaborative or win-win negotiations. It cannot yet be determined whether these new approaches will work or whether they really will contribute to greater efficiency and productivity. This arises at a time when the national economy is having a difficult time competing with foreign products and producers. Most of the economy is made up of nonunion workers. One cannot but wonder if there is a more collaborative approach that might be used in this individual employment area to reduce the apparent amount of distrust and animosity that is displayed in the cases. Perhaps the answer lies more in the nature of human relationships than it does in subjects that are more amenable to legislative or judicial resolution. As the analysis of the at will doctrine and other historical staples of the individual employment relationship gets underway, attention might be given to broader issues of economic or social security that may do more for our economy than simply changing the forum or the balance of power between two contenders in a bitter and divisive dispute. At a minimum, the debate should be over factors relevant to the workplace rather than over factors involving the nature of common law contracts or untested views of what really promotes economic development and efficiency.

Index

American Arbitration Association. *See* arbitration

arbitration: American Arbitration Association, 28–29; at will reform, 241; balancing interests, 85; burden of proof, 241; cause, 210; EAP, 160; efficiency, 74, 76; exhaustion, 26; external law, 26; generally, 21–22, 23, 36, 176, 213, 251, 261; individual contract, 21, 25; in house, nonunion grievance mechanism, 29; judicial restraint, 22; judicial review, 23; last chance agreements, 163; limitations, 26; mitigation, 25, 206, 241, 255; procedure, 25; revitalization, 244; settlements, 162; special employment relationship, 63; testing, 154. *See also* cause; forum

at will: cause, 187; demotion, 211; EAP, 161; job security clauses, 144; language, 166; presumption, 20, 28, 33, 59, 78, 102, 105, 106, 111; public policy, 159, 234; reform and statutes, 27, 42, 222, 230, 233, 237, 240. *See also* cause; contract; contract clauses

balancing employee, employer, public interests: 84, 85, 112, 149, 157, 159, 176, 224, 259, 260

bias, personality dispute. *See* evaluation

burden of proof. *See* contract; forum

cause: arbitration, 200, 204, 210; at will, 187; changing economic conditions, 82; courts, 210; covenant of

good faith, 205; demotion, 211; discharge, 43, 68, 103, 131; efficiency, 136; employer rights, 189; explicit-implicit, 200; factual-reasonable, 202; federal service test, 74; generally, 136, 187, 244, 251; higher level employee, 61, 62; in house grievance mechanism, 30; no basis whatsoever, 204; no fault, 209; one of several grounds, 77; procedure-substance, 189; public sector, 207; role of jury, 202; special job characteristics, 252; specific offense, 203, 207. *See also* arbitration; employer; evaluation

collective bargaining. *See* arbitration; forum; *individual and collective contracts*

consents. *See* waivers

contingent fees. *See* courts

contract: ambiguous-specific terms, 105; authority of agent, 105; balancing interests, 84, 159; bargaining power, 59, 117, 164, 251, 254; basic element, 2; beyond contract, 4; burden of proof, 104, 177; consideration, 107, 108, 116; definite term, 3, 102, 244; efficiency, 136; employment application, 109; ending, constructive discharge, 8, 9, 31, 242, 257; ending, generally, 7–8, 9, 129–131; ending, statutes, 130; general or special rules, 132; handbook, 118, 190; indefinite term, 3; integration clause, 113; long-term extraordinary, 105; modification, 124, 127, 128; mutuality, 111; negotiation,

ABOUT THE AUTHOR

DONALD W. BRODIE has been teaching labor and employment law at the University of Oregon School of Law for more than twenty years. He graduated from New York University School of Law and has written extensively in the field of labor and employment law. Professor Brodie has written two books on labor law and numerous articles, two of which have been cited by the United States Supreme Court.